BABY DOLL

My Mother, My Secrets

MEMOIR BY CHARLOTTE ROSSLER

BABY DOLL: MY MOTHER, MY SECRETS
Charlotte Rossler

Cover and Design: Jodi Bogart

All photographs are the property of the author.

ISBN: 978-1-7377560-2-6 Paperback Edition
       978-1-7377560-3-3 Hardcover Edition
       978-1-7377560-1-9 Digital Edition
       978-1-7377560-0-2 Audio Edition

Library of Congress Control Number: 2021916304

10 9 8 7 6 5 4 3 2 1

Printed in the United States of America

xx-v10

For my amazing siblings, Mary Lou, Theresa, Shirley, David, Suzanne, and Kathy, and in memory of our deceased sister, Jacquie.

Also for my two sons, Mark and Andrew. May you live the life I always envisioned for you.

Secrets are untrustworthy allies.
They provide a sense of security,
all the while they threaten to betray you.

Contents

(L-R) Charlotte, Mary Lou, Shirley, Theresa, David, Jacquie, Suzie, Kathy

PART I

ANNIE OAKLEY GONE MAD

Teary-faced and gasping, Suzie, my five-year-old sister, raced across the backyard to our corral where I stood brushing our chestnut mare, June.

"They're back! The boys came back again," she said. "The big kid pushed Kathy down, and her knee is bleeding!"

A stinging flush started at my face and burned down my chest as I listened to Suzie describe my youngest sister, four-year-old Kathy, sprawled on the pavement with a bloody knee. I took a slow deep breath and let it out in a whoosh. My hand shook as I lay the grooming brush on the corral fence, trying to keep cool. I gazed up at the blue California sky.

I was fifteen, the oldest of eight kids, and I held back my urge to charge into the street, swinging a baseball bat and pummeling those kids into the ground for hurting my little sisters. I'd defended my sisters many times, but this time, it wasn't our mother I defended them against.

Suzie kept talking while a new wave of fury rose within me. I thought about Dad on tour in Vietnam for a second term and Mom away in Las Vegas so often. We had lots of fun without parental guidance, including riding our two horses, but so many crises came up with eight kids left alone.

I bridled June, hopped on bareback, and reached down to grab my brother's BB gun propped against the water trough.

I trotted June out to the far end of the dead-end street, which ran next to our old country house. There, a group of young thugs was harassing my sisters. One yanked the jump rope from my seven-year-old sister, Jacquie, and another pulled her hair. I couldn't make out what the boys shouted, but I heard my sisters' screams. Kathy turned and gave the boys hell while another kid shoved her from behind. The biggest kid grabbed her by the hair and swung her around like I saw Dad swing our dog, Speedy, by the collar.

Time for these boys to find out what it felt like to be bullied.

June responded brightly to the nudge of my bare heels. She galloped toward the ruckus, hooves stamping the pavement.

I waved my rifle in the air like Annie Oakley-gone-mad and bellowed, "I'll smash you kids to a bloody pulp."

The boys froze, staring at the enormous horse and rider charging at them.

They yelled and ran for cover in the orange groves. I chased them through the trees until they split up, staying on the heels of the biggest kid—the one who'd knocked Kathy to the ground. He stumbled and fell face-first into the mud of a small irrigation ditch. I reined in June, three feet from stomping on him. So mad at the world of mean people, I almost let June kick him. He rolled over to his back and gazed up at me. I towered above the cowering boy.

I raised the BB gun slowly for effect, peered through the sight marker, and took aim directly at the kid's snotty face. He shielded his eyes to block the shots sure to come. I cocked the gun.

"Get ready to die, crybaby."

His pleas and tear-smeared face made me hesitate long enough for him to scramble to his feet. He took off running through the trees.

I held my aim steady and shot him bullseye on the butt. He hopped like Charlie Chaplin, yelped, grabbed his rear, and kept going.

I walked June out of the orange groves to join my sisters. Suzie and Jacquie saw us coming and cheered.

Kathy sat on the pavement, nursing her scraped knee and scowling. "I hate those boys. I hope you killed them all."

"I didn't kill them, but I don't think they'll be back for a while."

I wished I hadn't shot the kid. Not because I had any sympathy for him, but because his parents might contact Mom when she returned from Vegas. I'd be in big trouble for shooting him, no matter the reason.

That night, relieved because the kid's parents hadn't called, I lay in bed holding a flashlight close to my side. All the light bulbs had burned out, so the family room TV provided our only light. We feared getting up at night, even for the bathroom, because rats scurried freely around our house after dark. They had a rat festival that night.

Whenever Mom went away, she left plenty of food for the animals and us—cereal, milk, spaghetti, peanut butter, and jelly—but never any money. After buying food, Mom needed what scarce money was left for her trips to Las Vegas.

YOUR MOM IS LIKE, REALLY PRETTY

I was playing with a Raggedy Ann doll my grandparents had sent for my fifth birthday when Mom called from my bedroom. "Come sit with me."

She closed the door, sat on the edge of the bed, and took my hand in hers. With the other, she used one finger to turn my chin toward her and look me level in the face. "There's something important you need to know. You're five now and old enough to understand." She tucked my hair behind my ear, and I swallowed hard, wondering what was wrong.

"Your brother and sisters are only half yours," she said. "Dad is not your real father."

"I'm not like the other kids?" I held Mom's eyes, not understanding and not wanting to understand. "You're different," translated to "You don't belong" or "You're not as good."

"This is a family secret." She lightly squeezed my hand. "We can't tell anyone your big secret, okay?"

"Yes, ma'am." A bottomless ravine cracked open inside me, and shame rushed in to fill it. "Am I still in the family?" My voice quivered.

"Yes, but never tell anyone what I told you, okay? Even though Dad isn't your real father, he chose you. You weren't born to him, but he chose you. Do you understand?"

"Yes." But I didn't really. He never acted like he chose me.

From that day on, I understood why my Christmas presents were less than the others. In the coming years, when my sisters got brand new shiny bicycles for Christmas, I pretended excitement over receiving my rusty old bike painted red to look new. Alone in bed, tears soaked my pillow. My presents proved I wasn't as good as the rest of the kids. I hoped my siblings wouldn't notice or find out I wasn't really their full sister, but they did find out.

I was around thirteen when one of my sisters discovered my birth certificate and ran through the house waving it, shouting, "Look what I found! Charlotte's last name's not the same as ours!"

I had leaped to my feet and chased her. Dad caught her before I did. He snatched the paper from her hand, laid it back on his desk, and pulled down the rolltop.

"You kids, stay away from my desk." He glared at me like I had done something wrong.

I ran to my room, dove into bed, and buried my face in the pillow to muffle my crying. My awful secret was revealed. I had loved being their big sister all those years. I had never wanted my siblings to see me as different from them, and now they did.

Starting around seven, old enough to reach the stove, Mom credited me for raising my youngest siblings and for being a good mother—the mother she didn't want to be.

The youngest kid was Dave at the time, a toddler. After him, Jacquie, Suzie, and Kathy were born, each one year after the other. Sometimes, we had multiple kids in diapers at the same time.

Although I adored my sisters and brother, I never took pride in changing the little ones' bulky cotton diapers using big metal safety pins. I held my breath and rinsed the dirty diapers in the toilet, then wrung out the toilet water before cramming them into the diaper pail.

Changing my sisters proved easy compared to my brother. When his dangerous little hose sprang free from the wet diaper, he sprayed everywhere and everything—especially me at close range. When he heard me squeal, his wide-open toothless grin broke into fits of laughter, and his chubby arms boxed the air.

I cradled the infants and fed them baby formula from bottles heated in a pan of warm water, testing the temperature on the inside of my wrist like Mom taught me. I loved my little siblings' puffy pink cheeks, sweet smell, and soft baby skin. I tickled them, making them giggle till they cried, little fists clenched and un-clenched, chubby arms waving and legs kicking.

In second grade, a girlfriend said, "Your mom is, like, really pretty."

It was true. Mom looked like a bleached-blonde Ann-Mar-gret, so when she wanted to charm a man, and she often did, she got his attention. I worshiped my mother.

"My mom says your mom can sail and scuba dive," my friend said.

So proud, I stretched and stood a bit taller. "Yeah, she can sail, scuba dive, ride the wildest horses, swim the fastest races. She stood on the back of her horse on one foot and jumped over a swing set! Everyone clapped like crazy!"

"You said that last time, but my mom said a horse can't jump over a swing set. It's too high."

"Oh, phooey," I said, placing my hands on my hips. "My mom's horse jumps that high, easy. I'm going to be strong and brave like her when I grow up. My dad says I'm already like her."

Mom looked different than the other mothers—prettier, shinier, and always more fun. But over time, my admiration eroded as I matured enough to distinguish her failings from her extraordinary character.

She didn't drink, smoke, or swear, but when the military sent Dad overseas, she hid a boyfriend in her back pocket.

Each evening while our parents were away, we cooked our own dinner together. Afterward, we knew our assigned chores.

We lifted Suzie and Kathy to the kitchen countertop and handed them each a towel to dry dishes and plastic cups. The pans weighed more than they did; too much for them to hold.

"Hurry up, you guys. Let's get this done so we can watch *Star Trek*," Mary Lou said.

I was two years old when Mom married my stepdad, so a three-year age gap separated me from Mary Lou, the first child born of Mom and Dad.

Mary Lou, at twelve, matched my height and still grew fast. Model thin, her thick blondish-brown hair hit the lower part of her back, and her eyes shimmered blue in her pale face.

The next sister down came Theresa, eleven and a platinum blonde. She looked a lot like me. Theresa wore her hair long, the same as the rest of us, and pointed her toes in a prissy manner when she sat. A natural flirt, she charmed everyone.

Shirley, the next sister—ten years old and born only ten months after Theresa—beamed an engaging smile. Her natural curls framed her face and fell to her shoulders. Her intelligence was evident from her sharp wit. Mom blamed and picked on Shirley a lot, probably because she articulated her thoughts clearly at ten years old. Mom didn't like us to challenge her authority or sound too uppity.

Our brother, David, came next. His eyes flashed the same shade of blue as the rest of us. He carried a muscular build for a little guy of only eight. Dave, as we called him, was our parents' pride, their only son. People often said things like, "Oh, poor boy, smothered by so many sisters," but the rest of us knew he got everything he wanted, even his own bedroom. It was hard to understand at the time, but I get it now.

Jacquie, seven, came after Dave. Her striking doe-like looks matched her grace and quiet demeanor. We often called her beautiful, with her creamy complexion, flowing hair, and tall, slim frame. She never took our praise to heart, brushed us off, which made her even more beautiful.

Suzie, five, with thick, wavy blondish-brown hair and a little round freckled face, reminded me of a baby doll with cupid lips and an impish smile. Her cheery demeanor and natural ability to dance and recite Disney songs made her shine like our little star.

Kathy, the youngest at four—with her straight hair, white-blonde like Theresa's, Jacquie's, and mine—shocked strangers when they heard a booming voice of authority come from such a skinny little kid. She refused to let us older siblings dismiss her because of her small size. She took part in everything we did, even riding the horses. She and Jacquie looked so much alike that people often mixed them up in photos.

We played games or performed plays for each other, creating our own world of fun.

Suzie and Kathy, mimicking fairy tales they'd listened to over and over on the record player, memorized every word to the running-late-rabbit song in *Alice in Wonderland*.

"Listen up, you kids. Suzie, get over there," Mary Lou said, pointing with authority. Mary Lou, my closest sister, naturally fit the director role. "You and Kathy play the two little mice. Shirley, you're the handsome prince. Theresa, you're the fairy godmother. When I give the signal, you mice start dancing."

Pretty soon, at Mary Lou's direction, I watched while they acted out a full-blown scene from her imaginary musical.

A few days later, Mom returned from Las Vegas. I found her unpacking the suitcase lying open on her bed. She took out several pairs of silky leopard-print panties, held them up to the light, and carefully set them in her dresser drawer. Seeing how happy those panties made her froze an uncomfortable image in my mind.

"Did you see the clothes Mom bought in Las Vegas?" I asked Mary Lou when we were alone.

"No, and I don't want to. Did you hear her say anything about bringing her new guy home next week?"

"Here? She's bringing him here?" I asked.

"Yeah, I think so," Mary Lou said. "I heard her talking to him on the phone. She makes me sick."

"Yeah, me too." I held Mary Lou's steady gaze.

We knew Mom dated men, but nothing she did seemed ordinary, even having kids. She had me at eighteen and gave birth to her eighth child at age twenty-nine.

After Mary Lou told me about the phone conversation she overheard Mom have with her new guy, I went back to Mom's bedroom and found her kneeling on her closet floor looking for something.

I blurted out, "Mom, are you bringing someone back with you from Las Vegas next week?"

"Yes, a friend of mine, and I want you kids on your best behavior."

"Who'd you buy those leopard panties for?" My breath caught in my throat.

She glared at me. "Can't I buy anything nice for myself for once?"

I turned to leave. "Can't you buy anything nice for us for once?" I said under my breath, clenching my jaw to stop from saying more.

"What did you say?"

"Nothing, Mom."

"If you're talking back to me, so help me, God—" She jumped up, lunged toward me, but I bolted out of her reach and out of the room before she could grab me.

Running down the wide staircase, I checked to see if she was chasing me.

I closed myself in the bathroom. Brushing my teeth didn't help the sour taste in my mouth. I didn't care that I wore the same outfits to school week after week while Mom wore beautiful clothes and lingerie. Well, maybe a little. It bothered me more to see my sisters run around in torn cotton underwear. Their stained, stretched-out panties hung down like they carried a load. My face turned pink in blotches as I stared in the bathroom mirror. Why couldn't my mother see her selfishness? I wanted to rescue my sisters and brother and somehow make a wonderful home for them like we'd seen on TV.

The following week, Mom brought home a tall, bushy-browed German guy from Las Vegas. She introduced him, several years her junior, as Pete.

We kids sat silently in the back seats of our family station wagon while he drove us to the skating rink. Mom rode in the front middle seat next to him, singing softly to the radio and caressing his neck while he drove.

Arriving home in the afternoon, we piled out of the car and ran toward the house, glad to escape from Pete and Mom cooing at each other.

"Charlotte, come back here. I want to ask you a favor." Mom lowered her voice. "Can you get me some diet pills from your friends at school? I ran out."

"I'll try."

Honored because Mom involved me and needed me for

something other than babysitting or cleaning house, I set out determined to help her. Her face fell in disappointment when I later reported back that I didn't find anyone who took diet pills.

I suspect Mom's mood swings from a creative, fun mother to a frantic, stressed-out demon were due, in part, to the popularity of diet pills at the time and her desire to look her best.

I hoped being a teenager in California would be cool. After all, the Beach Boys lived there, and they loved California girls. I entered my new high school as an almost-fourteen-year-old freshman, but I didn't own the right clothes. To make matters worse, I wore outdated, black-framed eyeglasses—not the cute wire-rimmed ones like John Lennon wore.

Embarrassed by the way I looked, I kept my head down in pre-algebra, but the A-list girl sitting behind me said out loud, "Are you wearing the same outfit you wore on Monday?"

My pent-up anger exploded. I zipped around in my seat, glared at her, and said, "Yeah, you want to make something of it?"

She responded with a nasty smirk, and I felt uglier and more alone than ever in my new school.

I missed living on the military base in Arizona, the twenty-five-cent movies, bowling alley, swimming lessons, and horse stables all within walking distance from our house.

Mom measured sheer white fabric for curtains in the living room.

"Mom, you said I could get contact lenses when I became a sophomore. Can I have them now?" I hated my stupid glasses.

"If you pay for them yourself," she said.

"How?"

"Save your babysitting money."

Mom responded the same way when I asked her privately if Dad, my stepfather, had ever adopted me. "No, but if that's something you want, save your babysitting money and pay for it."

"I get twenty-five cents an hour. It'll take a hundred years to save the money."

"Can't you see I'm busy? I said I'm not paying for contact lenses. I have enough on my mind without hearing about your problems. Are your chores finished?"

An artist and interior decorator, Mom loved to create a designer ambiance in our home. She'd make slipcovers or paint Goodwill furniture to match the items she saw in decorator magazines. Those projects carried more importance than school clothes for me or new panties for my youngest sisters.

According to Mom, Dad made a good income as an officer helicopter pilot in the Marine Corps, but it spread thin over our family of ten. Mom's spending created part of the problem. She spent money on anything and everything and continued to ignore our basic needs.

"Who broke my vase?" Mom threw the fabric on the couch. "God, I can't have anything nice in this house around you kids. I hate every one of you. I wish I'd never had you!"

Confused, I slunk away behind the rest of the kids.

Home after a day at school, the ruckus coming from Kathy's bedroom made me rush in to see little Kathy tucked behind Mary Lou, barely out of Mom's reach.

Mary Lou blocked Mom from hitting Kathy, so Mom beat Mary Lou instead.

Bent over at her waist, Mary Lou pulled back from Mom's blows, but Mom tethered her by the hair.

"Run, Kathy!" Mary Lou shouted.

"I'll be damned if I—" Mom sputtered, swinging a sandal and pounding Mary Lou on her ducked head and outstretched arms. "Damn it! I'll kill every one of you kids." Spit flew from Mom's mouth.

Mom spotted me, and her face twisted, eyes piercing into mine, daring me to get involved. I dropped my schoolbooks, sprang into action, and pried open her fingers clutching Mary Lou's hair. She let go long enough to swing the shoe at me but missed. Mary Lou leaped out of her reach.

Mary Lou's hair stood out in knotted tangles. Her face was tear-stained, and her nose flushed red from crying. She stood up to Mom with or without me around to help her. This time I stood beside her. Other times, we battled Mom on our own, defending our little sisters, or ourselves, from her rage.

"Stop it!" Mary Lou screamed when Mom hit her again. Her thin frame quivered.

"Don't you talk back to me. I hate you kids." Thick vertical lines stood on the bridge of Mom's nose, and she snorted.

Mom hit Mary Lou's arms again and again with a shoe. She fist-hit me with her other hand. Cowering behind us and safe out of Mom's reach, Kathy saw her chance and ran out of the room.

We took Mom's blows, letting her beat us until she tired. When she finally left the room, Mary Lou and I sat on the edge of the bed, heaving for air and wiping our angry tears until we found our voices to talk.

"Only three more years, and I can leave," I said.

I acted like the big sister Mary Lou admired, but most of the time, I secretly marveled at her. I watched her enormous inner strength when she stood up, faced my mother's brutal wrath again and again, always holding her defiance and taking her beatings a little too long. My heart broke to see her trusting sense of fairness get bruised and hurt.

I swore to myself I'd never turn out like Mom, a trapped woman taking it out on her children.

Early in my parents' marriage, Mom converted from Southern Baptist to Dad's Catholicism, per church rules, and they raised us Catholic.

When Dad was home, things settled into a family routine, sort of.

He poked his head in the bedroom door where we laced up our saddle oxfords, the ones he'd polished the night before. "Taxi leaves for church in ten minutes. You kids better be ready." Dad referred to himself as "the taxi." He hated arriving late for church.

For Christmas or Easter pictures, Mom and Dad lined up the eight of us, oldest to youngest, cherubs all dressed alike in puffy dresses our mother or grandmother sewed.

Parishioners turned to watch the eight of us kids waddle into church behind Mom and Dad like baby ducklings. The ten of us filled nearly every seat in one pew.

After church, Dad reclined in his easy chair, read the Sunday paper, and smoked a cigar. He savored his weekly cigar. The football game played in the background. I loved the smell of cigar smoke mixed with the fragrance of dinner cooking.

We ate a big supper early on Sundays, and Dad popped corn for an evening snack. We kids piled on the leatherette couch or chairs in front of the TV, watched *Star Trek*, and shared the massive bowl of buttery popcorn. I cuddled next to my sisters, a blanket thrown over us.

LONELY GIRL JUST WANTS TO HAVE FUN

Standing next to June on a sunny California afternoon, I inhaled the fragrance of oranges mixed with sweet hay and horses. Ducks quacked in our little pond. Speedy, our German shepherd, ran in circles and barked wildly when he saw me reach for the bridle. He loved to run with the horses.

"Hey, you're not allowed to ride after school," Dave said, raking manure out of the stalls. "You're supposed to finish your homework. I'm telling Mom when she gets home."

I gathered my hair into a ponytail. "Mind your own business, punk. Mom isn't coming back today."

He ignored me and kept raking.

Frustration ate at me when I thought about Mom leaving us alone for days at a time while Dad served in Vietnam, but I enjoyed the peace. "I'll be home to start dinner. It's your turn to take out the trash and feed Speedy."

I peered up at the rambling two-story house my parents rented. I loved to climb into our tree house or play hide-and-seek on horseback in the orange groves surrounding our home. Sometimes we'd line up and swing from the barn roof on a tire that Dad, my stepdad, roped to a high branch.

Mom decorated and divided our home's huge living room in half with a gigantic see-through bookcase, creating a formal living room on one side and a family room on the other. Built when country homes had wrap-around screened-in porches and horse stalls in the back, the beautiful house lived long past its glory days. With six large bedrooms, a formal dining room, a glassed-in breakfast room, and two staircases, the once-beautiful home needed many repairs and a fresh coat of white paint. The cracked windowsills let in winter drafts and summer dust, and the house creaked at night like in a scary movie.

The name Orange County fit the area. Miles of groves and acres of hills dotted by oil wells surrounded us. We boarded our two horses on the tree-shaded four acres that went with our house. A family friend, a GI we knew in Arizona, got orders overseas and gave us his horses before Dad got transferred to California. He made my dream come true. I loved horses.

I finished bridling June and stroked her long neck. Light-reined and sensitive to my touch, I spoke softly to her, sometimes even sang to her on a ride. I laughed out loud when her ears twitched back on my high notes. Sweetness and intelligence glimmered in her brown eyes that were canopied by long, fanned eyelashes.

Denise, my friend who attended a different high school but lived less than a mile away, emerged from the trees on her horse, Lady, riding bareback like me. She ducked to pass under a low branch. We'd become friends from riding together.

June neighed a greeting.

Denise's messy light-brown hair fell in tangles to her shoulders. She wore her usual ragged jean shorts and white tennis shoes with no socks.

She often struggled to control her feisty horse. Every time

Lady bucked her off, Denise hopped back on. I liked her more for it. Spirited like her horse, she reminded me of Mom and me.

"Where are we riding today? Not the oil fields again, pa-leease," Denise said.

"How about 7-Eleven? Get something to drink?" I climbed the corral fence and threw my leg over June.

"Cut through the neighborhood this time. See what's going on?" she asked.

"Mom won't allow me near there. You know the rules." I stroked June's neck and felt her skin twitch under my hand.

"You're never allowed to go anywhere." She lifted and dropped her shoulders in frustration. "Why can't you ride through the neighborhood?"

"Mom doesn't want me around a bunch of kids she doesn't know." I nudged and reined June away from the corral.

Denise followed. "She plays bridge with their mothers, doesn't she? And you go to school with most of them anyway."

"Yeah, whatever. I don't know why it's off-limits." I hated all the restrictions and rules, and I didn't like explaining to Denise every time we rode.

"You're a sophomore. Time to make your own decisions. Your mom's not even home." She moved ahead and reined Lady toward the road as if her decision carried the final word.

Denise and I galloped, staying on the dirt path alongside the road. My ponytail swung in time with June's gait. We slowed to a walk as we entered the blocks of tract houses with two-car garages and fresh-cut lawns. I spotted some kids from school mingled in a group on a corner. Mom taught me to dismount when approaching pedestrians, so I slid off, reins in hand.

"Hey, what's up?" I asked.

"Hanging out. Your horses are beautiful," Angela said, standing back.

Angela, my one friend from school, said she loved horses but never wanted to ride. She didn't say why, but I think horses scared her.

I dug in my jeans and pulled out a sugar cube. "Here, take this. Hold your palm out flat. She won't bite."

Angela looked tiny next to June when she opened her shaky palm and offered the sugar cube. "Oh, her lips tickle! Like velvet," she said.

A boy with full red lips, wearing a black T-shirt and faded jeans, asked, "Why don't you use a saddle?"

The edges of his mouth curled into a hint of a smile. His unblinking stare made me look away.

"I don't like saddles," I answered.

Denise giggled behind me. He gazed past my shoulder at her.

"Do you ride?" Denise asked, a bit too challenging.

"Nah, but I like horses." His attention swept back to me. "I've never seen you around here before. Where do you live?" His perfect teeth sparkled like he starred in a Colgate commercial.

"Down the road in the two-story house on the corner." I pointed with my baby finger, clenched my jaw, and waited for his reaction.

Our house sat more than a half mile away from other houses. I didn't think anyone heard the screaming from that distance, but I dreaded his response.

"You mean the house with a double-decker tree house in the back?"

My relief concealed, I said, "Actually, it's got three stories now."

A long strand of dark hair escaped his combed-back style and fell forward on his forehead like Elvis. He raked it back with his open fingers.

"My name's Danny. What's yours?" His focus was steady and confident.

"I'm Charlotte."

"Some of us are going to Kevin's house tonight to listen to the Stones' new album. Wanna come?"

Angela was stroking June's face after the sugar cube, but she stopped to listen for my reply. She knew my parents didn't allow me out of the house often.

"I can't. My mom's gone. I'm not supposed to leave." I hoped Danny didn't see my embarrassment.

"Sneak out. I'll wait for you," he said.

"I don't know." I tapped my lip, thinking.

"Come on. You said your mom's not home. Besides, what's she going to do if you get caught?" He shrugged.

I didn't respond. I didn't even want to think about it.

On the slow ride home, delirious and drunk with soaring glee, Denise trotted up and guided Lady to walk beside us. "There's something you should know about that guy Danny."

"What?"

"He got kicked out of school for smoking and fighting. He goes to a detention school now."

"Really?" I smiled to myself. Dangerous. This new information made him even cuter, but Mom would kill me if she knew I liked a Mexican boy.

After cleaning the kitchen from spaghetti dinner, my sisters and brother watched TV. I got my bedroom window unstuck and opened it wide enough to lean out and peer into the dark, listening for danger. Only the crickets chirped. I balanced on the sill and dangled my feet about four feet off the ground before dropping. Speaking to the horses in low, calm tones so as not to scare them, I tiptoed around the stalls.

Danny, like a shadow, moved out from the darkness of the trees.

"Hey, girl." My rebel boy stood before me in a black leather jacket.

My heart thumped like June's hooves stomping the trail in a gallop. We made our way to the neighborhood where I'd met him earlier that day.

Danny spoke about Kevin as we walked. "He's got a great stereo. Huge speakers. A bunch of us hang out there a lot. I can't believe you've never been."

The families who lived in this neighborhood weren't like our family.

A month later, after spending every moment possible with Danny, he met Angela and me at the bus stop after school.

We walked and talked, giggling. Out of nowhere, Angela asked me, "Don't you hate that guy, Rob?"

"Who's Rob?" Danny interrupted.

I tried to redirect the conversation. "A guy at school. Angela, don't—"

Danny ignored me and looked at Angela, still walking. "Why do you hate him so much?"

"He bugs me and Charlotte all the time. In Spanish class, he turns around and scribbles on her work. He bumps me in the hallway on purpose."

Danny's red lips turned white. He stopped and ground out his cigarette butt with the heel of his shoe.

A few days later, I spotted Danny and Angela next to the lockers outside my classroom.

"Danny, why are you here?" I asked. "You'll get in trouble."

I searched the hallway for the vice principal weaving through the crowd of students, but luckily he wasn't there. Danny would be thrown off campus if he got caught.

Kids streamed out of the classroom behind me.

Angela pointed. "That's him."

Rob, wearing pressed khakis and sporting a fresh crew cut, stood an inch taller than Danny.

Danny charged him in the crowded hallway, banging him against the lockers and twisting Rob's shirt collar so tight his face turned white. His face inches from Rob's, Danny said, "If I hear about you bothering Charlotte Gulling again, I'll come back and cut your fucking head off! Got it, asshole?" He twisted Rob's collar tighter, and tiny bubbles slid down Danny's chin from the corners of his mouth.

"I'm sorry, man. I didn't—"

Danny released his grip. The kids who'd stopped to watch took off grumbling, disappointed not to have seen a real fight.

Nobody had ever defended me like that, and in front of the whole mean school. I fell in love with Danny that very day.

A week later, I bolted down the street from Danny's house, late to make dinner. Terror drove me faster and faster. I stumbled and went down, my knees and elbows smashing into the pavement. Books and drawings flew from my arms and scattered on the asphalt. Shaking, with no time to check my elbows and knees for blood, I gathered my belongings together, sprang to my feet, and ran on. I could only hope Mom had stayed late at her part-time library job.

I stopped dead when I spotted her car in the driveway. *Oh, God, please. If I sneak in the side door, maybe she won't see me.*

I took a deep breath on the steps and slipped through the side door to the living room. My sister, Shirley, zipped past me toward the kitchen, whispering, "Mom's really mad."

I sprinted to my bedroom.

Mom yelled from the kitchen, "Charlotte, get in here. Now!"

I dumped my books on the bed. "Bathroom first, Mom," I called, making my voice sound casual as I darted to the bathroom, dizzy from fear.

Leaning on the sink, I stared in the mirror, splashed water on my sweaty face, and took another deep breath. *Why hadn't I been more careful about the time?*

Mom's pumps laid on the living room floor where she'd kicked them off. The smell of fried chicken hit me when I rounded the corner of the large old kitchen, the long, yellow Formica countertop littered with dirty pots and pans. Nine-year-old Shirley, running sudsy dishwater, stood on bare tiptoes to reach the kitchen faucet. She flashed me another warning with her expression.

Mom stood at the stove barefoot in her nylons and purple skirt-suit. She turned frying okra using a metal spatula. Fried chicken was piled on a brown paper sack to absorb excess Crisco. The gold brooch pinned to Mom's collar caught a glint of light, and strands of blonde hair escaped from her sagging French twist.

"Where have you been?" she asked.

"School, Mom." My voice cracked.

"Look at me when I'm talking to you. You got out of school two hours ago. Where have you been?"

"I stayed after—"

"Don't lie to me. You saw that damned Mexican boy again."

I ground my teeth, and defiance filled me. "You never let me do anything. Why can't I hang out with my friends?"

She lifted the last bit of okra from the frying pan and faced me. "You know the rules. Come straight home from school and do chores."

"I ironed all day yesterday. Why can't I see my friends?" My voice was whiny.

"Don't you dare talk back."

"This house is a jail, and you're the ugly old jailer." My loud words slipped out before I could swallow them.

Mom's face pinched into an angry squint that reminded me of a witch. I'd pushed her too far. She raised the spatula and came at me. I folded my arms over my face and head, ducked down, and turned away.

"Don't you talk back to me!"

She slammed my back with the spatula over and over. I screamed under the stinging blows and stumbled against the kitchen counter.

"Do what I tell you, or I'll kill you!"

The spatula crashed down again. I struggled to stand, but I turned toward her, my arms still protecting my head and face.

To my horror, I watched my arms take on a life of their own, deflecting her blows. *Oh my God, I hit her! I'm her size now, and I hit her back!*

Stunned, Mom's eyes widened, and her mouth stretched into a bloodless line. She beat me harder and faster, pausing when she saw the sharp edge of the spatula break my skin. In a flash, I pounded her arm with my closed fist, knocking the spatula out of her hand.

She lunged at me, battered me with her fists. I returned her punishment and pushed her back. Now she was crying too. Numb to her pounding blows, I hit back and shoved her away again and again.

"Mom! No!" I pleaded through my tangled, mucus-wet hair. Another hard push knocked her off balance.

We jostled our way out of the kitchen, propelling through the living room, both of us screaming through tears.

At the open outside door, the one I just entered, we lost our footing, tumbled down the cement steps, and sprawled onto the circular gravel driveway.

Stunned and lying beside Mom, my wits returned. I sat up and quick-checked her. She slowly pushed herself to a sitting position and examined her scrapes. She scowled at me, eyes flashing rage. Without speaking, she stood up, brushed off, and limped into the house.

I waited on the cement steps and took deep breaths to calm myself and clear my head. I gingerly touched my knees and felt my arms for bruises.

Minutes later, a black and white rolled into the driveway, tires crunching over the gravel. Two officers got out. Mom banged open the door and scurried down the steps to exchange words with them.

With her back to me, her words were muffled until I heard, "I think she's on drugs."

I stood on wobbly legs. "Not true! I'm not on drugs. You're lying, Mom!"

The first officer scribbled something in his notebook. The other cop opened the cruiser's back door and directed me to get in.

"I'm sorry, please don't send me to jail, Mom. Please."

"You think this is a jail?" She pointed toward our house. "Now you'll find out what jail really is."

"Get in the car, young lady." The officer held open the back door.

Suzie and Kathy, my two youngest sisters, watched from a window. I forced a weak wave at them from the back seat and wiped the tears running down my cheeks and into my mouth. I didn't want the little kids to see me upset and be afraid for me.

"What's going to happen now?" I asked the cops. *I can't believe Mom did this.*

Neither cop responded. The older gray-haired driver looked ahead at the road while the young subordinate cop with a pock-marked face wrote in his notepad.

After a minute, the driver spoke in a baritone voice without turning his head. "You gave your mother a lot of trouble. Now you're the one in trouble."

"Where are you taking me?"

"Juvie. They'll deal with the likes of you."

My heart slammed against my rib cage.

The police car rolled down an incline and slowed to a stop in an underground garage. Both officers got out, and the pock-faced one left me in a small room.

Alone and in a daze, I stood shaking next to the white plastic chairs positioned against the gray walls.

A half hour later, a big woman stepped through an electric door. A blue uniform shirt stretched tight across her huge breasts, the little white buttons straining.

"Gulling, this way."

I lost balance when the floor seemed to tilt sideways. I made myself concentrate on placing one foot in front of the other to follow her to the slaughterhouse.

She indicated a door. "Change in there."

I pulled on a light blue uniform like in the prison movies. But this was real. Far away, somebody yelled and something crashed. I willed down the sour saliva in my mouth and fought to keep from vomiting.

The same guard hustled me along a corridor lined with heavy metal doors. Each door had a small, rectangular window. Terrified of what I might see in those windows, I stared straight ahead. The walls bulged out and loomed over me, and the lights blazed down like *The Twilight Zone.*

We stopped at one of the doors. It made a loud *cli-clank* and opened.

"Here's your new home. If this doesn't straighten out your attitude, there's no hope," she said.

The door *cli-clanged* shut, leaving me alone in a small cell with bunk beds attached to opposite gray walls and a stainless-steel sink and toilet in the middle.

My spirit deflated, I chose the closest bottom bunk.

Soon the loudspeaker announced something staticky. A buzzer went off, and my cell door clanked open. I quick-swiped my hand across my wet face before two girls trudged inside.

A tall, honey-skinned girl with a shaved head glared at me. "Off my bed."

I sprang up and looked around, unsure where to sit.

"You pick the top one. I'm Phyllystyne with three y's. What your name? What you here for?"

"Um…" I choked. I didn't know what to think. I'd won spelling bees at Catholic school and wasn't sure that was the right way to spell her name.

"Can't you talk?" She moved close to me.

I stopped myself from stepping back. "My mom—we fought, and she called the cops."

"How long you here for?" Her wild eyes glistened and stared at my face.

"I don't know."

She rubbed her shaved head like she was searching for her lost hair. "My brother stay two years. You may be here longer if your mama don't want you no more." Her words faded as she looked away.

The other girl rolled over and faced the wall, silent in her lower bunk. I climbed to the top bunk, hoping Phyllystyne wouldn't murder me in my sleep.

"Play cards?" Phyllystyne asked.

"Sorry, I'm tired."

"Get your skinny ass down here and play cards," she said loudly, kicking the bottom mattress she'd claimed as her bed. "If I catch you cheating, I'll smash your head in."

"Fine." I slid off the top bunk, keeping my head down and mouth shut.

Over the next few days, I spoke only when necessary and tried to make myself invisible. I lay awake at night thinking about my grandparents. Mom probably had called and told them she put me in juvie. I never understood why she used me to cause them pain, but she did—any chance she got. She forbade me to talk to them ever since the fight over the bicycle tire my grandfather put on my bike several years ago.

I lay there drawing comfort from my favorite memories.

At one or two years old and learning to talk, my grandparents coached me on how to pronounce their last name, Beerman. They asked me to repeat "Mommy Beerman" or "Daddy Beerman." I had slurred Beerman into "Burr." From then on, I referred to them as Mommy Burr or Daddy Burr. So did my siblings.

As kids, we'd spent summers in Texas with Mommy Burr and Daddy Burr. Always concerned, Mommy Burr questioned me about home. I learned to hide my homelife from them and the rest of the world. They couldn't change things anyway.

"Mommy Burr, did you know my real dad?" I asked, almost in a whisper.

"Yes, sweetie. He came from a good family, and he adored

you." She stopped kneading the bread dough and wiped her hands on a kitchen towel.

"He's not mean?"

"Oh no. He and your mom had their troubles, but he loved you very much."

I latched onto this new information and savored the moment.

The summers with our grandparents were filled with juicy watermelon grown in their garden, honey from our grandfather's bees, and cool well-water straight from their windmill.

Daddy Burr hung rope swings on a number of trees on his parklike grounds that were bordered by rose bushes. We rode horses made of broom handles, or I drove the lawn tractor and towed my sisters behind in the wooden wagon Daddy Burr had built for us.

After dark, the fireflies came out and the crickets sang. I sat on Daddy Burr's lap while he pointed out stars and constellations. The sound of his voice warmed me. Those moments remained vivid in my heart for a lifetime.

On my third day in juvie, a lady-dispatcher called over the intercom, "Gulling, Charlotte Gulling, report to the front desk."

The clerk stamped a form and slid it across the metal desk for me to sign. I changed clothes before a guard escorted me to a crowded reception area.

Mom saw me the instant I saw her. She stood slowly, scanned me head to toe for injuries beyond the beating she'd given. Although she hit me at home, she defended me from the rest of the world.

I held myself back from running to hug and thank her for coming. Home was so much better than this place.

Driving home, Mom shot me a look. "I could have left you there, you know."

My gratitude vanished. "Thanks for coming, Mom."

False words tasted like stinky garbage in my mouth. I wanted to tell her I hated her.

"How'd they treat you?"

"Real nice."

I pushed my feet against the floorboard. She'd abandoned me, hurt me again, but now she wanted credit for saving me. A small sob escaped my throat. I hoped she didn't hear.

"Maybe you'd like to go back permanently?"

"No, ma'am." I held my breath. *Oh, God, please give me the right words to say.*

"I didn't think so. You brought this on yourself, Charlotte." Expectation weighed heavy in her scrutiny.

I turned toward the window and fought to stay strong, but teardrops escaped through my closed eyes, giving me away.

"Look at me when I'm talking to you!" She slammed her fist against the steering wheel.

My lower lip trembled.

"And stop feeling sorry for yourself. Now repeat what I said. Say, 'I brought this on myself.'"

"Yes, ma'am."

"Say it!"

"I brought this on myself." Not a hint of defiance in my tone.

"God, you're impossible. There's a pile of ironing waiting for you. I'm leaving for Vegas tomorrow, so you're in charge."

"Yes." I swallowed hard, glad she was going.

"Yes, what?" she demanded.

"Yes, ma'am." *I hate you.*

FORGET THE MAPS...
FOLLOW YOUR INSTINCTS

As soon as Mom's car disappeared around the corner, I sprinted to meet Danny.

Danny made me feel like I mattered to someone.

"Your sister told me your mother sent you to the Hall."

"She hates me, and I hate her too. We got in a fight, and I hit her back for once." I liked the thought of hitting her back.

"So, what happened in there?"

"Horrible. Scared every minute, especially of this crazy girl in my cell. And the food tasted awful."

"Oh man, your mom's really a bitch."

I shifted my weight from foot to foot, holding back a retort, a natural defense of my mother. I hated when someone said anything bad about Mom, even if they were right. My siblings and I had the right to bad-mouth her, but nobody else. It still felt wrong to tell on her to the outside world, even to Danny.

Danny cupped his hands and lit a cigarette, waved the match out, then looked up. "Let's run away."

"What?"

"Run away. There's a house, not far, where the family left on vacation. We can live there while they're gone. They probably have food and everything."

"What if they catch us? Mom will throw me in jail forever."
She'll beat me to death first, though.

Danny crumpled his empty Winston pack into a ball. "Think about it. You'll be free from everyone's stupid rules. Besides, anything's better than living at the Hall, right? We'll never come back."

I tugged at my embroidered Mexican blouse and imagined running away.

"I'm worried Mom will call Dad overseas. If she does that—" I stopped.

I didn't fear my mother as much since I'd stood up to her, but my stepfather presented a greater challenge.

I didn't see it at the time, but I mirrored my mother in many ways, good and bad. I rebelled against my circumstances like she rebelled against hers by running off to Las Vegas and having affairs.

"They won't catch us," Danny insisted. "The owners won't even know we stayed there. After a few weeks, we can find another place to hang out."

Sounded like heaven. Freedom from Mom's beatings, from all the work of taking care of seven kids, doing laundry, cooking meals—so many chores. Danny's plan gave us the chance to be together all the time and go wherever we wanted. I'd be free. I fantasized about growing up and leaving home at eighteen, but it could happen now if I left with Danny.

"Okay, but I can't go until Mom comes back," I said. "My sisters will be scared if they're left alone at night."

I needed to be there when the rats ran through our house after dark, but I didn't tell Danny that. His home always appeared so clean.

Three days later, Mom returned from Las Vegas. She walked in to find Mary Lou and me cooking dinner, Theresa making iced tea, Jacquie setting the table, and Shirley sweeping the floor. Dave had already emptied the trash. Suzie and Kathy sat perched on the countertop, talking to us.

Mom looked around and said, "Good job, kids. You're all big enough to take care of yourselves."

Blood rose to my cheeks. "Thanks, Mom." I controlled my words and made my voice sweet, not sarcastic.

That night, I hugged my sisters and brother, knowing that when I escaped, I'd never come back. They wriggled out of my arms and ran off.

"Ew," my brother said over his shoulder as he scampered away. He hated it when his big sisters hugged or kissed his rosy cheeks, but we found him irresistible.

When the house got dark and quiet, I climbed out my window to meet Danny and his sixteen-year-old buddy who had a car. His friend dropped us off at the empty house.

Around the back, I held the flashlight for Danny. The light jiggled with my trembling hand. He jammed the screwdriver in the backdoor lock, twisting and prying, then pushing his shoulder against the door until it gave.

My heart slammed so hard against my ribs, I thought I heard a bone crack.

We remained still in the shadowy laundry room, listening. Someone or something might pounce out from a dark corner any minute. An intoxicating rush tingled from my fingertips to my toes.

We crept through the house.

"Don't turn on any lights. Neighbors might notice," Danny whispered.

The filtered light from the streetlamp allowed me to see the L-shaped lime-green couch and mod circular designs on the silver wallpaper. The home looked like a house from a TV show.

We found Cokes and frozen food but nothing cool to wear. The family photos on the refrigerator showed kids playing badminton in their swimming pool. Guilt crept through me for invading their happy home.

Danny moved in close behind me and whispered, "Let's go watch TV."

I slipped off my tennis shoes and padded in my socks behind him to the living room.

We watched *Godzilla* reruns. It was almost daybreak when the National Anthem woke us. We made our way down the hall to the master bedroom. Danny bounced onto the large bed. He lay back with his fingers interlaced behind his head, legs crossed at the ankles, fully clothed. My nerves jumped. Was I ready for this?

"We better stay dressed in case we have to split during the night." A tiny smile played on his full lips.

"Yeah, good idea," I said quickly.

I lay on my back next to Danny, relieved. I wasn't ready to take off my clothes. I found his hand and held it.

Danny smelled like his leather jacket even without wearing it. Leather mixed with the smell of Juicy Fruit gum. I drank him in and let his scent intoxicate me. The weight of the world spun away, and I drifted off in a twilight sleep, floating in the fantasy of achieving my freedom at last.

The next day, sitting cross-legged on the beige living room carpet, Danny lit a strange cigarette.

"You ever seen pot before?" he asked.

"Pot? No."

"Check this out. It's a joint. Marijuana. Do it like this." He took a deep draw on the hand-rolled cigarette, held the smoke in his lungs, then coughed ferociously. "It'll make you think you're walking on clouds." He barely squeaked out the words before coughing again.

I smoked it like he did and coughed so hard my throat burned. I rubbed the sting of smoke from my eyes. A few minutes later, the living room curtains, patterned with large orange and green geometrical shapes of circles and triangles, took on a richer, brighter hue. My first high felt like I'd sailed through a child's storybook.

I glided over to the stereo and cranked up Jefferson Airplane's "White Rabbit" but quickly turned it back down, fearing the neighbors might hear.

Danny pushed back on the brown leather recliner, wearing a big grin. Life had never felt so good. I laughed hysterically at everything.

"I'm starving," Danny said. "There's TV dinners in the freezer, or we can walk to Taco Bell."

"You always have money. Where—"

"I was saving my allowance for a new stereo. I brought all my money to take care of us." Pride resonated in his voice.

He pushed out of the recliner, and we lay together on the shag carpet. He rolled on his side, pulled me close, and kissed me with his mouth closed, shaking. We stretched out to full body contact, even our toes touching.

The album ended, and the house went silent as if waiting for us to do something. I'd never kissed a boy before Danny. Sinking into him, I let my kiss linger on his puffy lips like I'd learned from watching TV. The smell of Juicy Fruit blended with boy sweat made me delirious.

"Let's do it," he whispered in my ear.

I stopped myself before saying, "Do what?"

He unbuttoned his shirt and waited. I traced my trembling fingers along his hairless chest before pulling back. Not the daring girl I pretended to be, I whispered, "I'm scared."

"Why?"

"Just am." *Maybe it'll hurt or I'll bleed on the light-colored carpet. What if I hate it?* Mom had never told me anything about sex. What little I knew, I'd learned from Angela at school.

Danny ran his hand under the back of my sweater and fumbled with my bra clasp. I sat up, twisted away from him for privacy, pulled the sweater over my head, and shook out my hair like a shampoo commercial. Unclipping my bra, I let it slide down my arms. Completely naked from the waist up, I hesitated.

I finally faced him. A crack of diffused streetlight shone through the curtained picture window and lit his face. He stared at my chest like an eager child but flinched when a neighbor's dog barked, which made me flinch.

Face to face, laying stretched out on the living room shag carpet, goosebumps trickled where he touched my breasts. He lightly pinched my nipple, causing me to twitch, then trailed with his index finger down my stomach to my crotch where he rubbed the outside of my jeans. I rubbed the outside of his jeans but stopped, wondering what to do next. The air got still, as if the house held its breath anticipating our next move.

"Take off your pants," he said.

Now our naked bodies stretched out side-by-side in full contact. I felt his body tremble—or was it mine? His erection, raw and exposed, pressed hard against me, smooth and dangerous.

"I love you," I whispered before he kissed me.

Danny and I played house for two weeks. We spent every second together, shared every thought, and I fell more deeply in love.

Even still, I worried about my sisters.

"I've got to see Mary Lou," I told Danny. "She must be going crazy doing all the extra work. I want to make sure she's all right." I missed her more than anyone, except maybe the horses.

Beyond the chain-link fence which bordered Mary Lou's school's soccer field, I spotted one of her friends. "Hey, can you get my sister?" I asked.

Minutes later, Mary Lou trotted around the corner of the building. Her face lit up when she saw me, leaving me with a tender feeling in my chest and a vague prickling in my eyes. I rushed to the gate and grabbed her for a hug.

"I've missed you, Boosie," I said, using her nickname.

I pulled back and took in her bounce and energy. Seeing the familiar gleam in her crystal-blue eyes made mine well up and threaten to spill over.

"Yeah, me too. You've been gone so long," she said. "Where'd you go?"

"A nice house not far from here." I hoped I sounded grown-up, but a twitch of longing pulled me toward home.

Her voice got low. "Dad's home."

I jumped back. "What? He came home because of me?"

"Uh-huh. After you left, Mom went nuts and called him in Vietnam. He's home on emergency, but he'll go back soon. He said if I saw you, I should tell you to come home while he's still here, and you won't get in trouble."

With steady eye contact, I asked her, "Do you believe that?"
"No."

I never wanted to go back to my homelife with Mom's demands and abuse, but deep down, a steady tug pulled me like an ocean undertow. I imagined Mom running back to Las Vegas after Dad returned to Vietnam, leaving the kids without anyone at night.

Danny said he missed his friends from the neighborhood, but I think he missed his home too.

"Let's go to Kevin's house and see everybody," he said.

Everyone at Kevin's had welcomed me when I'd snuck out to meet Danny that first night. His friends had naturally included me, something I seldom felt except with my siblings.

"Cops might look for us there," I said, "so let's wear disguises. You can wear the wig we found in the closet, and I'll dye my hair black."

Two nights later, in our new disguises, we received a happy welcome from our friends. Danny's younger brother, Julian, stopped his dart game when he saw us enter the recreation garage. Danny grabbed him in a bear hug. "Wow, good to see you, bro!"

Julian shook him off. "Dad's pissed at you."

Danny snorted. "He'll get over it."

Julian looked from Danny's wig to my dyed hair, shook his head, and left.

"Do you think he'll tell your dad we're here?"

"No. My brother's a jerk, but he's not a snitch."

Julian brooded a lot, always resentful of Danny. I didn't share Danny's faith in his loyalty.

For a half hour, we sat around the rec room and enjoyed watching our friends' mouths drop open when they heard stories of our adventure, how we "borrowed" a house, ate the food we found, and lived free like daredevils.

Headlights flashed through the flowery curtains covering the glass sliders.

"Cops!" Danny said. "Julian ratted us out."

We raced out the back door. Danny's wig flew off and landed in the pool. A spotlight flashed on behind us, making our shadows huge on the cement-block wall fencing the yard. I gripped the top of the wall to hoist myself up. Danny scaled to the top, but a cop grabbed his leg and yanked him to the ground.

"Okay, kids. Game over."

I never saw Danny again.

They put Danny and me in two different police cars and drove us to the station, where we waited in separate rooms for our parents. Worried about Mom's reaction to my dark hair, I chewed my bottom lip till it hurt.

Mom's eyes grew big. "Oh no! Your hair!"

I touched my head. Dad stepped from behind Mom. I caught my breath and bit my tongue so hard I tasted blood. He moved with his usual determination, face solemn and eyes pressed together seriously. I swallowed my blood down.

Why is he still home from Vietnam?

I could handle Mom's abuse, sort of, but Dad's? Take me back to juvie. Anywhere except home with him.

A polite, intelligent man to the world, Dad thanked and shook hands with the officers who'd found me.

On the way home, silence swelled to fill the inside of the car. It smelled hot like bad breath. Mom said a few words I couldn't make out from the backseat. Dad remained quiet. Dark outside, a million pebbles of rain hammered down on the car. The windshield wipers fought the downpour when a crack of lightning spidered across the sky, and a boom of thunder rolled behind it. Lightning and thunder often occurred at my grandparents' place in Texas, but never in Southern California. It was strange to hear it now, like God was warning me of my fate.

The headlights from other cars briefly illuminated Dad's face in the rear-view mirror. I withered under his stare. Chills crawled like ants over my body. I hadn't seen him in months, but it wasn't long enough. He looked the same. Tall and lanky, with dark receding hair, a narrow face, and hollow cheeks. Clothes draped on his bony frame, though with the way he ate, you'd think he'd be overweight.

A responsible, helpful father to his own seven children, he spared little approval or attention for me, his stepchild.

In the backseat, I moved as far from him as possible, wedging myself into the crack between the seat and the door.

At home, I hurried inside to see my siblings. I got hugs all around and questions about my hair.

"Charlotte, look! Dad brought us a pinball machine from Vietnam."

They all talked at the same time, excited to show me the upright pinball machine. So close to each of them, I never told them about my fear of their Dad. They loved him, and they'd feel confused or maybe not even believe me if I told them.

Now is the best time to take a shower. Nobody will miss me in all the competition playing pinball.

I escaped to the bathroom. The steam rolled as the shower sprayed needles of hot water on my back, warming me to my bones.

Sounds came from outside the bathroom door. More thunder?

The bathroom door banged open.

"Hey, I'm in here!" I shouted.

Dad yanked back the shower curtain.

"Oh my God! Dad!" I wrapped my bare arms around myself, trying to cover up.

He swung his belt, whipping me again and again. I crouched in the corner of the tub, shrieking and trying to hide my privates. Face grim and eyes piercing, he stared at my crotch and breasts, which I hid partially with my hands. He swung his belt against my back, my buttocks, everywhere. Folded in a ball, shower running, I made myself as small as possible.

Even after he left the bathroom, my sobs continued from the shame of him seeing me naked.

Covered in welts, I crawled into bed, hardly able to move. The tip of a red pocketknife stuck out from under some clothes on the dresser. I carved my agony into the old, chipped headboard: "Help me, God." God couldn't miss my plea because I dug the words deep. I prayed for an angel to fly me far away from this hideous house.

I eased over to find a sleeping position that didn't hurt. I'll never forget Dad's rage, his beady eyes staring at my naked body. I hated him for beating me, but I wondered if I deserved it.

He'd first beaten me at a much younger age. My earliest memory was of him beating me. I was around two or three years old. Sometimes I didn't make it to the bathroom before I wet my pants.

I remember tiptoeing to the kitchen and squinting up at Mom. So terrified, my words refused to come.

Mom looked down from the kitchen sink, where her hands hid beneath the suds. "What, Charlotte?"

"I wet my pants." I whimpered and rubbed my teary face with the back of my hand. Mom leaned against the sink toward the window, searching the backyard.

"I have to tell your father."

"No, please. Mom, no." My voice faltered. A jumble of desperate feelings roared through me. Mostly fear for my life. Nothing scared me more than that tall man.

"I promise I won't do it again. No, Mom. Don't tell him. Please."

She wouldn't look at me.

"Mom!"

The screen door banged closed behind Dad.

My fear was so strong it distorted Mom's words. The huge stranger towered over me, eyes fixed on me, his mouth pressed tight and his dark eyes full of hatred for me.

He jerked me up by one arm.

I screamed, "Mom!"

He hauled me to the bathroom. He yanked my clothes off, suspended me by my skinny arm over the tub, and beat me with his free hand. My eyes traveled upward to see his huge hand covering mine in midair. The force of his blows caused me to twist and turn as I kicked air. Mercifully, I went numb, somehow removed myself, but the picture of my body dangling over the tub was fixed in my mind forever.

On that day, when I lost control and wet my pants, my mother—my only security in the world—stood by while her new husband beat her only child. I knew I must have been bad, that I had deserved it. My body became my shame.

Even lying in the bed more than a decade later, I could still hear the sound of my little-girl screams echoing in the bathroom.

Mommy!

I've wondered about my mother's state of mind during that time, in the mid-1950s. She married at eighteen, divorced my biological father, and jumped quickly into her second marriage, bringing her two-year-old daughter with her. In those days, women found few alternatives after leaving their parents' home. Their expected pathway. Marriage and children. Not much had changed.

In the twenty-first century, the idea that women have choices is illusory. We do compared to women in developing countries, but our oppression is subtler, hidden under the notion that we can have it all. Sure, we can balance children, cooking, household duties, and a full-time job while making less money for doing twice the work of our male counterparts. Is that what "having it all" means?

My young mother, a product of her environment, needed her parents or a husband to survive. If things got uncomfortable for the subordinate partner, so be it. Capable of more but finding no opportunity to contribute her creative energy, earn validation, or enjoy herself outside her role as a wife and mother of eight kids, she eventually found another outlet. She used her looks and charm to attract affairs.

My stepfather beat me other times throughout the years. At around thirteen, he pulled my underpants down, laid me across his lap, and spanked me. Nothing so severe as the first time as a toddler or as a fourteen-year-old girl naked in the shower, but I knew this six-foot-three marine would kill me if given the opportunity.

I burrowed deep in my pillow and found relief thinking about my grandparents, their warm embrace and quiet home. I never told them about these beatings, not even during those summers we stayed with them in Texas while Mom and Dad spent time away.

The summer I was seven, I remember watching my grandmother through the mirror of her vanity while she stood behind me. She braided my hair in pigtails and tied the ends with pink bows. Five of us had been born by that time, and my sisters waited their turn to get their hair brushed and braided. David, not yet a year old, slept in his playpen nearby.

"Charlotte, how are they treating you at home?" Mommy Burr asked, her voice so soft only I could hear her.

I bent my head down and didn't answer. I didn't want to talk about it. I didn't want to disturb my grandparents' gentle spirits. I never told anyone about life at home. Why had she asked me that?

Lying in bed after the beating in the shower, waves of quiet sobs rolled through me. I tried to replace the picture of Dad's angry face with the memory of Mommy Burr brushing my hair—her throaty chuckle—and Daddy Burr's kind demeanor. I yearned for them. They lived far away, and I didn't dare use the phone. Mom had forbidden me to speak to them. I fell asleep through tears and hiccups, holding their memory close, knowing I'd see them again one day. They loved me, and nobody's hate could destroy that.

LA-LA LAND

The next day, back and legs tender, I woke from an agitated sleep. Humiliation filled me as I remembered Dad had seen my naked body. The image of his face and the leather belt lashing me again and again refused to leave my mind. I dreaded seeing him and having to pretend everything was okay when it wasn't. I wished he'd die in Vietnam.

I got out of bed and gingerly slid on my T-shirt and jeans, every movement painful. The dirty breakfast dishes waited while I finished eating my cereal. I scrubbed the dishes in a tangle of confusion and flinched when Mom called me from the bathroom.

"Charlotte, get in here."

My throat constricted, holding down fear vomit. *What did I do wrong this time?*

I dried my hands on a dishtowel, dragged myself to the bathroom, temples throbbing.

Mom and Dad faced me from inside the bathroom.

"In here, now," Dad said, holding the door open.

I made myself take a tentative step. Dad yanked me in and shut the door behind me. They sandwiched me between them. Mom held up scissors.

"Oh no, Mom, what are you going to do?" I begged her

silently to help me and not betray me like she had her two-year-old child.

I backed up against the closed door, but Dad grabbed me, pushing me to the floor.

I kicked at him. "No!"

He knelt across my legs and pinned my arms. His weight hurt. His knees dug in, almost breaking my bony shins.

"Hold still or we'll cut off your ear." He snorted.

Mom chopped my hair close to my scalp like they did in insane asylum movies. She pulled and cut. I screamed in pain. Dad stood up. I scooted away and kicked.

Snot and tears smeared my face, but I managed to utter words through my horror. "I hate you."

I froze on the floor watching Dad's eyes grow into a dark, slit-eyed stare. He made a growling sound. "When are you going to learn to keep your mouth shut, little girl?"

"Pick up this hair. Clean the bathroom," Mom said before they walked out.

Shorn black hair lay all around me. I stood up, avoiding the mirror.

Let me die. Even Mom wanted me dead, so why didn't they go ahead and kill me? Why did they hate me so much? Because I resisted their crushing control? Dad hated me because I was another man's daughter. Why did Mom hate me? Because her parents cared about me?

I woke repeatedly during the night, sobbing each time I felt my butchered scalp. The next morning, a scarecrow with jagged hair and swollen eyelids stared back at me in the mirror.

How can I go to school like this?

Mom entered my room, catching me staring at myself. I didn't dare utter a word.

"You're not going to school today," she said. "I'm taking you to the beauty shop to get your hair cut right and colored back to blond."

Thank God she didn't make me face the mean girls with chopped-off black hair.

Did Mom feel guilty and want to make things right? I suspected she took me to the beauty shop to hide what she and Dad had done. Even if someone had discovered what happened, what could they do? Neighbors, teachers—not even my grandparents had the right to involve themselves in a family's private issues in 1967, so they looked the other way.

The following day at school, Angela took in my short, blond hair. "Wow, you never said you wanted to cut your hair. It's so short."

"Yeah, I wanted a change." I rubbed my neck and looked away.

Angela, sensing my discomfort, dropped the subject.

We walked to class.

I yearned for Mom to act like she cared when Dad beat me. I lived without Dad's love—he'd always been distant anyway—but I hated to think Mom had known about every beating and stood by, complacent. There was no denying she knew about the first beating when I was two. Maybe she thought she had to stand by her man and show a united front with her new husband, even if it meant betraying her only child.

Sometimes Mom called me by the nickname she gave me, Charlie. She said it with affection, and sometimes she said it in front of the whole family, even Dad. Mom often expressed her gratitude to me for helping raise my sisters and brother, but she never acknowledged that oftentimes, I raised them on my own.

When I was about nine, I fell while playing outside and broke my left arm in two places. I stumbled through the front door, wailing and propping my arm up using my right hand. The bone stuck out through my skin. As if for a small bird with a broken wing, Dad brought me a pillow, but he lacked sympathy beyond that.

We were a single-car family, so Dad called the beauty salon and ordered Mom home to take me to the base doctor.

I stared at my exposed bone and wailed so loud, Dad couldn't hear Mom on the other end of the line. He raised his flat hand, ready to hit me if I didn't shut up. He forbade me to be a helpless little girl who needed him. Dad had kept the commitment he made to Mom to care for me when he married her, but he never promised to love me.

I stood outside on the front steps waiting, arm pulsing with pain. Within minutes, Mom's tires squealed around the corner. The car bounced into our driveway. She sprung out, big curlers in her hair, and raced toward me.

After the shower beating and chopping off my hair, Dad returned to Vietnam, but not before he and Mom put me on restriction for a month. "Restriction" meant I stayed home after school and on weekends and wasn't permitted to ride the horses. I did my chores in silence, counting the months and years until I turned eighteen and could see Danny again.

I sometimes confided in Mary Lou, but she had her own problems with Mom and Dad. We seldom talked about being beaten—except the time Mary Lou described how Mom had almost choked her to death. Dad, hearing Mary Lou's screams, rushed to the bedroom and pulled Mom off a blue Mary Lou, almost too late.

I lived in silence and secrecy. Maybe Mary Lou felt the same way because sadness shaded her bright blue eyes more every year.

A few months later, Mom noticed my ragged appearance and the dark circles under my eyes. "What's wrong with you lately? You're always down. Are you okay?"

"Mom, I think—" My hand flew to my stomach.

Her eyes followed my hand down to my middle. Her jaw dropped as realization spread across her face. "Oh, God, no. You're pregnant."

"No! I don't know, Mom. I missed one period so far."

"By God, I'm not raising another kid."

I prayed for a way out of this mess. I wanted my life over or to wake up from this bad dream—anything but this. During classes at school, my absent period dominated my thoughts.

Mom took me to the base doctor for an examination. I waited for the test results, barely able to breathe, hoping the doctor would discover an illness had stopped my period. Instead, he confirmed my pregnancy. I followed Mom out of the doctor's office in a blind trance. My life would change now, but how?

In the car, Mom said, "I'm taking you to Danny's house to talk to his parents." She sounded like a Southern Belle.

"Mom, no. I don't want to see him."

"Danny's the father, isn't he?"

"Yes, I've never been with another boy."

She stared at me from the driver's seat. "This happened when you ran away, didn't it? Well, you're not living at home around the kids, walking around pregnant."

"Where will I go?"

"I don't know. Don't even think about keeping this kid. A baby will ruin your life like you kids did mine."

"Maybe Mommy Burr and Daddy Burr will let me stay with them." *Oh, please.*

"You're not calling Mother and Dad. They're too old to take on your problems."

The next day, after Mom telephoned Danny's mother and asked to come by for a face-to-face meeting, I sat beside her on the edge of the dark plaid couch in the Ruiz's living room. Danny's parents sat in overstuffed chairs across from us. No Danny. I didn't ask his whereabouts. He was probably hiding out somewhere. I wanted to run and hide too. My teeth ground together and knees bounced.

The Ruiz's suburban home always appeared tidy, like the brick-red crocheted blanket lying folded and draped across the back of the couch. I had visited their home several times with Danny, but everything looked different and magnified under these circumstances.

"I told you on the phone, my daughter's pregnant by your son," Mom said.

"We understand." Mrs. Ruiz wrung her hands.

"What do you suggest we do about this?" Mom asked. "Abortion's illegal, and I haven't found a sympathetic doctor who'll do it anyway. We have another appointment to see a different doctor in La Jolla next week, but if you know someone—"

"Abortion's illegal, and it's also against our faith. Yours too, I believe. Abortion is out of the question," Mr. Ruiz said.

Mrs. Ruiz leaned forward. "Is that what you want, Charlotte?"

"Well, no, but I'm not sure what..." I said what they wanted me to say, but I really wanted my mistake erased. That's what Mom wanted too.

Mom raised her hand to silence me. "It doesn't matter what

she wants. I'm trying to help my daughter. Her life will be ruined if she has this baby. What other solution is there?"

"They can get married," Mr. Ruiz said.

"Absurd." Red blotches appeared on Mom's face. "She'll be sixteen when she gives birth. How will they live? Where will they live?"

"We got married at fifteen, and it all worked out," Mrs. Ruiz said.

Mom ignored her remark, grabbed her purse, and stood up. "This is a waste of time. I need solutions, an abortion doctor, not ridiculous ideas. Let's go, Charlotte."

On the way home, Mom said, "If you want me to help you, keep your mouth shut—unless you want to ruin your life by getting stuck raising kids."

After the La Jolla doctor refused to perform an abortion, Mom drove me to meet her friend, Evelyn Landry, who lived in Laguna Beach.

In the car on the way down the coast, Mom said, "Evelyn and I met in Yuma at a military function five years ago. Her husband's in Vietnam like Dad. You'll live with her and her eleven-year-old son until you deliver."

"Why can't I live with Mommy Burr and Daddy Burr?"

"Because I said so."

It was her usual response. I knew better than to question her further.

We snaked our way through the hilly neighborhoods above Laguna Beach as expansive views of the coastal village spread out below. Bordering Laguna, the blue Pacific Ocean stretched across the horizon. The pastel stucco houses all looked alike with perfect lawns, hedges, and two-car garages—like Danny's neighborhood.

We stopped near the crest of the hill. I got out, turned my face to the sun, and inhaled the clean scent of ocean air mixed with honeysuckle.

A large lady with an open, toothy smile, frizzy blond hair, and beige slacks stood at the front door. "You found it."

We sat on Evelyn's flowered fabric sofa while she and Mom drank coffee fresh from the percolator. An Irish setter bounced in and chewed on a dirty fabric doll.

"This is Clancy," Evelyn said. "He gets worked up when he meets new people, but he's friendly."

On the light blue carpeted floor, Clancy and I played tug-of-war. His long red hair, brushed to a shimmer, smelled like vanilla cookies.

"I need someone to take care of Joey when I'm not home, help him with his homework, keep the house in order, do laundry. Do you cook, Charlotte?" She looked directly at me and waited.

Before I answered, Mom said, "She can cook, clean house, iron, and everything else. She's helped me raise her brother and sisters ever since she could reach the sink."

Evelyn watched and waited for me to answer.

"Mrs. Landry, I'd love to take care of your son. I'll learn your favorite recipes and cook for you both every night."

Mom's shoulders relaxed, so I relaxed. I had said the right thing. Everyone looked pleased.

Would this nice lady really let me live with her in this clean, quiet home? If I did a good job, maybe she'd let me stay forever.

Weeks later, I set my brown suitcase in the hallway of Evelyn's house. Not sure what to bring, I had packed my drawing pad, pencils, jeans, and T-shirts. On the way, we'd stopped at the PX where Mom bought me several items she thought I'd need.

Evelyn chatted and guided us through the house. She opened the door to present Joey's bedroom. Model fighter jets hung from the ceiling, and matching plaid bedspreads covered his bunk beds. I'd met Joey a few weeks earlier when Mom first brought me to meet Evelyn. His reddish hair, braces, and freckled face made it easy to like him. He reminded me of the dog, Clancy, with the way he carried himself in a gangly, loping manner.

He saw me admiring his model jets and grinned from ear to ear. "My dad and I built them together." The reverence in his tone when he spoke of his dad was palpable.

Evelyn opened the door at the end of the hall. "Here's your room, Charlotte. I picked up this bedspread at the PX last week. Do you like it? If not, we can return it and get something else."

I stepped in and caught my breath. "I love it." I didn't want to sound too excited, fearing Mom might resent my happiness.

"This is adorable," Mom said under her breath.

My bedroom, smaller than the others, had a large, framed poster on the wall above a double bed with a purple paisley bedspread. The poster featured the silhouette of a girl standing next to her upright surfboard, the water sparkling in the sunset behind her. A shiny white dresser with gold pull handles and a large, curved mirror completed my room. I'd never seen a bedroom like this. It looked as though it belonged to *Gidget*.

Joey shuffled down the hallway in his lazy, lanky gait, followed by Clancy walking the same way.

"I'm going to Roger's house," he said to his mother.

He didn't ask for permission but just told his mother his plans. Seemed strange.

Most nights, Joey and I did our homework facing each other across the kitchen table. Mom notified my high school, inquired about a home-study program, and arranged a tutor to show up once a week to assign me schoolwork. The tutor, a soft-spoken woman in her twenties, often stayed after our session, and we talked about the horses I'd left behind at home or my brother and sisters. She was my only friend, and I never wanted her to leave.

Unloading the dishwasher, a reflection caught my eye. "Your dishes are so pretty, but the drinking cups are made of glass. What if one breaks?"

Evelyn shrugged as if my question baffled her. "I'll buy a new one."

Her voice sounded casual, as if breaking things were no big deal, unlike Mom. Evelyn's patient demeanor reminded me of Mommy Burr, and I liked her more for it.

When we went grocery shopping at the commissary, Evelyn didn't buy fifteen gallons of milk to cram in the freezer like Mom did. Evelyn bought one gallon to slide into the refrigerator. I didn't fault Mom for buying so much milk. After all, we were a bunch of growing kids. We were permitted milk only on our morning cereal, but that amounted to at least a gallon per day. It magnified the difference between the simplicity of a small family versus a large one.

"Charlotte, smell this bubble bath. Do you want some?" For the hundredth time, Evelyn surprised me when she cared about my opinion and even wanted to buy me things.

Every day I expected stress or anger to pop out of Evelyn like a crazy jack-in-the-box and destroy our tranquility. But she didn't get mad or even raise her voice at Joey or me. She never told Joey she wished she'd never had him or that he'd ruined her life. If Joey did something she didn't like, she sat him down and talked to him face-to-face. Joey respected her and never talked back, but he tested the boundaries from time to time.

I spent the day alone while Joey attended school. Evelyn didn't work but routinely left the house to run errands, play bridge, and do other things. Travel programs and teenage beach volleyball shows filled my time. Clancy and I became friends, but loneliness dominated the day.

I wrote to Mommy Burr and Daddy Burr and gave them my new address. Mom called them and complained about the embarrassment I brought to the family by getting pregnant.

Many nights, I lay in bed fantasizing about Danny finding me and tapping on my bedroom window. Not because I wanted to run away again, but because I wanted to see him. I wanted him to rescue me from my emptiness and my fear of having his baby alone.

I rubbed my belly in circles, wondering about the tiny life growing inside me. Babies meant diapers, chaos, crying, and tons of work. I couldn't imagine why anyone chose to birth a kid, let alone raise one. What did I want? A normal teenage life like the girls on TV who had nice parents and one brother or sister—not that I didn't want my siblings. I loved each and every one of them.

I heard about miscarriages and sometimes wished for one so all this would be over. Then I could return to school, see Danny, play games with my siblings, and ride the horses.

Mommy Burr wrote me every week, and I wrote back. Since I hadn't been permitted to contact my grandparents for several years, many things were left unsaid. I never told them I'd rather be with them more than anywhere else in the world. My loneliness would only sadden them.

Another big box arrived in the mail from Mommy Burr containing billowy blouses she'd sewn for me that doubled as maternity clothes. So excited to receive something new, I wrote back, thanking her repeatedly. I told my grandparents about the subjects I studied, looked for anything to write about, but my life contained no new news. She wrote about their garden, canning green beans, and the fact they needed a good, slow rain to nourish the Texas hill country.

Mom drove down the coast to take me to my doctor's appointments, and sometimes we'd go to lunch afterward. I cherished every moment with her. I hoped she'd forgive me for causing her so much trouble, but I didn't voice my feelings. I wasn't sure how.

"I'm playing bridge today and will go on to happy hour. Will you please fix dinner again?"

"Sure, Mrs. Landry. We'll play Monopoly after we eat. Right, Joey?"

Joey threw his hands up and let them drop. "What about my science model, Mom?"

"Charlotte can help you. I'll take you to the beach this weekend to make up for it."

Joey blew out a puff of air. "You said that before. You promised—"

Evelyn grabbed her purse and keys off the counter. "All right, Joey, stop."

On many evenings, Joey and I ate dinner alone, did our homework, and played board games. I understood. He missed his mother like I missed mine.

"Hey, I want to ask you something," Joey said one afternoon. He stared at his feet, avoiding eye contact. "The school dance is next month. Will you, um, be my date?"

He rocked onto the edge of his shoes then back to the flats, still not looking at me. This kind of question from a bashful sixth-grader took me by surprise. His long, blond-tipped red lashes hid his downcast eyes.

"Have you asked your mom?"

"No, but I will. She'll say yes…if you want to go."

The next day, Evelyn pulled me aside. "Charlotte, I told Joey you're too old for him to take to the dance. Truth is, when the dance comes around next month, you'll be seven months along and might show. Now he's mad at me."

"I'll talk to him, Mrs. Landry."

"Good, and please call me Evelyn."

I wasn't accustomed to an environment where a kid's feelings mattered, or where you addressed an adult by their first name. But after a time, I relaxed into the ease of living with them.

I watched the ocean waves spray and swirl over the sand as Evelyn and I drove north along Highway 1. Teenagers played volleyball on the beaches like nothing else mattered in the world. I longed for a life like that—carefree, hanging out with friends, and reveling in the sun.

Evelyn turned down the Beach Boys' song playing on the car radio. "You look far away. What's on your mind?"

"Oh, not much. Did you ever get ahold of Mom?"

"No. I called a few times this week, but whoever answered said she wasn't home. Don't worry. I'm sure she'll be happy to see you."

The closer we got to the house, the faster my legs jiggled, partly from excitement to see my brother and sisters and partly because Mom didn't like guests to drop by unannounced.

"I hope Mom's okay with this visit." My voice cracked.

"She'll be happy to see you, Charlotte."

We rounded the corner and saw Mom's car gone. Relieved, I barged through the front door and stopped, waiting for my eyesight to adjust to the dim light inside. The house smelled funny, like mold.

"Mary Lou," I shouted. "Theresa, Shirley, David, Jacquie, Sue, Kathy! Anyone here?"

"Charlotte!" Mary Lou rushed down the stairs. I grabbed and gathered her into a hug.

"I've missed you, Boosie," I said. "This is Evelyn, the lady I live with."

"Hi." Mary Lou eyed Evelyn.

"Where's Mom?" I said.

"Vegas. Don't know when she'll be back."

My other sisters ran in, followed by Dave. Evelyn scanned the dirty floors, torn carpet, and three-foot pile of clothes on the sofa waiting to be folded.

I tensed up again. As awful as our homelife looked, it was all we had. We kept our house business to ourselves, and I didn't want judgment or sympathy from anyone.

Mary Lou brought me out of my thoughts. "Are you back for good now?"

"Not yet. Oh no. What happened to Speedy's back leg?" I kneeled, wrapped my arms around our German shepherd.

"Amputated. Infection. Vet said we waited too long."

Anger at Mom's lack of empathy bubbled up in me. She didn't care about Speedy's leg, our house, or the kids—only herself and her boyfriends.

"Can he still run with the horses?" I coughed past the lump in my throat, afraid of Mary Lou's answer.

"Oh yeah. He's fast as ever." She crouched down beside me and stroked Speedy as if to reassure him and me.

Like Mary Lou, I said good things to outsiders about our family. But when we locked eyes, I glimpsed past her guarded words. Her eyes glimmered with things she wanted to say. Evelyn studied each of us as we talked. I avoided looking at her, embarrassed by our home. It was none of her business.

I stood in the center of our smelly living room, looked around, and noticed my sisters' bright, hopeful expressions contrasted against the stretched-out T-shirts and droopy underwear they wore, and Speedy's amputated leg. Evelyn and I would head back to Laguna Beach soon—to an airy, beautiful home, clean and brimming with love. *I want to take all the kids with us. Speedy and the horses too.*

Evelyn woke me from my thoughts when she said, "We better go. Your appointment."

She meant my monthly adoption agency meeting. I didn't want to leave—even to go back to Evelyn's beautiful house. A strong undertow pulled me toward my brother and sisters with their sweet, expectant faces.

Mary Lou motioned, pretending she wanted to show me something in the dining room.

"About Danny," she said, her voice low. "Um, he has a new girlfriend."

"What?" I stared at her trying to comprehend.

"He's got a new girlfriend, Charlotte."

My head spun. I swayed and leaned against the wall, feeling as though all the air had been knocked out of me.

I held a frozen face as though this information didn't matter, but Mary Lou looked deep into my averted eyes and saw right down to the truth.

Evelyn found us in the dining room. "Are you ready? Let's not be late. What's wrong?"

I sputtered out the words, "I'm okay. Just a little dizzy."

A picture of Danny loving another girl was plastered to the forefront of my mind on a giant screen. He said he loved me more than anything, but now he'd betrayed me. I gave him my deepest love, trust, and even my virginity, and he abandoned and humiliated me while I carried his baby. I didn't want to believe what Mary Lou had told me. Maybe someone lied to her. But I felt the truth of her words, and they deflated me. An unbearable disgust rose in me. I hated Danny as much as I'd once loved him.

MY ANGEL BABY 6

The adoption counselor wore lightly tinted glasses, and her white hair puffed out like milkweed. She sat behind her gray metal desk and scribbled in a yellow manila folder.

She glanced up when I took a chair. We exchanged greetings and got down to business.

"My notes say you saw the doctor last week. How did your visit go?"

"Fine, nothing different."

She scribbled in the folder again. "Any new thoughts since we last met? How do you feel about giving up your baby now that you've carried him or her for seven months?"

I picked the lint off my sweater and avoided looking up. Her words found a way through my jumbled mind and forced me to focus. "I don't know. I don't think about it because I can't change anything. My mother and I talked. There's no choice."

"There is a choice. Is it your choice to give up your baby?"

"I really want this all over." Mom coached me on what to say when anyone asked these types of questions, but I needed no coaching this time. I visualized Danny holding his new girlfriend without a thought for his baby or me. "I don't want this baby." My voice came out clipped but definite.

I didn't want to talk to this lady anymore either. Nobody understood my mixed-up feelings, especially not now. Not even me.

The counselor peered at me over her glasses. "Once you sign the papers, you can't change your mind. You'll be forbidden by law to contact or ever see your child. Do you understand?"

I tried to picture a happy homelife caring for my infant, but I wanted fun, not more responsibility.

I blew out the deep breath I held, slumped over, and stared at my hands, defeated. "I want my child to live a good life. I hope you find a home with parents who love kids, who really want kids. That's what I wish for my baby."

"Many couples want—"

I barely heard the rest. She said the same old stuff about finding a nice Catholic family, with a hardworking dad and a caring mom who wanted a child.

Months later, something woke me in the silent dark. I eased out of bed and slid my hand along the wall feeling for the light switch. I remembered that Joey was staying overnight at his buddy's, and Evelyn had gone out to celebrate someone's birthday.

I'm not due for another week, so it can't be the baby. But when a second, then a third wave of pinching, punching cramps grew more intense and rolled through my stomach and lower back, the realization hit me. *The baby is coming!*

It felt like a giant steel vise squeezing my insides. I fought down the pain, but it overtook me just as I made it to the kitchen phone. I sank to my knees.

"God help me!"

Using the counter for support, I pulled myself up and found the contact number that Evelyn scribbled on a scrap of paper.

It rang but no answer. Another long, deep gut pinch swelled bigger and bigger, then stopped. I called Mom.

"Mom! Mom, come quick! I'm having the baby!"

"Oh, God. Where's Evelyn?" Before I responded, she said, "Hang on, Charlie—getting clothes on. Thirty minutes, tops."

My overnight bag, packed and ready for a week, waited near the front door. I drew aside the vertical blinds on the picture window and watched for Mom. More pain roared through me. I hugged my stomach, trying to control the feeling of a giant bird clenching its talons deep into my gut. Unable to sit or stand, the pain hurt a hundred times worse than the most horrible cramps ever.

"Mom!"

The kitchen floor spiraled beneath me. I awkwardly lowered myself and lay flat on my back, fighting the spin.

Sweat and tears rolled down the sides of my face and dripped on the cool tile, but my teeth chattered. *God, let me die right here!*

I bent my knees to search for relief. The angry jaws gnawing my insides released a bit and faded. I rocked myself to one side and noticed the time. It'd been twenty minutes since Mom hung up. The pain subsided for a few moments, allowing me to clear my head enough to struggle to a standing position. I wobbled to the window and watched for headlights on the deserted street. Minutes later, a car squealed around the corner without braking and bounced into the driveway.

"Mom!"

She bolted from her car, leaving the engine running and the driver's door wide open.

After she helped me in, she jammed the car in reverse and raced down the winding hill, screeching around corners and running stop signs all the way to the hospital.

Mom's normally coiffed hair looked like a mass of yellow cotton candy, and her blue eyes bulged out in her pale face. Gratitude flooded through me in place of all my hate for her.

In the delivery room, I whispered, "Mom—" She read my mind and yelled down the hallway, "My daughter needs pain medication!"

The nurse scurried in and examined the drip bag.

"Ma'am, she's already on strong painkillers. I can't give her anymore."

"I don't give a damn what you put her on," Mom said, "she's in a lot of pain. Look at her."

The nurse ran her hand along the thin rubber tube the doctor had previously stuck in my lower back.

"Okay, here's the problem. The tube came dislodged and is leaking her medication on the bed."

Mom glared at her. The nurse quickly reinserted it, and the pain disappeared.

After she left, I whispered, "Thank you."

Mom exhaled and released her tense shoulders. She patted my arm, consoling me. "I'm here, Charlie." She eased into one of the leatherette chairs, lay back, and closed her eyes. "Now we wait."

Comfortable at last, I noticed the two chairs, a monitor, and a metal tray covered with a sheet of white paper. A baby-weighing scale and a white canvas hamper waited nearby. An orderly rolled another metal tray in the room, greeted us with a grunt, and left.

My labor went on and on, nearly painlessly, until the doctor finally came in, laid a sheet over my bent knees, and examined me. He pulled the arm of the bright metal-shaded light directly over me.

"Okay, Charlotte, it's time. Let's do this. Give me your best push," he said.

Mom squeezed my hand. I gulped then pushed so hard I thought blood would squirt from my pores. The anesthesia worked so well, I wondered whether my body was reacting to my pushes at all.

Exhausted from hours of labor and sweating, a squeal then a tiny wail signaled the end. The baby was real! After so many long days and weeks, it all ended suddenly.

"A healthy boy," the doctor said, removing his gloves.

"A boy? Can I see him?" I used my arms to push up but fell back.

Mom shot me a warning look. "Charlotte—"

"I want to see him." *Something must be wrong.* "Please! Let me see my baby!"

The nurse whipped around, and her face squeezed down into the same look of authority I saw on teachers about to throw a kid in detention. She glanced at Mom, then walked out.

"It'll make it harder to let go if you see him," Mom said. "I want to make it easier on you."

The constriction around my chest felt like a thousand tears held captive.

A thoughtful look flashed across Mom's face. "It's for the best, Charlie."

I hated her force and control, but I clung to the belief that she protected me from more suffering. Caring for a baby would change and restrict my life the way it had hers.

Where would my little boy end up in this world? Maybe he would get adopted by a good family with a dog and horses. Maybe he'd have brothers and sisters and receive a brand-new bicycle at Christmastime. I envisioned him and his dad climbing trees and building a three-story treehouse together. Maybe he'd have funny little quirks like dunking his toast in orange juice or forgetting to double-knot his shoelaces and jumping off his new bike to tie them over and over again. I hoped he'd have the childhood I never had.

At my lowest points, Mom showed up to help me. My love for her grew from our bonding during those difficult times. She met my problems with deep concern and care. Mom saw my life going in the same direction as hers—young, pregnant, and burdened with child-rearing. So, she did everything in her power to prevent my destiny from mirroring hers. Mom often warned us, her children, never to have kids. She did what she thought was right for me. Later in life, her tutelage coupled with distrust of my stepfather left me no foundation from which to build my own healthy relationship and family.

A week after giving birth, with my few belongings already packed in Mom's car, I embraced Evelyn and Joey.

"I'm not good at goodbyes." Evelyn sniffed and touched her eyes with a Kleenex.

"Thank you so much for your help. For everything," I said. "I'm going to miss you—and Clancy."

On the way home, Mom said she enrolled me in a different high school where no one knew me. We buried my shameful secret together, never to speak of it again.

On my first day at the new school, some students gave me curious glances, not recognizing me as a regular. I hoped this school had nicer kids than my other one. Using a Xeroxed diagram the counselor had given me, I tried to look confident when I walked into my first class and sat in the back. A couple of students glanced around.

One girl actually nodded a bit and said, "Hi."

I returned her greeting and silently exhaled relief.

I often rode June or sometimes our other horse, Apache. Only Mom or I took Apache out for a workout. A tri-colored pinto, high-strung and difficult to control, he sweated to a lather from prancing. If he heard the slightest rustle or a branch crack, he'd spook sideways, and at times, he'd lose his rider. It took constant awareness to ride him without falling off. Abused before we got him, he shied whenever I raised my hand with the bridle. I spoke in low, even tones until he stopped tossing his head and calmed down enough to fit the hackamore.

Sometimes I watched Mom work with him. Apache quivered and pranced side to side, always ready to bolt. Mom held tight with her thighs, reins poised properly in her left hand, and stroked his neck.

"I wish I handled him like you do, Mom," I said.

"You do, Charlie. I don't ride him enough."

I rode him a few miles from the house to the dried-up river bottom where rabbits scampered and lizards hid under tumbleweeds when they heard us coming.

Apache loved the riverbed. He tossed his head, fighting to break my tight control. He wanted to run. I loosened his reins, and he bolted forward like he was shooting out from the starting gate. Hunkered down close to his neck, I listened to the drum of his hooves pounding the hard-packed dirt. His mane blew straight back, whipping me in the face. The heat of his powerful muscles straining beneath me worked up a lather. He snorted and huffed as we galloped away from the cruel past that chased us both.

My haunted memories disappeared during those wild escapes with Apache. I wanted to capture the freedom we shared on those rides and hold on forever.

Then I met a guy.

Studying my notes for an afternoon quiz, the library wall clock alerted me to the time. A blond, tanned boy wearing an army jacket stepped into my line of sight. He dropped his books on the study table, then slid into the chair across from me. We exchanged friendly greetings in low, library tones, and I asked about his stack of zoology books.

"I'm trying to identify the baby owl in my garage," he whispered. "I found him in the oil fields, and I'm raising him until he's strong enough to fly."

"A baby owl? Really? Cool." I noticed the time again. "Oh, I have to go. Got a test."

"Hey, you want to meet here for lunch tomorrow?" He grinned and tapped his pencil eraser end on the table, waiting.

By the third week, we spent every moment together. We played, chased, and wrestled like kids on a playground. He loved animals and said he loved me. I fell for this wannabe veterinarian and his Honda 350 motorcycle in a big way.

"My mom thinks you're a bad influence," he said one afternoon while walking to his motorcycle.

"Why?" I asked.

"Remember the wooden block you painted for me with peace signs?"

"Yeah. 'Flowers, sex, drugs, and rock 'n' roll' painted all over it?"

"Yeah. She found it in my backpack. Now she thinks you make me smoke pot, have sex, and listen to the Stones." He choked out an embarrassed chuckle, but I didn't think it funny at all. I wanted his mother to like me.

I loved riding on the back of Tim's Honda motorcycle. The wind on my face and the sense of freedom thrilled me as much as galloping along the riverbed on Apache.

One day, while riding on Tim's motorcycle behind him, he

took a detour on a dirt path through the oil fields. We bumped over the potholed trail. I hung on tight, my arms around his waist and my notebook wedged between us.

My Mexican sack-purse, slung too low, caught in the back wheel. The purse yanked off my shoulder and wrapped in a tangle around the wheel, causing it to freeze up. Makeup and ink pens flew everywhere as the motorcycle skidded to a stop and a dirt cloud enveloped us. We jumped off. While Tim untangled my shredded purse, he spotted something near the trees.

"Look! Wow!"

"Oh my God! Don't touch it!"

He knelt, picking up a black snake at least three feet long. He held it beneath its head and watched it slowly curl in the air.

"I want to take him back to my house."

"What? How?"

He grinned at me.

"Oh no. No way. I'm not touching that thing," I said.

It was Tim's lucky day. He found a large piece of old shirt near the same trees. He folded it into a sack, bringing the ends together at the top.

"Look, carry him like this," he said.

"No way!"

"He won't bite you. Keep your fist closed around the opening, and hold it away from your body."

"I swear—"

We took off. The snake nudged my fist. I yelped and reached around Tim, almost dropping the sack on the gas tank. "It's getting out!"

He stopped, pushed the snake down, and handed the wretched thing back to me. We sped away.

Tim cleaned out an old aquarium from his garage, filled

it with sticks and grass, and carefully placed the snake in its new home.

"You did a cool thing helping me get him home. Thanks."

He put on a Pink Floyd album, lay back on his bed, and patted the pillow next to him. "Come on, lie down," he said.

We got comfortable, kissed, and made out. When he pulled up my shirt, I pushed back, startled.

"No, I don't want to get pregnant," I said.

"You won't get pregnant from doing it one time."

I wanted to feel his warmth, his closeness, but fear held me back. Even after having a baby, no one told me anything about birth control—not Mom, not a doctor, not Evelyn, not anyone. Sex outside of marriage was considered immoral by the church and frowned on by society. I guess they thought I learned my lesson. Only bad girls—sluts—had sex. *Roe v. Wade* hadn't been passed yet, so there was no going back.

Tim rolled up on his elbow. "I heard rubbers stop pregnancy. I'll get some, but let's do it this once without one."

"I don't want to risk it."

I loved him and didn't want to lose him. *Maybe the first time I got pregnant was a fluke. What if I did it this one time?* I had so many questions but didn't know whom to talk to.

"My brother and his girlfriend do it all the time, and she's never gotten pregnant," Tim said.

I wanted to tell him about my baby boy but choked. I didn't want him to think of me as a "sleep-around-type girl." Ashamed of my past, I kept quiet and let him assume my virginity.

"No, I don't want to risk it," I said again.

"Shit. Whatever." He stood up, walked to the aquarium, and lifted his snake to admire it.

"What are you going to do with him?"

"Feed him mice for a few days, then take him back to where we found him. My mom won't let me keep him."

A few weeks later, Tim and I made love in his bedroom after school without protection. I convinced myself getting pregnant was bad luck and couldn't happen again.

On Tim's stereo, the Zombies sang "Time of the Season."

Every time we made love after school, I remembered Mom's words: "Charlotte, you're like me. You'll get pregnant from thinking about sex, so don't do it again. Ever."

Worry about getting pregnant ate at me until I could no longer stand it. The torment drove me crazy. I never told Tim about Danny or my previous pregnancy. He'd heard about some of my problems at home, but he couldn't possibly imagine how much I feared my parents' reaction if I got pregnant a second time.

"Every time I tell you I'm worried about getting pregnant, you don't want to hear it. You won't even listen, and I'm sick of saying the same thing over and over. You don't give a crap about me anymore. I'm done." I stared down at the class ring he'd given me. I'd wrapped the ring in angora yarn to make it fit. I pulled it off and held it out. "Take it back."

Instead of taking the ring, he moved toward me with open arms, smiling like I was joking. I pushed him back.

"What's the matter?" he asked, not smiling anymore.

"I'm done talking to you. Take your ring." I hurled the class ring at his chest and heard it clink on the pavement. "I don't want it anymore. I'm breaking up with you."

He left the ring where it laid, straddled his bike, and looked back at me before roaring off like Steve McQueen.

The lonely ring lying on the street filled me with regret. Crying, I left Tim's ring behind.

MARRY JERRY

When I spotted Tim walking to class, I went the other way. Focusing on schoolwork helped me avoid thinking of him, but I still did. At least I breathed easier without worrying about getting pregnant.

A month later, I jumped off the school bus behind a senior boy from the neighborhood.

Like a swimmer emerging from the water, he flipped his hair out of his face, saying, "Hey, Charlotte, wanna go to the Eagles concert this Saturday with me, my girlfriend, and my cousin, Jerry?"

I shaded my eyes and looked at him. "You mean like a blind date?"

The four of us danced, whooped, and hollered all day at the crowded outdoor stadium concert. Sunshine filtered through the clouds of pot smoke. For the first time in a month, Tim left my thoughts.

Jerry, a quiet and sometimes shy fellow, wasn't daring like Danny or funny like Tim, but I liked him. Like me, he parted his blond hair right down the middle and tucked it behind his ears. He walked with a bit of swagger, swaying his shoulders from side to side, like a teenage cowboy. From his looks, you'd think he was a laid-back surfer, but he didn't surf. Instead, he worked long hours as a gas station attendant and assistant to the owner, fixing cars.

My menstrual week came and went without evidence of blood. The pressure in my head increased every morning when I leaped from the bed and raced to the bathroom only to discover my period hadn't started. Instead, the vomiting began.

Hanging my head over the toilet, heaving, I whispered out loud, "Please, God, don't punish me again. I'm sorry." I sat on the toilet, covered my face with a towel so my mother wouldn't hear, then leaned forward and bawled.

I found it impossible to focus on schoolwork, ride the horses, or do anything except sit in our tree house and obsess over the possibility of another pregnancy. My teachers' words sounded garbled. I dragged from class to class in a trance. Day after day, I sat alone on a grassy hill at lunchtime, apart from other students who ate sandwiches or played guitars in the sunshine without a care in the world. With my arms wrapped around my bended knees, I bowed my head to hide and think of a way to prevent the storm brewing in my future.

The next time I spotted Tim walking to class, I caught up and fell into step beside him.

"Charlotte," he said, surprise written on his face.

I blurted out, "I think I'm pregnant."

"What?" He jolted to a stop then guided me out of the student traffic by my upper arm. "How do you know?" he whispered, his face inches from mine.

"I haven't had my period since we broke up."

"Wow." He looked at his shoes. "What do you want to do?"

"I don't know."

"I still love you. Maybe we should get married."

His words surprised me, but I considered his solution. I still loved him, too. "Your mom doesn't like me. She'll never let you marry me, and you need her consent."

"Yeah, probably right. She won't allow the marriage." His buddy called to him from a group of kids. Tim ignored him. "What are you going to do?"

"I'm not sure. I'm too scared to tell my parents. I'm telling you because it's your baby, and whatever happens, you should know."

I've wondered what my life would have been like if Tim and I found a way to convince his mom to let us marry. At the time, I needed a solution fast, and convincing her would take time and maybe never happen.

Besides, subconsciously, I knew if I married Tim—a boy I dearly loved—and had his baby, there was a clear possibility I'd end up like my mother, frazzled from raising kids too young.

I avoided Mom. If she saw my face, she'd read my secret, but the suffocating pressure forced me to tell her before she saw the signs.

After dinner, I slipped into my parents' bedroom. Mom stood barefoot in front of her mirrored dresser, fastening her pearl necklace around her neck. Chanel No. 5, Pond's Cold Cream, and Aqua Net hair spray crowded her cream-colored dresser.

"Hey, Charlie, hand me my brown patent leather purse from the closet. The one with the gold trim."

I dug through her tousled walk-in to find the purse.

She glanced at her little gold watch. "Where's your dad? We can't be late for this parent/teacher meeting."

My stepfather had returned from Vietnam months earlier.

When Dad stayed home, Mom stayed home too. My siblings and I knew better than to mention anything about her trips to Las Vegas. I avoided Dad but always knew his whereabouts in the house.

Mom took her purse from me, and I sat on the edge of her king-sized bed. My eyes drifted around the room to avoid meeting hers. I smoothed the burgundy velvet bedspread and noticed the gold metallic design woven through it. Tiny dust particles twirled through the beam of sunlight streaming through the window.

My attention rested on the back of Mom's glossy French twist. I listened to her chat without hearing what she said as she applied makeup. I wanted to say something, but my throat swelled shut and no words came out.

Fear pulsed through me and threatened to burst from my throbbing temples. I wanted to crawl away and hide.

When I didn't respond, Mom stopped to watch me in the reflection. "What's the matter, Charlie? You look so serious. What's wrong?"

I snapped out of my trance to meet and hold her stare for long moments. I silently conveyed my secret and touched my stomach.

Realization dawned across her face. Her expression changed from lightness to disgust. "Oh no—"

"Mom, I'm sorry."

Mom banged her purse down on the dresser, knocking over the Chanel No. 5. "Damn it! This can't be happening again."

She swung around, waving her arms like she was ready to hit me. I leaned back on the bed. She stopped midair and clasped her palm over her mouth to stifle her frustration.

"I give up. You're determined to ruin your life and mine.

What's wrong with you? I can't stand you anymore. Get out. Get out of this house!"

"Mom, no. Please. I'm so sorry."

"Do you go around having sex with every boy you meet?"

"No, Mom. I'm—I was in love."

"You only met him a few months ago. How could you possibly be in love? You're ridiculous," she said.

"It's not Jerry's baby. It's Tim's."

"How do you know it's not Jerry's?"

"Because we haven't had sex."

"Get out of my sight. I'm so sick of you. I can't even look at you."

The next day, Mom called me to her bedroom again. "Your father and I talked about it. We're sending you to a home for unwed mothers. Don't even think about keeping the baby. If you do, you'll be another single teenager starving on the street with a kid."

"I know I can't keep it."

My parents didn't want me, and I knew nothing about unwed mothers' homes. Mom described them as teenage orphanages full of disease. Mommy Burr and Daddy Burr might take me in, but Mom said my condition would embarrass them in their small, country town. Besides, I hadn't seen them in years and felt too ashamed to tell them I was pregnant again.

"You've been seeing Jerry for two months. Are you sure the baby isn't his?" she asked.

"No, not possible. It's Tim's baby. What if I got married, Mom? I'll tell Jerry I'm pregnant and see if he'll marry me until the baby's born. Then I can put the baby up for adoption and annul the marriage."

"Well, if that's your decision, do it soon. You're not living here with everyone finding out you're pregnant again. What would the neighbors think? Anyway, if Jerry doesn't want to marry you, an unwed mothers' home will serve you right. You can have your baby with the other deranged girls."

She almost broke my shaky control, but a glimpse of hope held me together. Maybe getting married to Jerry and giving up the baby was the best solution to escape this mess.

Jerry and I sat next to each other, rocking on the porch swing. I turned off the outside lights to create a peaceful setting. The crickets chirped nearby, and an owl hooted in the distance. A soft breeze blew in the scent of night jasmine.

I wore jeans and Jerry's favorite light blue blouse sprinkled with tiny yellow flowers. I'd gathered my hair in a barrette to one side, showing my small gold earrings.

"I like this screened-in porch. It reminds me of houses you see in old southern plantation movies," Jerry said.

When I didn't respond, he turned and looked at me.

"Is everything okay? You're so quiet lately." His eyes flicked to the top of my head. He plucked a ladybug out of my hair, then held his palm out flat to let her fly away.

"I need to tell you something."

"Shoot," he said.

"I'm a little nervous, but here goes." I paused.

He waited.

"I'm pregnant."

He planted his foot and stopped the swing from moving. "Oh?"

"Yeah. My parents want to send me to a home for unwed mothers." I let my words sink in. "But there might be another solution." Before he responded, I blurted out, "I could get married."

"Married?" He met my eyes.

I swallowed. "Yeah, if you'll marry me, I won't ask you to raise my baby since we both know it's not yours."

He stared at the floor. "What will you do after it's born?"

"I'll put the baby up for adoption and annul the marriage. I won't hold you to it after the baby's born. Will you help me through this?" I bit my bottom lip and held my breath.

He spoke in a low tone. "I know how it is here for you, Charlotte. I want to help you, so yeah, I'll marry you. Heck, my car insurance will go down." He gave a short laugh, and I attempted a weak smile.

"I'll make it good for you, Jerry, I promise."

We hugged. My heart swelled. I exhaled relief and wrapped my arms around him.

"Um, hold on," he said. "There's one thing we got to do for this to work."

"What?"

"My parents and yours will need to sign consent forms because we're underage. If my parents think it's my kid, they'll sign; otherwise, they won't. It's important we keep it quiet. They're serious Jehovah's Witnesses."

Two weeks later, after all the arrangements were made, my parents drove me to Jerry's family home in Arizona. In route, we stopped for lunch at a country diner outside Show Low.

We sat at a window table covered in a sticky, red-and-white-checkered tablecloth made of plastic. I watched the middle-aged server chat with the customers at the next table as she took their orders. Nausea churned in the pit of my stomach, so I concentrated on the year-round Christmas lights strung behind the lunch counter.

Mom scanned my face. "You're perspiring. Are you okay?" she asked.

I used my paper napkin to wipe my forehead.

"If you're having second thoughts about getting married, it's not too late to back out."

She read my mind as she often did. *Is she offering me another way?* I didn't see any other solution.

Dad stopped eating, set his fork down, and stared at Mom. "Ann, what—"

Dad wants me gone.

"I don't feel well. Excuse me." I slid my chair back.

I found my way to the bathroom, braced myself against the graffiti-covered wall, and racked my brain for a different solution. I wasn't sick from the three-month-old baby growing inside me, but because I was on my way to marry a boy I barely knew. I took a deep breath, blew it out in a swoosh, and straightened upright.

Mom examined the directions she'd received from Jerry's mother, then pointed for Dad to turn onto an unpaved road. Dirt and rocks pinged the bottom of the car as we bounced through the ruts, but soon a small, tree-shaded farmhouse came into view.

A middle-aged man wearing overalls emerged from under the hood of an old gray sedan. He removed his cap, wiped his head with his forearm, and squinted at us through the midday sunshine. He wore a curious expression that looked vaguely familiar.

He must be Jerry's father.

"Okay, here we go," Dad said as he killed the engine.

Jerry and his mom came out the screen door, letting it bang shut behind them.

Dumbstruck as introductions were made, I watched the event take place before me as if watching a play.

Jerry had told his parents he wanted to marry his pregnant girlfriend but didn't mention the baby was not his. My parents, Jerry, and I concealed that fact from Jerry's folks in order to get their signed consent. We kept a big secret from these nice people.

Standing on the farmhouse porch, Mom behaved as she always did in a social gathering, but her fun demeanor fell flat, forced. Dad acted polite, though aloof as usual.

By nature, Jerry's dad seldom spoke. His mom gathered me into a big hug and patted my back, upbeat and happy.

"My sister, Jerry's aunt, lives in Orange County too. Once you kids get settled, I hope you'll attend her weekly Bible study," Jerry's mother said.

"Um, okay," I said.

The next day, I put on the short, white velvet dress and veil my mother sewed for the occasion. With the documents signed, the ceremony proceeded. I took Dad's arm, pretended to look happy, and stepped into the tiny living room to face Jerry and the Justice of the Peace. I would turn seventeen two weeks later.

Within a few weeks, Jerry and I settled into our one-bedroom apartment in Anaheim, a few miles from Disneyland. Our unit, located on the bottom floor of the two-story apartment building, sat among twenty units. The complex, shaped in a rectangle, wrapped around a small, grassy courtyard where the neighbors gathered for barbecues. A pay phone conveniently located on the back alley provided tenants a way to make calls.

We furnished our place with a brown corduroy couch from Goodwill, a table, and a bed Mom gave us. I cooked and kept our apartment immaculate, finding it easy to care for the two of us after coming from a family of ten.

Appreciative of everything I did, Jerry worked hard pumping gas and fixing cars. We lived in a traditional marriage, but I wasn't a traditional girl and didn't come from a traditional family. He'd come home from work tired and hungry, and I had dinner prepared for him. Happy to eat, watch TV, and have sex every night, Jerry didn't say much and seemed content.

"I want to find a job and get a car," I said. "I'm tired of walking to the market and having nothing to do all day."

"What happened to waiting until the baby's born to start work?" he asked.

Jerry had never mentioned the baby before. I didn't show yet, and we never spoke about it, but I wondered how he felt knowing I carried another guy's child.

At a neighborhood barbecue, Jerry and I stood next to the grill talking to our landlord while he flipped hamburgers.

"You kids must be excited about your new baby on the way," he said, waiting for one of us to respond.

Jerry made eye contact with me over his beer bottle as he took a long swig.

"We don't know what to expect," I said, quickly changing the subject. "Are either of you ready for another beer?"

While alone, I rubbed my stomach in circles and talked to the little baby inside me. What will the baby look like? Did the tiny thing feel lonesome like I often did? Something else resided in me too. I wanted freedom from this suffocating confinement, from the baby, the situation, everything. I wanted to live like I saw other teenage girls living, playing, and having fun.

While cooking dinner, I turned to face Jerry from the stove.

"I spoke to my grandparents today, Jerry. I want to go see them in Texas."

"Oh? When do you want to go?"

"Next week, but I wanted to talk to you first," I said.

"Wow. How long are you going for?"

"At least a month." *I want to go for two months, but I might start showing by then.* "They're sending a prepaid ticket."

He waited for more explanation.

"I miss them so much." I yearned for the security I used to feel in their home, the comforting way they lived, and the aroma of bread baking.

"Hey, there's something I need to tell you too. My mom's driving here from Arizona this weekend," he said.

"Why?" I asked. "Is this about converting me to a Jehovah's Witness? Because I—"

"I don't know." He shrugged.

"Crap. I'll bet that's it. Your aunt probably told her we showed up twice for Bible study and never went back."

My mother-in-law, upbeat as always, arrived carrying shopping bags. She scanned our new place and stared at my flat belly. I self-consciously laid my hand across my stomach.

"Can I get you something cold to drink, Mrs. Freeman?"

"No, thank you. You're not even showing. Are you okay?"

"Yeah, I'm over the morning sickness. I feel normal," I said. "Riding my bike every day."

"Good to hear. I brought you some maternity and baby clothes. That's not why I'm here though." She set the bags on the couch before addressing me directly. "Is there somewhere we can speak alone?"

"Alone?" I asked.

Jerry looked confused. "Mom, what—"

"This is between Charlotte and me. Give us a moment of privacy."

I motioned to our bedroom, uncertain what to say about not going to Bible study.

Mrs. Freeman followed me in, Jerry close behind. He leaned against the doorjamb. His eyebrows were stitched together as if he was trying to figure this out.

"Leave and shut the door behind you," his mother told him. She turned to me.

Jerry didn't move. His bewildered look matched my feelings.

"We'll be a few minutes, now go." She shooed him away.

She sat on the edge of the bed and patted the spot beside her, inviting me to sit. "I bring good news."

It didn't feel like good news was coming. My body tensed up, ready to bolt from the room.

She took my hand in hers. "It's about the baby. I can't think of anything else, Charlotte. I've always wanted another child, and we tried. Anyway, when I heard you and Jerry planned to give away my only grandchild for adoption… Well, I want to adopt the baby!"

My mouth dropped open. "I'm so sorry, but—"

Her smile faded, but her words kept coming. "Let me explain. This is the most important decision I've ever made. I'll love your baby as my own. You and Jerry can come see the child anytime you want."

"I can't give you the baby," I said, voice shaking. *Ask me for anything except this.*

She searched my face, absorbing my refusal. Her eyes watered, and her voice climbed to a high-pitched, desperate plea. "Don't give away my grandchild to strangers."

She blinked over and over. A tear escaped the tip of her eyelash, threaded its way down her face, and dripped on our entwined hands. She let go and plucked a Kleenex from her purse.

Guilt overwhelmed me.

My own mother often said she had never wanted any

children at all, but this woman begged me for the opportunity to raise her grandchild. *Strange.*

I looked down at her hands fidgeting with her small, diamond wedding ring, which caught the light and sparkled.

She grabbed my hand again and leaned in closer. "Let me adopt Jerry's baby, please, Charlotte."

My face stung hot. *Where's Jerry? He should be in here helping me.*

"No, Ma'am. I plan to go through with the adoption," I said firmly.

To my horror, she slid off the edge of the bed, knelt on the floor in front of me, and cupped my hands between hers.

"Oh please, in the name of God, don't give away my grandchild. I'm begging you. It will break my heart."

When I witnessed the naked motherly love on her face, I nearly blurted out the truth. She possessed the kind of motherly love my baby deserved.

I bent down from the bed, slowly embraced her, and wept with her. She shook free from me, pushed herself up, and rushed out.

Jerry darted in. "What happened? What did she say?"

"She wants to adopt the baby."

"Oh my God."

"Why didn't you come help me?" I asked.

"She told me to stay out. When I called Dad a few days ago, he said she planned to come see us but didn't say why."

"It was awful. I didn't know what to say," I said.

"You didn't tell her, did you?"

"No, but I wanted to. She's really upset."

"I'm not sure what to do anymore," he said.

The image of Mrs. Freeman's pained face kept returning to

me. *Did all women feel like that about babies?* I wanted to see and touch my baby, sure, but keep it?

It wasn't my place to tell her the truth. It was Jerry's duty. If she knew the truth, would she still want to adopt my baby?

SUN-DRENCHED COTTON

A week later, the plane lifted off for San Antonio. I reclined the two inches the seat permitted, shut my eyes, and thought back to the last time I'd seen my grandparents. Around ten years old, I'd skipped into our kitchen right after hurrying home from school.

"When are Mommy Burr and Daddy Burr getting here?" I bounced up and down, impatient for Mom's response.

"Change out of your uniform. They'll be here any minute."

I clapped once and ran to my room to change.

Once they got settled after their long drive from Texas to our house in Virginia, Daddy Burr joined me in the front yard. I took his hand, felt his hard callouses, and peered up at his tanned, weathered face. The neighbor kids rode their bikes in circles around the cul-de-sac, chattering and yelling.

"How long has your tire been flat?" Daddy Burr asked.

A kid pedaled by and shouted, "Since my birthday, September 14th."

"Mom said she's too busy to fix it," I said quickly. "It's okay. I ride on the back of my friends' bikes a lot."

My grandfather winced, and his shoulders slumped. Without saying anything, he dug in his pants for his car keys and left.

He returned with a new tire, and I watched him put it on my bike. I stroked the handlebars and chewed the inside of my mouth, worrying about the resulting explosion if Mom or Dad discovered the new tire.

The group of neighborhood kids kept riding by, waiting for me to join them.

Mom pulled into the driveway, then climbed out of our family station wagon clutching a bag of groceries. She set the bag on the porch steps and stomped over to Daddy Burr and me.

"Dad, what are you doing?" she asked.

"Putting a new tire on Charlotte's bike."

Her face squished into a mean witch-glare. "I asked you not to show favoritism to her." Mom's face was a red balloon filled too full and ready to pop.

The neighbor kids sensed trouble and pedaled away.

"All the kids have bikes except Charlotte." Daddy Burr wiped chain grease off his hands.

"I don't care. Nick planned to fix it."

"I didn't know Dad wanted to fix it, Mom," I said, trying to take the blame off Daddy Burr.

"Her bike's had a flat for months," Daddy Burr said.

"I don't give a damn!" she bellowed at him, hands on her hips.

Humiliation for my grandfather flooded through me. My grandparents were gentle, soft-spoken people, always respectful of others. They never raised their voices. My parents hated when my grandparents treated me nicely, but I never understood why.

The front door swung open. Dad took long, determined strides to investigate the source of the yelling. Mommy Burr scampered behind, trying to catch up.

"If you won't do as I ask in my own home, then leave. Go

and don't come back!" Mom jerked her hand through the air and pointed down the street.

"No, Mom, don't make him leave!" I burst out bawling, mouth wide open.

"Get in the house. Now." Mom swung back to face Daddy Burr.

Worry lines creased his forehead. He and Mommy Burr moved inside the house together with heads bowed.

I stood at their bedroom door and watched them repack their suitcases.

"Go on now. We don't want to cause you more trouble," Mommy Burr said.

I ran to my room, stood on the bed to see out the high window, and watched Mommy Burr and Daddy Burr loading their suitcases into the car. Then they backed out of the driveway.

I had caused this. Me and my stupid bike. I cried as they drove away.

"If you don't shut up, I'll give you something to squall about," Mom shouted from the hallway.

I fell flat onto the bed. My pillow muffled my wailing. I didn't ever want them to leave. I wanted to go with them.

That day, Mom forbade me any contact with them.

During the eight years since seeing them, we'd received a big Christmas box from Mommy Burr and Daddy Burr, a peace offering. We kids jumped up and down, excited because we knew the huge box was full of clothes sewn by Mommy Burr—clothes not just for my siblings and me, but my mother and stepfather too. In the past, Mommy Burr had even embroidered a small, red star on the back of each pair of panties she made so the little kids would know the front from the back when they dressed themselves.

Years later, Daddy Burr told me that Mommy Burr had taken a part-time job at the local fabric store to afford the material to sew those badly needed clothes.

But Mom didn't see the big box of clothes as a gift. In shock, I witnessed my mother write "Go to Hell" and "Return to Sender" on the box in angry, black letters before sending it back, unopened.

Mom's hostility toward her parents had no limits. She adored her father but objected to his loyalty to his wife. Mom claimed her mother came between her father and her.

Mom was their only child and was accustomed to getting everything she wanted. She wielded enormous power. When she discovered her attempts to divide her parents had failed, she resented them both.

After Mom married my stepfather, she claimed my grandparents interfered with our family dynamic, accused them of disliking my stepfather because he was "a Yankee, Catholic, and military." When I got older and questioned my grandparents, they denied it. They told me they'd seen him mistreat me when I was little, and that's why they didn't like him.

I hated Mom for hurting her children all those years ago by returning that generous Christmas box from Mommy Burr and Daddy Burr. I hated her even more for hurting her parents. I resented my parents like Mom resented hers, but that didn't make us the same. I loved parties, fun, and escape like she did, but our similarities stopped there.

The plane bound for Texas leveled off in the brilliant sunshine. I admired the puffy clouds sweeping by below. I had wanted to make this trip for so long.

After we'd landed, I hurried up the San Antonio jetway and scanned the crowd. When I spotted my grandparents, I hid my shock at their appearance. They'd aged so much since that day they'd driven away from our home. I beelined through the greeters and embraced them.

Mommy Burr smelled of pure love blended with starch, sunshine, and cotton. Daddy Burr, at five-foot-eight, stood proudly on his bowed legs, patiently holding Mommy Burr's black, patent-leather purse. She and I giggled through our wet eyes while Daddy Burr guided us out of the crowded terminal, still holding her purse.

Years earlier, my grandparents bought a piece of land about seven miles outside a town in Texas called Fredericksburg. Fredericksburg was located in the hill country about seventy miles from San Antonio. They cleared out the underbrush and leveled and groomed the property, leaving all the beautiful shade trees. Daddy Burr worked full-time in civil service, and Mommy Burr worked in a fabric shop while living in their garage and building their 3,000-square-foot home around it. They did all the work themselves.

We drove through the fence gate bordering their five acres. The long driveway wound between the trees and through the manicured grounds. The towering water windmill came into view behind their ranch-style home, a snapshot from my childhood memories.

The next morning, Mommy Burr tapped on the door, a mug of steaming tea in her hand. "Good morning, sleepyhead. Do you want breakfast? Is there anything you can't eat?"

"Breakfast sounds good, thanks. And I can eat anything." I pointed at the wall. "Are those silhouette cutouts of me?"

"Yes. Don't you remember when we took you kids to Disneyland?"

"Oh yeah. Wow, you kept them all this time," I said.

"Well, sure. Look closer. This room is yours. Everything in here is something you made or that reminds us of you. We knew you'd find your way back to see us. Your room's been waiting."

I struggled to keep my emotions under control. They loved me so much, but they didn't know me anymore. I hadn't earned their love. I fought and sassed Mom, hated Dad, had run away from home, and gotten pregnant—twice. Though I hadn't seen my grandparents in years, I missed them every single day.

The smell of sizzling bacon floated in from the kitchen.

"I made bacon, eggs, grits, biscuits, and gravy," Mommy Burr said, glancing up from the frying pan. "What do you normally eat?"

I padded over to join her. "Don't go to the extra work. Here, let me help."

"Let me do what I can for you," she said.

After breakfast, the three of us remained at the kitchen table near the large picture window overlooking the backyard. Two furious birds warned the squirrels away from their nest. The birds squawked and dive-bombed the squirrels that scurried up and down the trees. Daddy Burr's windmill caught a small breeze, glinted in the sun, and turned a lazy rotation.

Mommy Burr stretched to reach a box of photos on a high shelf. Daddy Burr stood to help her.

"Look at this one. Your mother in high school."

I'd seen the photo before. It was an eight-by-ten-inch professional shot of Mom holding her baton and posing in full drum majorette's uniform.

"I'll never forget when she led the whole high school marching band down the length of the football field at halftime. Her dog slipped onto the field and entertained the spectators by running circles around her, barking wildly. She ignored him and never missed a beat. She tossed her spinning baton high overhead and caught it as she marched. She loved her dog." My grandparents exchanged sweet glances, sharing a fond memory of their only child, my mother.

"She had enough fun in her for three people," Daddy-Burr said as he pulled out a chair to join us. "When she turned twelve, I built her a sailboat and taught her to sail. I understand she's the captain of a women's racing team now?"

"Yes, she is," I said.

"How in the world does she find time?"

I didn't respond. Mom made time for her priorities, and her number one priority was having fun. Mine too.

"Your Mommy Burr sewed all your mother's clothes from pictures they found in fashion magazines—even her prom formal gown," Daddy Burr said proudly. "Ann wore the latest styles and was declared the best-dressed kid in her high school." He paused, deep in thought. "I don't know what happened to make her turn out like she did." He leaned back in the chair, his stomach swelling as he sighed.

I thought of how Mom sewed herself fairy-tale gowns to attend the Marine Corps ball each year on the arm of my stepfather. My grandmother taught her to sew, and she'd teach me, too, in the years to come.

Daddy Burr and I walked the grounds together. He adjusted his drip system for the dozens of trees and showed me his grafting work and garden. We paused for a drink of cool water from the windmill. As always in his presence, peace radiated from him and created a calm balance in me.

We entered the kitchen through the back door to the smell of sautéed onions and garlic.

"Are you ready to start working on your cape while lunch simmers?" Mommy Burr asked.

On her foot-pedaled black Singer sewing machine, my grandmother and I sewed a deep red velvet cape for me to wear with long dresses on chilly California evenings.

My grandmother, her head bent over the fabric, pinned the seams in place, and without looking up, she said, "Ann called and told us about your pregnancies. I know they made it hard on you. Do you want to talk about it?"

Blood stung my face. "No—I mean, there's nothing to say. I don't want to talk about it." I'd rather be in denial and pretend I was a little girl once again cared for by my grandparents.

The kitchen felt packed full of elephants, but I refused to acknowledge any of them. I used a needle to remove my stitching mistake and stole a glimpse of Mommy Burr. Her face crinkled, lost in thought, but she didn't look up. She appeared to be battling her own inner demons.

Finally, she asked, "Why didn't you come stay here during your pregnancy? We've always wanted you to live with us."

"It's too late now, Mommy Burr."

"Through your early years, Daddy Burr and I talked about taking you away from Ann and Nick. We knew they didn't treat you right."

They thought about rescuing me from my parents? She voiced my favorite fantasy as a kid. All the abuse would never have happened if they'd taken me.

I sprung up from the sewing machine. "So why didn't you?" I looked around for a way to escape my frustration.

"Charlotte—" Mommy Burr said my name so nicely it hurt. "Sit down. Please don't leave upset."

Her voice calmed me. I went to the stove and stirred the turnips and black-eyed peas from their garden.

I fantasized a million times about living with them. What about the other kids? Who would rescue them if I weren't there when Dad went overseas?

"It would entail a long court battle. Taking a child from her mother is not an easy thing for anyone involved," Mommy Burr said.

I wanted to tell her I understood, but I didn't. They feared my mother. I feared her too.

"I'm nauseated. Morning sickness, I think. I'm going out for a walk."

I wanted to confide in Mommy Burr and tell her about the confusion around my pregnancies, about Dad beating me, and so many other things. But why cause her more anguish? Mommy Burr and Daddy Burr carried great sadness for me already.

I strolled through the trees. My flight was scheduled to return to California soon. I hoped to make the last few days of my visit joyful for us all.

BABY MAKES TWO

9

I shook Jerry. "Wake up! I'm having a miscarriage!"

He rolled over to face me. His hair was sticking up. He blinked rapidly, trying to understand. My words sunk in and he leaped out of bed, yanking on his pants.

"Call the hospital. Oh my God. What's happening?" I gasped for air and wrapped my arms around my belly bump.

Wide awake now, he asked, "Can you get up?"

My arms around his neck, he pulled me from the bed, but my knees kept giving out. I fell back. He picked me up, but I couldn't bend at the waist. The vise crunched my insides harder and harder.

"Oh, God, I can't do it. I'm scared! Hurry! Get help, Jerry. Call Mom. Call an ambulance!"

He ran to the payphone in the alley, leaving me alone. While he was gone, something happened. As if possessed, my body heaved and pushed all by itself, and an unearthly scream blew out from somewhere inside me.

Panting, Jerry sprinted into the bedroom. His face was covered with a sheen of sweat.

My body heaved again. "What's happening? Help me!"

Jerry leaned over me, visibly shaking. His eyes traveled down my stomach and grew wide in his pale, horror-stricken face.

I gave a long deep moan accompanied by a hard push using every ounce of my strength.

Get it out of me!

Sweating, I concentrated on breathing in and out, trying to take my mind off the pain.

At six months, the baby refused to stay inside me another minute, battling its way from my womb. We fought together, mother and child, and with one more enormous push, it ended, and like a miracle, the pain stopped.

A little voice squeaked in the stunned silence. My eyes fixed on the wonder of the wet, bloody little baby, the tiniest human I'd ever seen. Jerry supported the baby's head and held him over my stomach so as not to stretch the dark, mysterious cord connecting me to the newborn.

The baby's tiny arms waved, and his legs kicked furiously. I understood him. I wanted to punch and kick at life with him.

"It's a boy," Jerry whispered.

"Yes, I know. Lie him on me."

He lay the little boy face down on my chest. *Is his heart beating in rhythm with mine?* I cried and laughed through my wet exhaustion.

"It's okay. It's over now," I whispered to the top of his fuzzy blonde head.

Ambulance attendants rushed into the bedroom, and one of them yelled at the gathering neighbors, "Stay outside!"

Mom's voice rose from somewhere, "But I'm her mother!"

She appeared beside me, knelt to my level next to the bed, and stroked my wet forehead.

"I'm here, Charlie. Are you okay?"

"Yes, thank you for coming, Mom." She always showed up when I needed her most.

The ambulance roared down Ball Road, my baby and I resting inside.

"Ma'am, let me see my baby—"

"You know the rules," the nurse said.

"I birthed him in my own bed at home. I've already seen him."

The nurse hesitated but lowered my child. He was quiet and sleeping. They'd wrapped him in a light blue blanket.

"He has his father's lips," I said. "He's so small."

"He's four-and-a-half pounds," the nurse replied.

I stared at the small bundle in her arms, then watched her place him back in the rolling incubator. "Please don't tell my mother I saw him."

Jerry said that several neighbors left bags of baby clothes on our apartment doorstep. I dreaded the thought of running into these nice people. *What am I supposed to say to them? I gave up the baby for adoption because he wasn't Jerry's kid?*

The day after I arrived home, I opened the door to find a neighbor wearing a bright smile and holding a fresh-baked pie in her outstretched hands.

Oh, God, quick, what do I say? I sputtered out, "The baby died."

Shock then sadness raced across her face. She spread the word because no one mentioned the baby again, and the sacks of clothes disappeared.

My breasts were huge and painful, and they felt like they could burst with pressure. I called the doctor several times but could not get help. A nurse said to soak my breasts in a bowl of ice water. I did that for days, but it wasn't enough to stop the pain. I didn't know there was medication to stop the milk production since the doctor had never mentioned nor prescribed it. I don't remember how long it took for the leaking to stop and the swelling to subside, but the pain kept me awake night after night.

Mom claimed that kids had ruined her life. She told her friends that Dad wanted a big family, and since she'd converted to Catholicism for him, she didn't use contraceptives. The Catholic Church permitted the rhythm system, but that system never prevented Mom from getting pregnant. Even though I was a married woman, I didn't dare ask her about birth control, and she didn't offer any suggestions.

It was horrifying to imagine having a kid every year for the next decade like Mom had. No matter what the Catholic Church said, I needed birth control, especially since Jerry wanted sex every night and never brought up the subject of an annulment.

I braced myself and asked my doctor about birth control. I detected no disgust in his voice when he explained my options. He even mentioned the IUD. I went through the procedure to have an IUD inserted right away.

I was under eighteen and without a car. Searching for work seemed hopeless. Other than occasional visits to my family's home with Jerry, I spent my days alone.

We adopted a small dog from the pound to keep me company and called him Smokey after the first horse my mother had as a young girl.

I loved Smokey and treated him the way I hoped my babies were treated, but he wasn't enough to keep me grounded. Going from a big, noisy family to this silent environment meant each day the confinement closed me in more.

Is this how Mom felt raising us?

Thoughts of my boys shifted day-to-day, from wanting to

know them to relief for not keeping and raising them. I said a prayer for each to live in a safe and loving family environment.

"Charlotte, wake up!" Jerry's voice came from a distance.

I woke to find myself clinging to him. The effect of my dream lingered.

"You had another nightmare, but I couldn't understand your words." He cradled and caressed me until I pulled away and wiped my face on the sheet.

"I'm okay. It's over. Let's go back to sleep," I said.

"It's not over. What's your dream about? Same as last time?"

"Yeah, same." I pushed my messy hair back from my face. "I ate too much ice cream before bed."

"It's not the ice cream, Charlotte. Tell me the dream."

I sniffed. "It sounds stupid."

"I won't think it's stupid. Tell me."

"It's my mom," I whispered and swallowed. "I dreamed my mother was a car, and she kept running over me." I gulped back the sorrow. "Every time she ran over me, she crushed me down further and further until I lay flat with the pavement. I screamed for her to stop, to see me. The worst part is I loved her anyway. This sounds stupid. I want to go back to sleep, Jerry, and not talk about it anymore."

Two days later, I came home to find Jerry cooking his own dinner. "Hey, you got home early," I said. "What's up?"

He followed me to the bathroom and stood in the doorway. "Where have you been?"

"I went out with Amy, her brother, and another guy."

His voice got louder as he spoke. "So, you've been out with Amy, the slut, and two dudes I've never met—all day?"

"I hardly ever go out, Jerry. How can I?" I shrugged. "I don't own a car. I'm going crazy waiting for you all day with nothing to do except cook and clean."

He slapped the bathroom door with his open palm, making a loud bang. "I work seventy hours a week so you can run around with your freaky, loser friends, right? God, you're like your mother."

"My mother? Loser friends? At least they party, Jerry. You're the loser because you don't do anything except work." I stood up from the toilet.

His lips pulled back from his teeth like a snarl. He lurched forward and backhanded me in the face. I lost balance and stumbled backward in the tub, my pants tangled around my ankles.

Jerry turned on his heel and left.

His remark, "You're like your mother," stung me more than the slap.

His slap seemed insignificant at the time because I'd experienced so much more at home. Still, I recognized violence. My mother and stepfather used it to control me, and now Jerry did too.

On his drive home from work the next day, Jerry stopped along the road to pick wildflowers. I cooked a spaghetti dinner and had it waiting for him. I normally prepared dinner for Jerry, but I missed out on life by staying home every day. I played Led Zeppelin albums so loudly, they nearly crashed the speakers. I grabbed Smokey, danced around the living room, and tried to create my own fun.

I talked to my grandparents every Sunday, and they sent me a prepaid ticket to come see them every few months. While I was in Texas for my next visit, Jerry took the engine from a wrecked car and put it in a '65 Camaro with a blown engine. He waxed the car to a shine and parked it in front of our apartment to surprise me when I returned home.

"Oh my God! This is amazing! Thank you! Thank you. I love it! I love you!"

"I love you too, baby. You know that, right?" He reached for me, and I jerked back. He turned away and combed his hair back with spread fingers. "Sorry. I don't know what I'm doing anymore." His voice sounded throaty.

I circled my arms around him, looking up into his face. "Thank you again for my car, Jerry. I don't know what I'm doing either."

Mom used her influence to help me get a part-time job at the bookmobile library where she worked. Things calmed down for a few months, but I stewed. *Give me freedom and control over my own life.*

I walked into our apartment and found Jerry sitting on the couch eating a hamburger while watching TV. I gulped air.

He scanned me head to toe and frowned. He wore the mechanic's blue shirt and pants I'd ironed for him. His once-new work clothes always appeared dirty from oil and grease—even when clean.

"Where have you been?" he asked, still chewing.

"Out with Amy."

"Are you loaded?"

"We got stoned. Is that a problem?" I opened my palms.

"Yeah. I come home exhausted after work. I expect you to cook dinner. Too much for you?"

I ignored him.

Sometime later in the night, Jerry got up, stood at the foot of the bed, and yanked off my covers.

"What are you doing?" Bleary-eyed, I squinted at the alarm clock. It was 12:30 a.m.

"I'm sick of you running around with freaky Amy. You've lost it."

"Fuck you! I'll hang out with whomever I want. And don't expect me to wait around all day every day for you."

His face turned blood red in splotches. A vein pulsed in his neck. "Then get out!"

We yelled at each other while I packed. Outside, he clutched my upper arm and pulled me toward his car.

I jerked my arm away. "All right, I'll go."

"Damn right you'll go." He grabbed me again.

"In my own car," I shouted, but he shoved me in his.

We drove a mile in silence when I realized the direction we were headed. The hair rose on my arms. Goosebumps peppered the back of my neck.

My words choked out. "Please don't take me there."

He kept driving.

"Take me to the bus station. Anywhere but there. Don't take me back, Jerry. You don't know what it's like there."

He refused to stop. I grabbed the handle and pushed the door open. Wind pounded my face as the pavement rushed by.

"What the fuck? Close the door!"

The speed we traveled stopped me from jumping out. But what was worse, broken bones from hitting the pavement or reentering my parents' home?

We stood in the dark outside the house, a suitcase in my hand. Jerry banged on the door.

Dressed in bathrobes and wiping away sleep, my parents opened the door together. They took in my disheveled appearance and Jerry standing beside me. I witnessed Dad's grim anger simmer. I shrunk lower. Mom stood beside Dad, a concerned expression on her face, but she remained quiet.

"I'm leaving her here." Jerry nudged me forward.

"Oh no, you're not." Dad closed the door in our faces.

My shoulders relaxed as I released my breath. At least they didn't trap me back in their house of nightmares.

I tried to get in the car, but Jerry shoved me back out and locked the door.

"Jerry!" I yelled at his car as he drove off.

The night air, black and inky dense, closed in around me. I didn't know where to go, but I'd rather sleep under a bush or tree than stay in my parents' house.

Trudging along the empty road running in front of our house, I shuddered from the leftover shock of Jerry forcing me to go back home. Crickets sang in harmony. Clouds moved, and the moon illuminated the surrounding oil fields and hills where I frequently rode our horses. An owl hooted from the shadowy treetops. No cars passed. After a twenty-minute walk, I spotted a small, red neon Budweiser sign marking a lonely tavern sitting off the road.

I dragged open the creaky wooden door and peeked inside. A rush of cigarette smoke and booze-breath hit me. An Alabama song played on the jukebox. Another Budweiser sign hung over a huge mirror behind the bar, and a cash register sat against the wall beneath the mirror.

A bald and aproned man, his tattooed, muscular arms bulging under his T-shirt, operated the register with his back to me. He banged the cash drawer closed and met my eyes in the mirror. He turned to face me. Something in his expression caused the three patrons on barstools to turn and look too. I'm sure a seventeen-year-old girl with long, wild, tangled hair, faded jeans, and a tattered suitcase appeared strange at 1:30 a.m. in this remote place.

I lifted my head and moved with purpose to the bar. "Can I borrow a dime to make a phone call?" I hated the way my voice came out, trembling and squeaky.

I called Jerry at the apartment on our new phone. "Please come back for me. If you'll pick me up, I'll find a place to go until we figure this out. I'm at Vick's bar on Macmillan."

I stood outside the bar, shivering. Someone in a silver pick-up truck with tinted windows slowed down. I froze, afraid he'd stop. I moved closer to the tavern door, and he cruised on. After twenty long minutes, Jerry arrived.

I stuck my head in the passenger window. "I need a dime to pay back the bartender."

He dug in his jeans. We barely spoke to each other on the ride home.

The next day, I met Amy in the local park. "Jerry and I can't live together anymore. I've got to figure out what I'm going to do."

"Maybe time apart will help. Why don't we hitchhike some-place?" she said.

Three young hippy-types strolled close by, two guys and a girl.

"What's up? Do you ladies get loaded?" the guy with a long dark ponytail asked, eyes traveling back and forth between Amy and me.

"Yeah, if you got the weed." Amy giggled.

We smoked, joked, and told the group of our plans to hitch-hike somewhere.

"We're leaving for San Francisco on Friday. We'll make room if you pitch in gas money," ponytail guy said.

Planning a trip to San Francisco was another attempt to

find freedom. My life up to that point had been reversed. The circumstances of raising kids when I was still a kid drove me to yearn for the childhood fun I'd missed. My sense of confinement continued by getting married too young.

My free-spirited character was influenced by my mother. Her craving for freedom, fun, and escape from marriage and kids had led to her affairs and irresponsibility. She'd missed her party years by giving birth to eight children during the time she was eighteen to twenty-nine. The Catholic Church forbade birth control until her health was threatened following the birth of her eighth child. By searching for an abortion doctor, my mother had attempted to change the trajectory of my life. She hadn't wanted me to suffer her fate.

The mores of the time dictated that an illegitimate pregnancy was the girl's fault, and so it became her responsibility to raise the child. I'd brought shame on myself and my family, but with my mother's help, I found a way to bury the secret. At sixteen years old, I'd married a boy I didn't know to give the dirty secret some legitimacy. To keep the lie buried, I hid the identity of the real father from my mother-in-law and told our neighbors the baby had died. The secrets multiplied, but I locked them away deeply and never told anyone that I gave birth to two sons as a teenager.

Throughout my life, when someone asked me if I had children, I answered, "No." If I said, "Yes," inevitably, the next question would be, "Where did he/she go to school?" Any question cornered me, forcing more lies, or worse, confessing my complicated past to a stranger.

Jerry didn't respond when I told him my plans to leave for a few days.

Six of us piled into a white VW van with an orange peace symbol painted on the back and homemade tapestry curtains covering the windows. The guy with the long, dark ponytail drove while the rest of us rode in back, got high, played guitars, or listened to the eight-track tape blare out the new song by The Who, "Won't Get Fooled Again."

The guy who played guitar was declared legally blind. He saw light and dark shadows but couldn't drive. A small, exuberant fellow, he wore shoulder-length brown hair and talked about becoming a music agent. He planned to make contacts while in San Francisco.

The third guy traveling with us came from French-Canadian Quebec and spoke with a thick French accent. His short, blond hair curled around his head like a halo. He'd hitchhiked throughout the U.S. for several months but planned to return home to Quebec after this trip.

The woman with us was the same girl we'd met in the park. Her heart-shaped face was framed by a tumble of bright red curls, and her skin, white as cream, had the barest hint of freckles. She wore a floor-length white gauze skirt and a low-slung macramé belt. She didn't say much but giggled a lot.

Anticipation electrified me, and I loved feeling included in this cool group of hippies. I had no one to answer to and no responsibilities. Life was all fun and music, and we were on our way to San Francisco.

However, thoughts of Jerry never completely left my mind. He knew some of my family's history of abuse, yet he'd dumped me back in that nasty nest of misery. As I saw it, marriage meant depending on the mercy of another person. I had to find a better way.

Someone passed me a joint, and I took another deep draw,

holding in the urge to cough. Soon my worries floated away like mist on a breeze.

Our van friends knew people in San Francisco who lived a few blocks from Haight-Ashbury. We hauled our sleeping bags up the stairs of the old Victorian house situated only inches from the houses on either side. The homeowners, a young San Francisco couple, welcomed us to throw our sleeping bags on their living room floor.

Neil Young's voice poured from the huge speakers, singing "Cinnamon Girl." The six of us rolled out our sleeping bags on the floor. After the lights went out, the ponytail guy lay beside me and reached for me.

"Come on, let's get it on," he said in my ear.

"I told you I'm married," I whispered. Surprised at his advances, I scooted away, positioning myself closer to Amy.

"Come on, don't be so uptight."

I liked feeling accepted as part of this free-love scene, but not by having sex with some guy lying between a bunch of strangers in the middle of the floor. I ignored him but felt out of place now.

Why are women expected to be available to men just because they're women? Is this the price I pay for exercising my right to freedom? Do I even have the right to freedom?

I still cared for Jerry but didn't want to be married anymore. I chose to escape into stony highs instead of thinking about it too much.

For the next few days, Amy and I walked around San Francisco, amazed by the talented chalk art everywhere. Guys wore very long hair, bandannas, and faded bell-bottoms. Young women wore belly-dancer belts that jingled when they walked. Others wove flowers in their hair, so Amy and I braided daisies into each other's hair too. Musicians gathered on the corners playing guitars and bongos. People wore tie-dyed T-shirts with Tricky Dick cartoons painted on them and handed out anti-war flyers.

The whole city sparked and crackled creative energy and smelled like marijuana combined with patchouli oil. People lived life freely, however they chose. Compared to this, my predictable life married to Jerry seemed mundane.

"Jefferson Airplane is playing in Golden Gate Park this weekend free," Amy said.

"I have to go back."

"Why? You talked to Jerry?"

"No, but I will tomorrow. I've got to figure things out."

That night, I avoided the ponytailed creep by moving my sleeping bag to the other side of the room, but he moved too, rolling out his bag beside me again. I loved San Francisco, but I no longer felt free or independent, just cheap lying next to this guy. I called Jerry the next morning.

"I'm in San Francisco," I said.

"How did you—"

"Amy and I caught a ride with some people we met in the park. I'll tell you about it when I get back. I miss Smokey. Can I come home?"

A woman tapped on the phone booth door to rush me.

I ignored her.

"He waits by the door for you every night. Yeah, come home," Jerry said.

"I'll catch a bus back if these guys aren't ready to leave soon."

A few weeks after I returned from San Francisco, Mom called. "Hey, Charlie, how are you doing?"

"I'm fine. We're all fine."

Although deeply hurt about her and Dad slamming the door in my face, I didn't confront her. I feared she'd tell me I deserved it. Our phone conversation consisted of mostly small talk about work at the bookmobile library until I told her my plans to annul the marriage or divorce Jerry. I waited, but her response didn't come.

"Are you still there?"

"I'm here. Did you talk to Jerry about this?" Her voice was clipped.

"Sort of. He knows I want to leave."

I escaped my parents' leverage over my life, yet the bond—the unspoken parallels between my mother and me—deepened the importance of her opinion, her shame of me as well as her pride. I wanted to untangle myself from her and do what she never did for herself, which was achieve fulfillment. She lived her life under the weight of religion, lots of kids, and a lack of formal education. She was burdened with society's expectations. She'd helped free me from raising kids in the only way she knew how, but it was up to me to take it from there.

I put my thoughts of divorce on pause as the holidays came around. Jerry and I planned to meet my family for Midnight Mass on Christmas Eve. They'd already left for church when we arrived at their home, so I put Smokey in their basement with Speedy.

After Mass, we drove back to pick up Smokey. Jerry and I arrived first.

"Oh my God! Look!" I pointed.

Flames and rolling clouds of dark smoke billowed out of the living room windows. I leaped from the car before we stopped rolling, darted through the front door but got blasted backward by a hot draft and the smell of burning wood. Fire blazed up the front staircase and up the chiffon curtains fast, like a crazed animal. I raced back outside and called for Smokey. My family's car slid to a halt on the gravel. Everyone scrambled out, and Mary Lou yelled, "Suzie and Kathy are asleep upstairs!"

"Don't go back in there, Charlotte," Jerry shouted.

But my two youngest sisters were trapped in a burning house. I bolted around to the rear of the house, inhaled a big breath of outside air, then banged through the kitchen door and raced up the narrow back staircase, two steps at a time. Dad closed in behind me. I stopped at the top of the stairs. Dad shoved past me and disappeared into the smoke-filled hallway, grabbed Suzie from one of the bedrooms, and ran back down and outside.

Back in the hall, I covered my mouth with the tail of my shirt. I was sweating and my eyes stung. I called for my youngest sister, six-year-old Kathy. She whimpered, but I couldn't determine which of the four upstairs bedrooms she occupied. I panicked, picturing her crouched in a corner engulfed in thick smoke with flames closing in.

With no time to think, I slid my hand along the wall searching for the first bedroom door, yelling, "Kathy, run! Run to the back stairs!" I coughed, feeling like I was suffocating but called to her again.

"I can't! I can't! I'm scared," she cried.

Dad shot past me and vanished into the blinding smoke. He reappeared a moment later with Kathy in his arms, and without a word, ran down the stairs and outside. I trailed close behind.

Thank God Dad had come home from church when he did.

Dad set Kathy on the grass. Dark ash coated her skinny body. She whimpered and quivered. Her white-blond hair looked like ropes of black vine. Someone wrapped a towel around her.

I searched for Smokey again, called and called, sure he'd run to me any minute. Speedy came charging out of the smoke, but no Smokey.

I stumbled around the outside of the burning house, searching and calling until I went hoarse. My broken heart overwhelmed me. I covered my face, determined not to see this reality.

What kind of God allows this? Kills the innocent.

I shouted to my parents that Smokey was missing, but they were busy comforting my brother for the loss of his parakeet.

Jerry and I called Smokey together. Misery erupted from a deep abyss inside me. My heart imploded when I pictured him dying in the fire. I kept thinking of him in pain, terrified, and so alone. I cried out for him then started sobbing. Jerry put his arm around my shoulders.

Neighbors spoke to my parents about dividing the kids in pairs and taking them to their homes for the night, Christmas Eve.

Through my tears, I watched the firefighters spray our house with their massive hoses. I hoped with all my power that the years of awful events that had taken place in that house would burn away with the fire. The house, and the cruelty which pulsed from it, had found one last way to reach out and stab me in the heart before its own demise. It took my little Smokey down with it.

I stuffed the horrors that the place represented down to the depths of my soul, and then I prayed for it to burn in hell.

Jerry and I drove home without Smokey. My stomach churned and made me want to vomit. I prayed Smokey died of smoke inhalation instead of the pain of burning alive.

The babies and now Smokey. No one in the world cared more for them than I did, yet I was the one who'd put them aside and left them either with strangers or in a cold basement. They looked to me with the trust of a baby or the innocence of an animal, and I'd failed them. I hated myself.

"Stop the car. Quick. Let me out." I opened the door and vomited. After those few words, I didn't speak for days.

Jerry and I, married a year and a half, seldom fought anymore. After the baby was born and the fire killed Smokey, nothing anchored me to our marriage. I wanted to escape the memories and explore the world. I was eighteen, fearless and careless. Nothing the world dumped on me frightened me anymore.

"I've been thinking about it a lot. I'm moving out," I said.

"What? I don't get it. Why?" Jerry asked.

"It isn't anything you did. It's me."

With a part-time library job and no plan, I packed my few possessions. I'd stayed married longer than I'd expected because I had nowhere else to go.

"I'm leaving the Camaro. I love the car, but it really belongs to you." I set the car and house keys on the Formica kitchen table.

Jerry stood by in silence, looking everywhere except at me, then stomped out, slamming the door behind him. My leaving hurt him, but the pull of independence outweighed my empathy.

PART II

MIGHTY MIKE

During the first several weeks after leaving Jerry, I crashed on a friend's couch and even saved a little money.

Since I no longer had the Camaro, Amy and I routinely hitchhiked to the beach towns. One weekend, we stayed overnight in a friend's RV at a campground near Laguna Beach and went to a nightclub that allowed eighteen-year-old kids inside but didn't allow us to drink. The music blared through the dim, smoky place. Teenagers and twentysomethings crowded the dance floor.

I sat alone at a small table, gasping for breath after dancing nonstop for at least an hour. I watched a guy who looked like Jim Morrison of the Doors but with light brown hair stand amidst the crowd. His appearance intrigued and reminded me of the artists and musicians in San Francisco. He scanned the room, and his gaze rested on me. I smiled.

He took my smile as an invitation, pulled out the chair at my table, and leaned in. "Do you live around here?"

"No. Here for the night."

Yelling above the music, Mike introduced himself with the relaxed Midwestern accent of an educated country boy. He and two friends spent the summer at a Laguna Beach hotel. During the rest of the year, he attended college in Northern California on the East Bay, across the Bay Bridge from San Francisco.

After that night, I hitchhiked to Laguna Beach every weekend to see him, glad to spend time away from my friend's couch.

We talked, laughed, and partied till the end of summer. I liked him a lot and daydreamed about moving in with him.

One hot August night, we sat by the hotel swimming pool, drinking and talking late. The small, two-story hotel looked more like a shabby motel with its peeling paint and white metal handrails, but the surrounding grounds made up for it. The pool glowed blue from underwater lights, and the night felt uncommonly balmy. Palm fronds fluttered and bent back and forth from the breeze. Sounds from a party drifted in from a distance.

Beads of water slid down my beer bottle. I took another swallow. "Didn't you say you went to Vietnam?"

"Yeah, drafted."

"Oh, wow." I waited.

"I got drafted in '68, during the most intense frontline fighting." His chest swelled from inhaling deeply, as if deciding whether to continue. "During one of our missions, my helicopter, full of GIs, accidentally landed on top of a Vietcong hideout."

I tapped my toes together, then interlocked and unlocked my hands. Dad never talked about Vietnam. What I knew, I learned from the San Francisco protesters and what I saw on TV.

Mike paused again, scrutinizing me from the pool recliner. "Do you want to hear this? You look uncomfortable."

"Yeah, I want to hear. What happened?" I stiffened at the thought of him on a helicopter flown by Dad.

"We jumped out, scattered, and ran for the jungle, becoming easy targets for snipers. Shots came from everywhere. Five of us dove into a deep canal for cover." He pressed his eyes shut as if trying to block out the memory etched deep in his psyche.

"One of the snipers, perched above somewhere, picked us off even after we dove in and swam deep." He paused, then quietly continued. "Bullet trails swooshed by me on all sides. My friends' bodies jerked and twitched from the bullets hitting them. Everyone who dove in the canal that day got killed, except me."

He stopped, rubbed his eyes, and pretended to yawn.

My throat tightened, and I waited for him to regain control.

"I got hit in the arm, and another round went through my helmet, barely missing my head. Another bullet grazed my scalp, but somehow my life got spared." He inhaled again and reached for his beer.

"My God." I sat on the edge of the pool, dangled my feet in the cool water, and waited to hear more.

"U.S. Air Support flew over and bombed the area. The sniper paused long enough to duck for cover. I scrambled out of the water and crawled on all fours through the jungle, searching for a place to hide. I found a dry canal, rolled in, and lay on my back in the ditch." He cleared his throat. "I hid in that fucking ditch in enemy territory. I'd never been so afraid in my life knowing I'd likely be captured." He glanced at me. "When a medic ran by, I jumped up and ran like hell, following him back to the remains of our—" His voice faded, and he looked away.

"Did you receive recognition for bravery?"

"Yeah. I received several medals, but the one I'm most proud of, other than the Purple Heart, is the CIB Badge. I often wonder why I was spared. The four GIs who dove in the water with me that day died along with so many others." His words dripped resentment.

Not sure how to comfort him, I remained quiet. Fear of his judgment prevented me from confiding anything about my own past.

"What's a CIB Badge?"

"Combat Infantry Badge." He took a big gulp from his beer. "I hate Nixon, and I hate Vietnam. I got railroaded into fighting for our American war machine. We're only there to protect U.S. corporate interests."

"My father went to Vietnam twice. He thinks we should fight and win. Otherwise, Russia will use Vietnam to take over the world."

Mike's face darkened. He peered at me and snorted like my words sounded ridiculous to him.

His character was different from Dad's, and I liked him more because of it. They'd both experienced unimaginable horrors in Vietnam, but the fabric of the two men differed on a deep level. Mike's character reflected justice and honor. In my mind, Dad's cold distance and sometimes cruel behavior overshadowed his honor, but Mike's history made me realize Dad's Vietnam experience probably affected him in horrible ways I'd never imagined. However, that realization didn't change my fear of him.

Mike believed in a universal spirituality—all connected to the same energy and all part of God.

"Karl Marx was right-on when he wrote that religion is the opiate of the masses," he said.

"But the Bible says Jesus is the way—"

He smirked and waved his hand. "I don't buy it."

I thought about my upbringing, attending Catholic school through seventh grade. At about ten years old, ready to make my First Communion and preparing for my first confession, the nuns taught us the sacred truth of Catholicism.

"Talking to Father O'Neill is the same as talking to God," Sister Louisa had said. "You must tell God every sin you committed during the week. If you don't tell, you'll go to hell and burn for eternity."

When I'd pulled back the dark, heavy curtain and entered the musty confessional to tell God all my sins, I imagined burning in hell. I knelt, but when a shadow—like a ghost or a devil—moved on the other side of the dark screen, goose bumps as big as BBs peppered my legs above my knee-high socks.

My voice squeaked, "Bless me, God, for I have sinned…" I continued, saying, "Yes, God" or "No, sir, God."

With no sins to confess, I covered my bases by making one up. I told God I'd talked back to my mother. I figured I'd probably done it because Mom had always yelled, "I'm so sick of you kids talking back!"

The shadow on the other side of the mysterious screen waved his hand in the motion of the cross. "Say three Hail Marys for your penance."

The nuns often talked about miracles. Every night, I prayed with all my heart for the Virgin Mary to grant me just one, which was to grow my hair long overnight. I'd wake up the next morning, feel my head for new long hair, and finding nothing different, I'd pray harder all over again.

On the day of my First Communion, I knelt at the altar, head tilted back, tongue out flat, and waited to receive the holy wafer, the body of Christ. The God-priest moved so slowly from the other end of the long communion rail that my tongue dried out and trembled. I held myself rigid with my tongue out, fearing my hair would fall out if I didn't do it right.

I peeked through one eye and saw the priest move in front of me, place the wafer on my shaky tongue, bless me, and move on. Was that it? I didn't feel different, and my hair didn't fall out or grow longer either. But the wafer tasted delicious like thin, sweet bread. I wanted to munch a bucket of them like popcorn.

Along with differences in our religious and political beliefs, Mike and I ate differently. I liked fast foods such as hamburgers and Cokes. He ate organic, healthy food.

His ideas made sense. By summer's end, I learned to accept and adopt many of his viewpoints as my own. I read books by spiritual leaders such as Baba Ram Das, Yogananda, and a few years later, the poet Rumi. Today, I read Eckhart Tolle. The books I read were popular during that time when young people looked outside their traditional upbringing to find new ways of thinking about politics, war, racial prejudices, women's rights, natural foods, and religion. Mike's logic won my respect, and his confidence led me to these new ways of thinking.

I fell hard for him over the time we spent together in Laguna. When I overheard him on the motel room phone making plans to return to northern California, a wave of panic rushed through me.

"You're leaving? What about us?" *Keep cool, hold steady, and don't cry like a baby.*

"Do you want to come with me?"

We locked eyes. "Live together?"

"Yeah."

I liked this conversation. "What will I do there? I mean—"

"Enroll in school. You like art. Take art classes, yoga, whatever. Take some political science courses and a sociology class with my favorite teachers. They'll help you understand what's actually going on in the world and in Southeast Asia."

"I know what's going on in Southeast Asia."

He frowned but didn't respond.

Although I didn't graduate from high school, I passed the GED. Mike said the junior college had relaxed acceptance rules, but maybe they'd require me to pass an entrance exam. This was the first opportunity presented that gave me a direction, a chance to pursue something worthwhile for myself. Besides, I was in love.

My divorce papers were signed, so nothing held me back.

The subject of money never came up. He knew I didn't have any, and I didn't care whether he did either.

On the way out of town, Mike drove me to the house in Carbon Canyon my parents had bought after the fire. I wanted to say goodbye. My parents knew of my plans to leave that day, but they'd gone out shopping. My relief at their absence was accompanied by melancholy about my mother not staying home to say goodbye. I told myself I didn't want them to meet Mike anyway with his long hair. My future belonged to me alone, and I wanted no taint of judgment shadowing my enthusiasm.

I embraced my brother and the few sisters who were at home. The ache of missing them tugged at me before I even left. As we drove away, I turned and waved until they were out of sight, then leaned back in my seat and looked ahead to my new life.

After arriving in the Bay Area, we stayed with Dan at his place. Dan was Mike's friend from college in Indiana.

"I need to go back to Indiana to buy pot before we hunt for an apartment," Mike said. "That's how I pay for school. I plan to leave and return before classes start."

"Do you want me to go too?"

"I don't have the money to buy you a plane ticket."

"Then let's hitchhike. It'll be an adventure!" I stopped breathing and waited. I loved the idea of traveling cross-country—or hitchhiking anywhere, for that matter. We'd be so free.

"I guess we could hitchhike." He didn't seem excited about the idea.

We planned to leave Mike's old Fiat at Dan's house since it needed work and had barely run well enough to deliver us from Orange County. Mike and Dan drove to town for parts. When they hadn't returned by late afternoon, I went out.

Dressed in a light pink sweater, jeans, and tennis shoes, I walked to a local park before sundown.

Bursts of laughter came from the other side of a long hedge bordering the park. Always ready to join a party, I pulled back the thick foliage, still unable to see anything. I wedged myself through a sticky, narrow opening and sprang out on the other side.

My smile faded when I found myself in the middle of a bunch of bikers and a single woman standing around their Harleys lined up along the curb. "Oh shit." I froze like a startled fawn. I'd crashed the wrong party.

It's never safe to be a woman alone, especially a young woman, who is perceived as fair game by many men. The risk didn't dissuade me from stepping out of prescribed boundaries, like walking alone at night or entering a bar without an escort. Although this was no bar, and the sun was still up, I sensed the danger.

The bikers turned, fell silent, and stared.

"Oh shit," I said under my breath again. Holding my head down, I made myself small to disappear and turned back toward the bushes.

"Where'd you come from?" asked the closest biker. He looked like a grizzly bear. He stroked his scruffy beard that reached the middle of his bulky round chest.

"I didn't—"

Another biker motioned to his friend. "Hey, Frank, check this out. Who are you, young lady?"

A few more of them closed in around me, smiling hard and brittle as if enjoying a particularly nasty joke.

"I heard a party going on and wanted to…" My voice died away. They stared at me like I was a sizzling steak.

The late sun cast long shadows. Ideas of escape flashed through my mind, like running past them down the street. But seeing no one around, not even houses, where would I go? Even the field across from the park looked deserted. If I bolted for the street, they might knock me down and drag me somewhere. I moved toward the hedge.

"You looking to party?" one of the bikers asked.

"No, I'm expected home. My boyfriend's waiting," I said too loudly.

"I'll take you home," a different guy said in a baritone voice.

The guy who'd spoken wore a sleeveless, black jean jacket that showed off his tattooed arms. Some of his greasy hair escaped his ponytail. Dark curls stuck out from under his arms. A big silver chain hung from a belt loop on his jeans and swayed down his side to his back pocket. He stared with dark, red-rimmed eyes. He wasn't friendly.

"My bike's right here." He pointed to a low chopper, its high handlebars towering over the tiny back seat.

"I can't—"

He swung his leg over the bike, sat down, and looked at me. "Get on," he said, his voice gruff.

Muffled laughter came from the bikers as they watched this play out. I swallowed. The motorcycle growled when Dark Eyes fired it up.

"No, I have to go home—" I bumped past the bearded guy

to go through the opening, but he grabbed me around the waist and lifted me from behind.

"Let me go!" I kicked and pedaled the air, beating and pinching his arms. He held tightly, crushing my ribs.

He laughed in my ear, swung me around, and carried me a few feet to set me on the back of his friend's bike. I barely missed kicking Dark Eyes in the back.

"Why're you so scared? You think we're going to steal you? He's giving you a ride home." The bearded guy chuckled again.

Dark Eyes revved the bike and zoomed away with me on the back. Behind us, the other bikes fired up, sounding like an army of assault weapons going off.

"Turn left here," I yelled and pointed. "My house is that way." He turned right instead.

We gained speed and raced down the road away from Dan's house. I thought of jumping off the bike into the street, but I'd get seriously hurt, maybe run over by the bikes behind us. I held on, not knowing the unfamiliar area or where I was going. My hair whipped back, and I squirmed on the tiny seat. Up close, with my face pressed against this guy's back, I almost gagged from his salty-sour smell.

"Take me home." I hollered in his ear.

No response.

I squeezed my eyes shut when we rounded a corner too fast, then opened them hoping to spot a police officer.

Mommy Burr and Daddy Burr flashed through my mind. Would I ever see them again?

We entered a neighborhood and slowed down. No cops anywhere. Dark Eyes maneuvered the bike backward against the curb beside several other bikes already lined up.

"Get off."

"Where are we? You said you'd take me home."

The bikers from the park rumbled down the street and backed against the curb, lining up next to us.

In the streetlights, the neighborhood looked normal, even affluent. The large homes, perched atop expansive, grassy hills, smelled of fresh-cut lawns.

Would anyone hear me if I yelled? What if I ran?

I had a sick notion these guys might like it. They'd beat me up, rape me, or even kill me. I sniffed and felt the beginning of tears.

"Give me a minute, and I'll take you back," Dark Eyes said, not convincingly.

"No."

A Rolling Stones song, "Sympathy for the Devil," blared from the house. He gripped my arm.

Moments passed. We stared eyeball to eyeball.

Think, Charlotte. If he planned to hurt you, he'd take you somewhere else, not here. Stay calm.

My stomach cramped.

He clenched my arm tighter, towing me toward the house. I bit my lip. We walked the long, inclined driveway and entered the kitchen through the garage. He nudged me ahead through the door. My eyesight adjusted as I scanned the smoky interior. Four biker-types sat at a kitchen table playing cards. A pale oval-faced woman wearing thick, dark eye makeup peered at me through her long bangs. She sat close to a guy who slapped a card on the table and hollered. Another biker studied me with a curious expression. I breathed in and got a lung full of pot smoke. Nobody else noticed me. At least it wasn't a setup.

The kitchen opened wide to a large living room with high-pitched cathedral ceilings. People stood or sat on the brown shag carpet talking. Some smoked cigarettes. One guy drank straight from a bottle of Jack Daniel's. Another guy smoked a bong, all while the music blared. A pretty blonde woman sitting on the floor next to a redwood coffee table threw her head back, laughed with mouth wide open, then leaned forward and snorted a line of white powder off the table using a short straw.

"Wait here," Dark Eyes said and disappeared into the crowd.

If the house gets any more crowded and people get drunker, I can slip out unseen. But what then? There were no pay phones in the neighborhood, and I didn't know Dan's phone number anyway. *Where would I go? To a neighbor's house? Maybe the neighbors are here at this party.*

A red-bearded biker with a huge belly and stringy hair parted in the middle took my hand and tugged me deeper into the crowded living room. Wearing a dirty red T-shirt, suspenders, and baggy jeans, he swayed my arms to the music.

"Hey, baby." Spit bubbled through his missing front tooth.

I got a whiff of urine, like pee ammonia. He lifted my arms, swung me wide to make me dance. When I didn't respond, he dropped my hands and his grin, grumbled, and moved away.

Large double front doors opened to the outside porch. The doors swung wide and a biker couple burst in like they were on a mission. They paced down the dimly lit hallway toward the back of the house where Dark Eyes had gone, not closing the front doors behind them.

I moved toward the entrance, but Red Beard blocked my exit. He closed the double doors and turned back to face me. His toothless grin returned, more determined to make me dance. He leaned back against the doors, moving like a drunk belly dancer, arms and hands waving in the air above his head.

Someone shoved me hard from behind. I crashed against

Red Beard. I swung around to confront the pusher. "Don't touch me, you filthy—"

In an instant, everything went dark.

The faint sound of howls came from far away and got louder until I realized it was me. My own screams helped me regain consciousness. Tiny white bubbles popped and burst while circling around my brain, and a sound like flies buzzed in my ears. Bloody saliva dripped in strings between my spread fingers covering my face. I struggled for complete consciousness and realized I was kneeling on the floor with people standing around me.

Over the music, someone yelled, "Go for it, man."

I kept screaming.

Someone's huge hand reached down through the crowd of bikers. He grabbed a bunch of my hair and pulled me up from the floor, almost off my feet, stretching the scalp away from my skull. He supported me under my arms. Leaning against him, I walked unsteadily to the bathroom, blood dripping in spots on the front of my pink sweater.

I fell into survival mode, silently numb like the countless times when Mom or Dad had beaten me.

Get this over with and let me go.

Bathroom lights blinded me but helped me further regain my senses. He banged the bathroom door shut behind us. I leaned against the counter and wiped the blood off my face by smearing it on my sweater sleeve.

The guy pushed me onto the closed toilet seat, tilted my head back by my chin. His brown eyes, piercing but calm, scanned my face as if he were assessing a puzzle. He wet a washcloth and wiped my nose.

"He gotcha pretty good. Knocked you off your feet against the wall."

"Wha—why—" I stuttered.

I jumped when another guy cracked open the bathroom door and stuck his head in. "She's going to bring the cops, man," he said.

"Close the fucking door," my hero guy said. "And get Frank—now." He kicked the door closed behind him, still wiping my face.

"Oh please, I promise I won't tell anyone what happened. Let me go, please."

I held eye contact. I implored this man to spare me. He saved me in the living room and was my only hope now, my hero. He still cleaned my face. When he didn't respond to my pleas, I sobbed out the beginning of new tears and pleas.

"Shut the fuck up. Why the hell did you come here anyway?" His voice was deep and harsh.

"I didn't want to. I—"

"How old are you?"

"Eighteen."

Someone tapped on the door again, opening it partway. Dark Eyes peeked in, his face grim and lips pressed tight.

"Take her back where you got her," my hero guy said.

Dark Eyes nodded.

My guy pulled me up from the toilet seat. I tilted my head back and covered my nose using the damp washcloth, then followed Dark Eyes through the living room, staying close behind. The house was more crowded now, but people barely noticed us. Music blared. The cool night breeze moved as we stepped through the double doors and made our way down the inclined lawn.

I rode while holding the washcloth on my face, my other arm wrapped tightly around Dark Eyes's cold leather jacket. I whispered prayers of gratitude to be alive.

Neither of us spoke when I slid off the Harley at the park. He gunned the bike and roared away.

Dizzy again, I tripped over a root and fell flat in the dark. I lay there, my cheek on the dirt, no tears, just grateful and getting stronger. I stood up and brushed off twigs.

RAGS TO RICHES

11

"My God, what happened?" Mike asked.

I told him everything.

"You got on a Harley?" he smirked.

"My God, Mike, I didn't want to. I was so scared. I—"

"Why didn't you call for help, run away?"

"I did holler and kick. No one heard me. It all happened—"

"So, you're saying no one else saw or heard you in the park?"

"Yes." *What is this? I feel like I did something wrong. Did I?*

Dan sauntered into the kitchen. His jaw dropped when he saw me. "Oh man, what happened?"

"She went to a biker party and some dude punched her in the face."

"Jesus." Dan's curiosity swept back and forth between Mike and me, but the crackling tension in the air made him turn and walk out.

"You're blaming me for what those assholes did?"

"It's hard to believe anyone can force you on a motorcycle. I think you wanted to go."

I gulped down my hurt and sank onto a kitchen chair, exhausted. "Can't do this. Going to bed." I got back up.

Later, Mike came in and sat on the bed beside me. He laid his hand on my arm in a consoling way. "I'm glad you're okay."

"I could have been raped or killed." I pressed my eyes shut against the memory.

He patted my arm, pulled his T-shirt over his head, and got in bed.

The next day, I woke feeling as if a bulldozer had run over me. The bathroom mirror reflected my matted hair, split upper lip, and rosy-red nose. The beginning of black circles had formed around my eyes during the night, along with a tender lump on the back of my head where I'd hit the wall. Nothing was broken.

Two days later, Dan dropped us on a well-traveled freeway onramp in Berkeley, a favorite hitchhiking spot where people lined the ramp and took turns thumbing a ride.

I lowered myself on the hard gravel shoulder, leaned back against Mike's army duffle bag, and hummed along with someone's transistor radio playing Janis Joplin's "Me and Bobby McGee." I wished I'd brought a harmonica to play in the pouring rain, even though there wasn't a cloud in the sky. We'd get splashed by passing trucks, shiver, cold and wet, then take a hot shower and eat a hearty meal at a truck stop. That was my fantasy about hitchhiking.

Instead, a guy named Eddie in a black Trans Am with a mega sound system picked us up and drove us all the way to Mike's childhood home in Indiana.

Mike grew up in a small Craftsman-style home in a one-stoplight town with one sister, a year younger than me. He comfortably interacted with his parents, referring to them respectfully as his "folks."

Mike took care of his business every day. After a week, he got irritable. *Was it the humidity, or did I annoy him somehow?*

"I'm flying back to California, and I don't have enough

money to get you a ticket." He rubbed the back of his neck. "I'm not sure how you're getting back."

A flush started at my face and burned down my chest and arms.

"Are you listening?"

"Yeah, I heard you." I lifted my head and commanded myself to breathe, not panic.

That night, I lay wide-awake in bed. Until now, I'd loved the way Mike handled problems with his level head and cool delivery. After coming out of a chaotic family where yelling and brute force occurred daily, I appreciated his innate sense of calm. But when he uttered those words of abandonment, my faith in him was shaken. I was in Indiana because of him, and this was bullshit.

First thing the next morning, Mike drove his mom's car to the auto shop for an oil change. I walked to town to find a pay phone.

"Mommy Burr, I'm stuck in Indiana. I don't have any money, and I want to go back to California."

"How in the world did you get to Indiana?" she asked.

"I came with a friend. I didn't figure out this trip completely, so now I'm here with no way home. Will you send me a flight ticket? I'll take a bus from here to Chicago and fly home from there. It'll be cheaper."

"Of course, we'll send you the money. We'll wire it first thing tomorrow."

No judgment or disgust in her voice when I told her I'd screwed up. I pictured her talking on the black wall phone in their kitchen, a pan of garden green beans cooking on the stove. They helped me regardless of my poor choices and did it with love.

My allegiance to my grandparents ran through me like the blood in my veins. I would never purposely let them down. Looking back, I realize the security and freedom I sought could not be found through the safe harbor provided by men, or even from the love my grandparents offered. I had to achieve it for myself.

"Thank you, Mommy Burr. Tell Daddy Burr thank you a million times. I'll come visit once I get settled. I love you both."

"My grandparents are sending me money for a plane ticket home," I said. "I need to find a Western Union."

Mike exhaled, and his shoulders relaxed. "There's one here in town. Are you planning to take the same flight I'm taking out of Chicago?"

"I plan to fly out of Chicago, yes. I'm not sure when, though."

Silence.

"I'll give you my flight information, so you can work it out and decide." He studied his handwritten list, not looking at me.

I gave no immediate response, then said, "I have a friend from California who's living in Chicago now. I called him after I talked to my grandparents. I'm catching a bus this afternoon and staying there until my flight leaves."

Mike's face hardened as he absorbed my words. "If you're traveling with me, my flight isn't for another week. You're planning to stay with him a week?" He caught my eye, unblinking.

"Yep, that's my plan."

My friend living in Chicago, Drew, had once resided in the apartment building where my ex-husband Jerry and I had lived. Always fun, Drew routinely gathered neighbors together for barbecues.

I'm sure he'd heard rumors about the baby dying, but he never asked us questions.

On occasion, I visited him at his apartment while Jerry went to work. I overheard him tell one of his friends to stay away from me because I was married. When Jerry got home, I told him what Drew said to his friend. As a result, Jerry liked him even more, and the three of us became closer friends.

Drew moved back to his home in Chicago after living a year in our California apartment building, but we remained in contact via postcards. I'd written to him about my divorce from Jerry.

Drew picked me up from the Chicago airport. After I'd gotten settled, I pulled the quilt over me and fluffed my pillow on his couch. I noticed a pornographic comic book within my reach. I grabbed it and flipped through the pages. I stared at the cartoons, having never seen anything like it. A strange sensation moved through me. I reached between my legs and touched myself but jerked my hand back. I was so sensitive.

My body twitched from my searching fingers finding their own way to my sex spot. I kept playing, unable to stop. Something built in me, filling me more and more like a stretched, overblown balloon ready to pop. My leg muscles contracted as the sensation intensified, curling my toes from the internal pressure running down my legs. I inwardly exploded and released. My vagina gulped in the delicious pulsing. When the intensity subsided, I relaxed into exhaustion.

My legs ached like I'd done five hours of calisthenics. I lay there on the couch, grinning, and marked my age in my mind—eighteen years old, 1971. I'd always remember when I experienced my first orgasm.

A week later, Drew dropped me off at the Chicago airport for my flight to San Francisco. I embraced and thanked him, regretting that I might never see him again.

I spotted Mike at the boarding gate wearing the jean jacket

I'd embroidered for him. His face brightened, and his light blue eyes set warmly on me.

However, he'd betrayed me when he'd left me stranded in Indiana. If I brought it up, his aversion to conflict would destroy any chance of us making it together. My love for Mike made me want this to work, so I pushed away my pride and said nothing. I didn't mention my orgasm either since I wasn't sure I could do it again.

Sitting next to each other on the plane to San Francisco, I stitched my latest embroidery project.

"Who's that for?" he asked.

"I'm making this for our new place. When it's done, it'll say, 'Home Sweet Home.'" I hoped my project hinted of a happy homelife ahead of us. "You still want to move in together, don't you?" I stopped stitching, my hand pausing midair.

He looked down, thoughtful. "Yeah, let's give it a try."

"Okay." *Inwardly, I exhaled relief.* I continued to stitch. "I called my sister, Mary Lou, yesterday. My dad received orders to Okinawa. My family is moving to Japan for three years."

I had no family left in my life now except my grandparents—though living in the Texas hill country would be a slow life. I craved excitement, adventure, and crazy fun, and I wanted to forget my past. And I wanted Mike. I'd never known anyone like him. Although he partied hard and had wild fun, he was grounded, too. He had a practical side to his demeanor and decision-making skills. Life felt safe with him.

I hoped that by attending college, I'd learn what he knew and become the kind of woman he wanted. It hadn't occurred to me to figure out the kind of woman *I* wanted to be since I never received any direction other than how to change diapers.

We moved into a dilapidated upstairs apartment in the Oakland ghetto, and we both enrolled in school.

"Why are you attending a junior college when you already have a four-year degree from an Indiana university?" I asked.

"To re-educate myself and acquire more political aware-ness," he said. "Change is happening in this country, and I want to be part of it. We've got to leave Vietnam. By the way, here's the list of classes I told you about. They'll help you understand what's going on in the world."

I winced at the hidden insult. "I'm not a nitwit, Mike. I'm aware of what's going on in the world." I expected him to pat me on the head. "Are you laughing at me?" I hated even the hint of someone mocking me.

"No. But you don't know what you're talking about—the domino theory and all that shit. Take these classes. They'll do you good. Speaking of classes, Dylan said Alyson signed up for a natural food cooking class."

"So?" I asked, miffed by his superior attitude.

"You want to take the class with her? It's given by Two Sisters Restaurant."

I liked Two Sisters, and I also liked Dylan and Alyson. "I guess so. Just don't expect me to cook carrot casseroles for you."

He chuckled.

I enrolled in art classes, the political science classes Mike suggested, and read books about spiritual growth and universal energy. In addition to landing a part-time job at the college library, I learned a new way of cooking using organic ingredients.

Meanwhile, Mike's small marijuana business grew. He set up and organized a nationwide network of close friends trans-porting marijuana coast-to-coast, and the pot business boomed.

Sitting on the floor in our living room listening to albums late one night several months later, a loud crack echoed from the street two stories below.

"Was that a gunshot?"

"Calling the cops," Mike reached for the phone. "Don't look out the window."

"Why not?"

"Somebody might use your head for target practice."

Our tiny apartment, one of four in a divided Victorian house, was so small it barely fit a single piece of a sectional couch in the living room, but I loved it because I loved Mike.

On the rare occasion we arrived home late, we ran from his rusty VW bug to our triple-locked apartment entrance. We'd scurry past the occasional drug addict asleep on the broken sidewalk and kick aside trash, but we got there.

"My supervisor asked me to work late tomorrow night. Can I borrow your car again?"

He shined an apple using his T-shirt. "I don't want you driving my car anymore. You're too irresponsible."

"I told you I'm sorry about those parking tickets at school."

"Why the hell did you keep parking in the same place after you got the first ticket?" He chewed the apple, watching me.

"I guess I wasn't thinking, but—"

He tossed the core into the kitchen garbage can. "I guess you weren't thinking when you stuffed every ticket under my front seat either, right?"

"I thought you'd get mad if you saw them."

"Damn right, I'm mad." He opened the refrigerator to search for something more to eat. Without looking at me, he said, "You need your own car if you're going to keep working."

Ashamed, I hung my head. Why was I comfortable with the role of a naughty child? Why was I so thoughtlessly negligent? Looking back, I saw my mother as a happy-go-lucky risk taker and my stepfather as a practical military officer, presiding over our family. I knew no other way of relating to a man other than to emulate Lucy and Ricky from *I Love Lucy*.

The next morning, we left our apartment for school and descended the sagging staircase to the street.

"Oh shit!" Mike pointed to his VW bug parked at the curb. Someone had bashed in the windshield during the night. "Goddamnit! I'm sick of this dump. We don't need to live here anymore."

I scanned the newspaper and found a house in Piedmont, the hilly, affluent area of Oakland.

We arrived early to meet the owner and stood in the front yard transfixed by the elevated, two-story home with vines growing up the outside. The fragrance of eucalyptus trees mixed with honeysuckle drifted through the air.

"I love this house," I said.

"You haven't even seen the inside," Mike said with a half-smile.

Ten minutes later, the Japanese investor/owner wearing dark sunglasses slid his black Mercedes into the driveway. Motionless and unsmiling, he sat and observed us from his car as if deciding whether to get out or drive off. He got out and moved toward us.

Mike held out his hand. "Mr. Kimura, I'm Mike Jarrett. This is my wife, Charlotte."

Mr. Kimura grunted a response, shook Mike's hand, and stared at his shoulder-length hair and beard.

We followed Mr. Kimura through the front door. My breath caught in my throat at the high ceilings, shiny hardwood floors, and large white-brick fireplace. I reached behind me, found Mike's hand, and squeezed twice.

Mr. Kimura opened the back door to a European-style patio. Eucalyptus trees grew up the slopes bordering the patio. To top off the fantasy, climbing morning glories ringed a wishing well. I almost jumped up and down and clapped.

We wandered through each room and attempted conversation, but Mr. Kimura remained silent. We stopped in the kitchen.

"We like it. How much do you want for the security deposit?" Mike asked.

"Wait," Mr. Kimura said, "I show many other families. No deal today."

His words echoed in my brain. Mike pulled out a wad of folded cash. In slow motion, he counted out hundred-dollar bills and presented them to Mr. Kimura in a neat stack on the kitchen countertop.

"Well, I don't think you'll find anyone who'll give you three months' rent in advance, plus security deposit, and pay you in cash every month—on time." Mr. Kimura's eyes grew wider watching Mike lay down each bill. "Our current landlord will verify our dependability."

I stood back, and my mouth went dry as dust. Waiting, I clenched my hands inside my jacket pockets.

Mr. Kimura tore his focus away from the stack of hundreds. "I call your landlord today. If he like you, I like you."

We moved from our ghetto apartment into our dream house a short time later. Mike made all my dreams come true. He provided a safe harbor, and he loved me. I'd do anything for him.

"Let's ask everybody over to celebrate your birthday tomorrow night," I said.

"I don't care about my birthday, but I want to try out the cocaine I got."

The next night, Mike broke out rocks of cocaine and chopped them in lines on the crystal slab using a single-edge razor blade. Our friends snorted with us. The eight of us joked, talked nonstop, smoked pot, and snorted late into the night. Coke became our new party-maker.

"I need to see my people in San Francisco," Mike said. "Wanna cruise up there with me tomorrow? We can discover another foreign restaurant."

"Sure. Everything okay?"

"Rethinking some things. Coke is easier to move than pot and way more lucrative."

The cool new party drug was in high demand, and business took off.

The smell of cumin and garlic enveloped me as we entered the Khyber Pass Restaurant through a curtain of beads. The host seated the eight of us on the floor at a large, round table. We sat on rich-colored pillows embroidered with seeds and small mirrored jewels. Woven rugs, naturally dyed in muted reds and yellows, covered the floor. The room appeared dreamy, like a flying carpet ready to float away. The dim light and carved wood screen provided privacy from other diners.

Servers arranged the fragrant food on our table. They liked us because Mike tipped them well. Dylan, sitting cross-legged on my right, rubbed his hands together like a greedy miser. His wife, Alyson, sat on his other side. She leaned toward him and whispered something that made him laugh.

They both wore hip-length straight-blond hair. Alyson once told me she ironed Dylan's hair when she ironed her own. Dylan, one of Mike's best friends, was his top distributor.

Mike sat on my left. Usually reserved and serious when in public, good food lightened him up. He clapped when the first belly dancer emerged from behind the curtain.

The dancer moved her hips and torso to the music. She bent backward, arms snaking above her head, always keeping time with the tabla players seated at her feet.

On the other side of Mike, Connie sat with her husband, Jared, next to her. Jared wore black engineer glasses like Clark Kent. In fact, he was an engineer by education, but working for Mike proved far more lucrative.

They were the only couple among our friends who talked about having a baby. Unwilling to change their party and traveling lifestyle, they decided to put the idea on hold. No one, including Mike, knew I already had two kids.

Eventually, I told Mike about my teenage pregnancy but didn't see the point in telling him anything more. He might see me differently.

The third couple was Steve and Cindy. Steve, about six-foot-one, wore a silver and turquoise inlaid belt and snakeskin boots. Mike often complained about Steve's tendency to flash his money.

When we finished dinner, Steve said, "I got this." He pulled out a wad of cash secured by a gold money clip.

"I'll get it," Mike said.

Steve put his money away. "There's something I want to talk about before we leave."

Mike gave him a sideways warning glance. No talking business here.

Steve caught the look but continued. "Regarding New Year's Eve this year, there's a small, undeveloped island off Miami called Bimini. There's no airport, but we can charter a twelve-passenger seaplane out of Miami."

"Amazing!" I blurted out, then looked at Mike for his reaction.

"What's on Bimini?" Mike asked.

"They say it's a cool island, very small, has places to stay and indoor plumbing, secluded. I'll check it out more if everyone's interested."

I traveled domestically growing up as a military brat, but traveling with Mike expanded the world in ways I never imagined. His appreciation of other cultures, cuisine, and languages rubbed off on me.

A sense of safety, purpose, and belonging settled over me. I was part of a select group of counterculture people who seemed more aware of important world issues than any people I'd ever met.

After a jerky driving lesson on the floor-stick sports car Mike had bought me, I watered my tomato plants on the patio and watched him brush the dogs nearby. Mike's love of our dogs made me care for him even more. He was my rock star, father figure, and best friend. My life was full of freedom and adventure because of him. What would I do without him?

The contrast between Mike's treatment of animals and my stepfather's came to mind. When I was about ten, my siblings and I played in the front yard with our mixed-breed dog, Pal. We held a jump rope taut about two feet off the ground and coaxed Pal to leap over it.

Dad came outside, watched, then said, "I'll show the mutt how to do it." He yanked Pal high in the air, dangled him by his collar, and swung him midair back and forth over the rope, choking him. Pal yelped, whined, and kicked his feet in the air.

I stopped breathing, clenched my teeth, and stared at the horror taking place in front of me. My sisters stood around silently.

Someone, maybe me, said under their breath, "No, Dad."

The neighbor kids ran away. I held steady, kept a stone face, afraid if I objected and he knew his treatment of Pal hurt me, he might do something worse.

After Dad finally left, I wrapped my arms around Pal, spoke to him, and reassured him. He coughed over and over. His soft brown eyes looked sad. His ears folded back flat, submissive, like he didn't understand. I didn't understand either.

FLYING HIGH

"Steve mentioned they may want to go to Maui with us this year, backpack down that dead volcano." Mike looked up from brushing our German shepherd, Spicey.

"I can't be away for more than a week this time," I said.

He winced as he cleaned the brush. "You aren't in school right now, so—"

"My job."

"It doesn't make sense for you to work anymore."

"You bought me a car so I could keep working without driving yours." I pinched dead leaves off my tomato plants. "Besides, I don't want to quit. I hate asking you for money like a kid."

"You don't earn enough to make any difference. Come work for me. I need some help."

"Doing what?" I filled the watering bucket with too much force, splashing everywhere, before turning down the spigot.

"Flying cash."

"What if I get caught?" Flying money coast-to-coast sounded thrilling, even scary.

"Can you remember anyone ever looking in your bag when you've flown? No one checks bags, especially not a woman's purse. Besides, it's not illegal to carry cash."

I quit my job at the school library, went to work for Mike, and had a blast flying. Someone always met me at the destination airport and gave me a large purse containing dozens of rolls of hundred-dollar bills. Never leaving the airport, I would board another flight home. It was an easy job, and I was helping Mike.

Two years later, we moved to a beach community south of Santa Cruz, glad to leave the crowded city behind. I found a house advertised in the newspaper under the vacation home section located on a hill overlooking Monterey Bay. The high ceilings and numerous tall windows looked out on full ocean views.

I couldn't think of a single thing I wanted. I lived every day happy and knew what made Mike happy: good food and good sex. I did everything in my power to make his life good.

"You're going back to Guatemala again?" I asked.

"Yeah, I'm putting more energy into imports. Looks like I can make money at it."

I exhaled relief. He'd been easing out of dealing and into other ventures. No more worry about him getting busted.

His business interests had changed, but our drug abuse hadn't. After another late night of partying, we said goodnight to our friends. Neither of us said a word. We'd developed a routine over the past few years. Our coke use increased from once in a while to two or three all-nighters every week.

I pulled the curtains and watched them silently sweep across the long, tall panes of glass running the length of the living room. Mike put on his bathrobe and took the phone off the hook. We blocked out the world and got into a different kind of party—a very private party.

We still had unlimited access to high-quality cocaine. I bent over the crystal slab and snorted a line. Euphoria rushed through me. The delicious high lasted about twenty minutes before my craving returned. I snorted another line, then another.

I want this feeling to last forever.

My urge intensified, and I was starved for more. The more our cocaine use increased, the more intense our sex life got.

"Go put on those spike high heels and the black garter belt."

I changed my name for the night to adopt a new identity for our fantasies.

Mike kept the coke coming. We kept the sex going hour after hour, all night, fueled by water and more coke.

We were still going at daybreak when someone knocked on the front door and used a key to open it. Alyson called the dogs for a beach run. We stayed quiet, letting her assume that we were asleep. After she left, we got back to our obsessive sex games.

Mike, seated on the couch, leaned over the gleaming burl coffee table and expertly chopped out more lines. I put on an Eric Clapton album. He offered me the rolled bill to go first.

Kneeling level next to the table, I wiped some coke on the inside of my gum, then took another snort from the long line of white powder.

"Oh my God, Charlotte! Can you hear me? Are you all right?"

Lying flat on my back on the shag-carpeted floor, Mike's face came into focus directly above me, inches away. His shining, glacial-blue eyes stared into mine.

"What happened?" I whispered. My heart thumped off the charts.

"You had some kind of seizure. Thank God you're okay. Your whole body shook like you got electrocuted. It scared the shit out of me. Can you sit up?" He put his hand under my back and pulled me to a sitting position.

Weak and confused, I felt vulnerable but didn't cry. He helped me to bed. I slept the rest of the day and through the night. The next morning, we drank coffee and read the paper on the deck. The ocean stretched across the horizon, sparkling in the sunshine.

"You need to see a doctor." Mike shook his paper and straightened it upright. "You had some kind of epileptic seizure yesterday."

"What would I say? I don't remember any of it." I stared at the newspaper in front of me without seeing the print, my mind so consumed by thoughts of the episode.

"You might have something seriously wrong."

"I want to forget it happened, Mike. If it happens again—"

"Make the appointment." He sipped from his steaming coffee mug.

After the neurologist ran several tests looking for anything that might cause a seizure, I returned to his office for the patient consultation to review the test results.

I sat across from the doctor's desk, shifted side to side in my chair, and twisted my hair around my finger while he perused my test results.

He finished reading then viewed me over his glasses. "All results negative."

"Thank goodness!" I snatched my purse off the floor and half rose from my chair.

"Hold on."

I sank back down.

He lay the test results on the desk, removed his glasses, and pinched the corners of his eyes. "You don't have a tumor or other obvious problems, but we still don't know what caused your seizure. What were you doing immediately prior to this happening?" His attention rested on me.

Oh no. Here we go. "Partying with friends, but—"

I stopped talking. I didn't want this conversation. Cognizant of the secrecy surrounding my life, I remained silent.

He waited. "What do you mean by 'partying'? Drinking?"

"Well, no." Cornered, I wanted to bolt out of his office. I feared he might report my heavy drug use to the police, bringing heat on Mike and me.

He persisted. "What were you doing?"

I swallowed and took a slow, deep breath. "Well, I was snorting cocaine."

"How much did you take—snort?" He made notes as I spoke.

"We'd been doing it all night." *I can't believe I'm telling him this stuff.*

His eyebrows shot up, but he still wrote. He stopped and set his pen down to lean back in his chair. "You overdosed. If you continue abusing cocaine on that level, you could die."

Driving home, I thought about the doctor's warning. I loved the high and the escape cocaine gave me, and I didn't want things to change, but I needed to slow down.

I arrived home and told Mike everything as I chopped garlic and onions while making dinner.

"He said I'm risking my life, Mike." I rinsed my hands and wiped them on a towel. I faced him, unsure of how to word the rest of my thoughts. "I—we're doing too much coke. It's bad for us, and it's ruining our sex life."

"It doesn't ruin our sex life."

I raised my arms and let them fall, exasperated at being contradicted. "Neither of us are interested in sex unless we're coked up."

"So stop doing it."

"Once I snort the first line, I can't stop. I don't think you can either."

"I'm not trying to stop," he said nonchalantly, then strolled out of the room.

"Can't we leave the coke in our storage unit so it's not so easily available?" I called to his back.

No response.

A month later, Theresa, my third sister down, and I finished our morning yoga practice and walked the dogs along the crashing shore. I felt the warm sand underfoot. I threw a stick and watched the dogs charge into the ocean for it. Theresa swayed her hips as we walked along in our bikinis. She pulled her waist-length blonde hair into a ponytail in the naturally prissy manner I loved about her.

"I might come back in October," she said. "Maybe celebrate our birthdays together—if you guys can handle me again after spending a whole month with you."

"Count on it. We'll celebrate your twentieth in style and send you another plane ticket when you're ready." I stopped talking. "Wait—scratch that. Things might be different then."

She pushed some breeze-blown strands of hair away from her face and glanced at me. "What do you mean?"

"I'm—I'm thinking of moving out of Mike's house." Hearing myself say it felt sad and real.

"Moving out? Why?" We both squealed and jumped back when the dogs, Sugar and Spice, shook off seawater right next to us.

"I guess I'm not happy anymore," I said.

"You guys been living together, what, six or seven years?"

"Six." *Was I really going to leave the man I'd loved for six years?* "Honestly, I don't know what to do. I can't stop doing coke. You've seen how often we party till dawn. It could kill me." I shrugged. "Anyway, I'm almost twenty-four. There's more to life."

"Like what, Charlotte? I agree, you've got to stop doing the coke, but you'd be giving up a great guy, friends, travel. How many cars has he bought you? He loves you. Think hard before you do anything."

Watching Spicy drop the stick in front of me, my resolve weakened.

"Have you talked to him about it?" She bent to pick up the stick, but Spicy jumped and snatched it from her hand before she could throw it.

"Spicy! Drop it! Yeah, I talked to him a bunch of times, but it's like talking to a brick wall. He doesn't listen. Coke's ruined us."

A vertical worry line appeared between Theresa's eyes and reflected my feelings. I plopped down on the warm sand.

Theresa eased down beside me and draped her arm over my shoulders. "Talk to him again."

"Yeah. We're going back to the Bahamas next month. I'll talk to him then." *Does talking about changing our lifestyle make sense when we're having a blast gambling and partying in the Caribbean?*

Months passed but I couldn't shake my worry about the coke.

Music by the Who blared through the house. I turned the volume down. Mike lay on the couch reading a book titled *A Heritage of Stone* about the JFK assassination.

"Let's put the coke in storage so it's not easily accessible."

"Nobody's making you snort," he said, irritation in his voice. "Just back off."

"I can't." My shoulders fell. I gave up. "I want more from life than partying, Mike." My bottom lip quivered so hard I thought my teeth might shake out. "I want to move out."

He lay his book down, open on his chest. "What the fuck do you mean you 'want to move out?'"

"I need to make it on my own now and have more control of my life."

He sat up, and the book fell. "You must be crazy. You haven't finished school, no job experience."

"I'll find a waitressing job or something. Until I do, I hope you'll help me." I tried not to sound whiny.

"You mean support you while you're out looking for new dick? Fuck no, I'm not helping you!"

I ran out the door, across the field, and stood on the edge of the cliff, watching the waves crash below.

He's right. How will I make it?

My dilemma was a common one for women like me who end up dependent on a man.

Mike didn't consciously hold me down, and he didn't abuse me. He reacted from hurt because I chose to leave our relationship. I flip-flopped because I loved him and didn't know what I was doing.

At that time, there were few clear pathways to independence for women. Society taught us from childhood our primary purpose was partnership with a man. Given the economic structure of society, stepping out of that role without an education was possible but not easy.

Girls received dolls to play with rather than chemistry sets. If careers were suggested, parents talked of little girls becoming flight attendants but never pilots, or nurses but not doctors. We were always in subordinate positions since a woman's ability to lead was always in question. Even our automobile driving was and still is joked about.

Eventually, we would pride ourselves on having more choices. At the time, *Roe v. Wade* had just passed after long years of battling for the natural right to make decisions about our own bodies. However, the notion that women owed men our bodies and our freedom didn't disappear. It still lingered just below the surface.

We never imagined how long women would earn less money than their male counterparts while performing the same jobs. We never imagined how the glass ceiling would limit women despite often working harder than men. We certainly never imagined the sexual favors less scrupulous men would demand of women in order for the woman to remain employed. I know I didn't. I was eager to make my own way in the world and naïve about what I faced.

What sort of message does this social environment send to future generations of women? Will things be much different fifty years from now?

Weeks later, I found Mike in the kitchen mixing the dog food.

"I found the perfect place to live. The lady's traveling for several months. She'll sublet to me while she's gone."

Mike set both bowls on the floor and looked at me.

I shrugged. "Only until she gets back."

He broke eye contact and shook his head. "I can't believe you're doing this. You've lost your mind."

"I haven't lost my mind. I'm leaving."

"Then get the fuck out!" He pointed to the door.

I ran to our bedroom and closed the door.

My new one-bedroom studio came furnished with a grandfather clock, an aquarium for which I took responsibility, and a red velvet couch. I liked it, but after a week without Mike, the dogs, or people coming over, it felt lonesome. I used my time alone to meditate, read books on spirituality, and try to discover my identity without Mike.

Mike paid my rent and gave me money to live on, which said a lot about the kind of man he was. I found a part-time job that allowed me to work around my classes at an oyster bar near the beach in Santa Cruz.

I spent the next several nights at Mike's place coking it up, having sex, and crying when we'd argue about my recent move. We never used to fight, but now it was part of our routine. I'd left the protective cocoon he offered, hoped to find my freedom, but my coke addiction seduced me back. In addition, I feared life without him, my best friend.

I have to do something about my coke habit, but what?

Coke drove me away, but I ran back and snorted as much as before.

During an extended stay at his place, I opened his closet to find another woman's clothing. "Whose clothes are these in your closet?"

"Some chick who stayed here a few days last week."

"Some chick? Who is she?" Light-headed, I swayed. I couldn't believe his words.

"Some girl I met right after you moved out. What do you care?"

Months flew by. I met a guy in one of my classes, and we often played pool together in the evenings. Randy had an athletic build from lifting weights and a tough-guy veneer hiding his sensitivity. To his questions about Mike, I replied vaguely or not at all. We spent time together but weren't lovers, which made my relationship with Mike merely a curiosity for him, at least at first.

Driving home from the pool hall one night, Randy turned down the radio and said, "There's something I want to tell you."

Crap, here goes. He's going to tell me he's married or gay.

"I spent time in prison."

I stared at him. "Prison? You're only in your twenties."

"At eighteen, I got busted holding two pounds of weed." He cleared his throat. "They locked me up for four years."

I'd never known anyone who'd spent time in jail or prison, except myself when Mom sent me to juvenile hall.

Someone banged on my apartment door. It sounded like they used a battering ram.

Mike slammed open the door and pushed past me, almost knocking me over. "Is that the punk's motorcycle?"

"Mike, what—"

Randy sat at my small kitchen table drinking a beer and leaning back on two feet of the chair.

Mike rushed at him, "Get out of here, or I'll bash your face in!" He cocked his fist, held it midair above Randy.

I grabbed Mike's arm and held it back with every ounce of my strength.

"Mike. No. I invited him. Don't—"

Randy glared at Mike. Smirk lines appeared around his mouth. Mike's fist hovered above him.

"Go ahead, hit me. I'll beat the shit out of you, asshole," Randy said.

"No! Randy's leaving," I said.

"I am?" His unblinking stare slid over and stopped on me.

I mouthed, "Please."

"Whatever. Fuck it," Randy said.

Randy stood and let the chair crash backward to the floor, then slammed his beer bottle on the table, splattering beer out the top.

Mike lowered his fist. "You lowlife. You live off her, and I pay the rent here. Get a job, gigolo. If I see you here again…"

"Does it look like I'm afraid of you, man?" Randy snatched his motorcycle keys off the table and stormed out.

Mike and I stood in place until we heard the bike roar away.

My shoulders came down, exhausted. My whole body exhaled. What a mess. "Just because you pay my rent doesn't give you the right to run my life, Mike."

"The hell it doesn't. Are you fucking that guy?"

"No. I swear, no. But that isn't the point—"

He stomped out, leaving the door wide open.

I paced around my apartment, turned on the stove burner, turned it off again, and cleaned up the spilled beer. What the hell had just happened?

Weeks later, Mary Lou left her boyfriend in Oklahoma and flew to California to stay with me. I divided my time between my place and Mike's, so she moved back and forth with me between the two places.

Randy joined us at my place. The three of us often listened to live music in the local park on the weekend. I watched the band members climb the tree-shaded stage and get ready to play. I tilted my head back and savored the afternoon sunshine on my face while Mary Lou lay beside me on the thin blanket we'd spread over the grass. Randy lay on his stomach propped on his arms, holding a four-leaf clover he'd spotted in a patch next to the blanket.

Happy dogs roamed freely through the crowd. A giant beach ball, hit like a volleyball, bounced from person to person. Mary Lou passed me a joint. When the band played a song we knew, we sang out loud and laughed at ourselves and each other.

"I have something to ask you guys," Randy said between songs.

His serious tone got my attention. I stopped giggling and waited.

"My best friend is in San Quentin for possession of pot."

"What a drag." I tried to sound interested.

"He helped me out of some tough spots. Always defended my back in the joint—a big deal in there."

"Okay, so what is it you want to ask us?" I smoothed down the leather halter top I wore.

"I promised him—his name is Arturo—that when I got out, I'd send him some pills, like acid."

After taking a long drink and recapping her water bottle, Mary Lou said, "Why do we need to hear this?"

"Arturo's my only family, and I owe him. I need a big favor." He paused. "Take a small balloon of pills to him."

I shut my gaping mouth. "Wait. Smuggle drugs inside a prison?" We locked eyes. "Wow, that's quite a favor, Randy."

Randy and I had become lovers, and I adored him. He'd taken some hard knocks in his young life, and I sensed his deep loneliness. I understood what isolation felt like, and I wanted to help him. But this?

"It's completely safe, I promise. It's done all the time. If it were dangerous, I wouldn't ask you."

Mary Lou got up from the blanket. "I've got to find a restroom."

"Yeah, me too." I leaped up and brushed off my jean shorts, glad to escape.

Randy looked up, squinting against the sun, "So you won't let me explain—"

"I don't think so." I loved dangerous adventures, but this sounded crazy, even to me. I trotted off after Mary Lou.

The next day, as we sat at the kitchen table, Mary Lou read the Sunday comic strip out loud to me while I scrambled eggs.

Randy had spent the night and sauntered into the kitchen, yawning and scratching his bare belly. "Good morning, ladies."

Within ten minutes, he brought up San Quentin again.

"I promise you won't get caught. I guarantee it. Do you believe me, Charlotte?" He poured himself coffee.

"Well, yeah, I believe you wouldn't deliberately put us in danger, but it's a prison and your plan might go wrong." I pushed scrambled eggs from the pan onto our plates.

"It won't go wrong if you do exactly as I tell you. The size of the balloon is small, maybe two inches." He used his thumb and index finger to show us. "Here's what you do. Sign in as family friends. After you greet Arturo, talk a few minutes, pass him the balloon, and leave. Done."

Mary Lou examined her toast, took a bite, and refused to look at me.

"We'll talk about it," I said.

The next day, Mary Lou and I tried on clothes in a Santa Cruz boutique and talked about Randy's idea.

"I can't believe he'd ask us that," I said.

The idea did excite me. After my childhood homelife, not much scared me. But did I really want to risk my freedom, my sister's freedom, and my relationship with Mike, all to do a favor for Randy?

"What do you think, Boosie?"

"I don't know. What do you think?" She pulled on a pair

of Faded Glory shorts and turned to examine the back in the mirror.

"It kinda sounds fun, like *Mission Impossible*. Like a wild adventure," I said.

"As long as we don't get caught and kept in prison like *Midnight Express*," she said as she slid the shorts off.

"I won't do it without you. Should we listen to his plan?" I hung up the sundress I tried on.

Mary Lou didn't respond at first, then said, "Sure. Why not? Fuck it."

The next day, while the three of us ate lunch at my kitchen table, I said, "Okay, Randy. Let's hear how easy it is again. We haven't decided."

Randy repeated the instructions many times and showed us a clear photo of Arturo.

"Where do I hide the pills?"

"In your panties. Wear a dress." He reached into his jeans pocket and retrieved a small red balloon. "Let's practice. Go put on a skirt, but not a long one."

The night before our prison smuggle, I rolled over again and again in bed, unable to get comfortable. Always challenging boundaries, I'd refused to obey rules. But now, I was hesitant and wished I hadn't committed.

Mary Lou's part in this scheme worried me too. She'd get in big trouble if we got caught. Her trust in me outweighed her judgment, and my decision to help Randy could let her down in the worst way.

I tiptoed to the hall bathroom.

"I'm awake," Mary Lou said from the guest room.

I sat on the bed next to her. "I'm scared."

"Me too."

"We can change our minds, you know," I said.

Instead of responding, she rolled over away from me.

SAN QUENTIN TO ESALEN

We left Santa Cruz early the next morning. There was a heavy silence in the car during the two-hour drive to San Quentin. Randy stared ahead at the road without blinking. He gripped the steering wheel so tightly his knuckles looked white.

When the prison guard tower came into view, reality slapped me hard. The blacked-out windows, like giant, shiny, bug eyes, stared down at our little car. I imagined guards inside watching us, machine guns aimed, waiting for us to make a wrong move. The white hair on my arms stood straight up like an electric shock passing through me.

Sitting in the backseat, Mary Lou spotted the evil tower. "Oh shit," she said under her breath.

"Don't panic," Randy said. "Do like I told you."

I wore a sundress which fell below my knees. Mary Lou wore her flower-embroidered bell-bottoms. We walked toward the entrance, and I reached for Mary Lou's hand, but she jerked it away, pissed.

The crispy cold reception area of the huge building smelled like Pine-Sol. My eye twitched and my underarms dampened. Every sound echoed and bounced off the cement floor and walls.

We got in the short line and watched a uniformed guard behind a plexiglass partition stamp a form for the man ahead of us.

As I signed the visitor's sheet, my hand shook so hard, my signature looked like a child's.

About ten of us waited in the small room. No one spoke. It felt like a dream—a bad one.

If I get arrested, they'll keep me in this place, a twenty-four-year-old drug smuggler. And what about Mary Lou? Oh my God.

An announcement crackled over the intercom. Mary Lou stood up, so I did too. We filed through the metal detector one at a time. Passing a guard, the cold balloon moved in my panties. Oh, please, don't let it fall out in front of this guard. I took tiny steps like a geisha, trying not to drop it on the floor.

Mary Lou entered ahead of me carrying her fringe leather purse, which set off the metal alert. She squealed, jumped backward, and crashed into me. I pressed my thighs together, holding my breath while I squeezed the balloon to keep it in place.

Mary Lou dropped her purse like a hot knife. It landed upside down, and pocket change bounced while makeup scattered everywhere. The whole thing shocked me into a severe case of hiccups.

I knelt to help scoop up her change. We bumped heads on the way down, causing me to hiccup twice in a row, which gave us an untimely fit of nervous giggles. Our hands shaking, we hurriedly picked up every penny while the people behind us shifted one foot to the other, waiting.

The guard kept our purses, and we made it through the checkpoint with no other incident. The double doors opened to a large visitors' room with four guards, each leaning back against one of the four walls.

"Are those cameras or fire sprinklers?" Mary Lou whispered, pointing at the ceiling.

I shrugged. We waited at a table for Arturo, planning to greet him with big, excited kisses.

I recognized him immediately from Randy's photo but wasn't prepared for his super-good looks.

"Charlotte, Mary Lou. So good to see you both. Thanks for coming."

He hugged me comfortably like an old friend, delight written on his face. We kissed deeper than I expected. A thrill of chills ran down my body, past the balloon of drugs, all the way to my toes.

This guy is a living doll.

His dark, wavy hair hung down on his forehead, making me want to push it aside. A picture flashed through my mind of him lying on top of me, propped on his elbows directly over me, enveloping me with his tanned, muscular arms. I ate him with my eyes and imagined biting his full bottom lip. I snapped out of it when he kissed Mary Lou first on her cheek, then a quick peck on her mouth. Her concerned face softened and turned bright pink. His good looks weren't lost on her.

"You look great. They must be treating you good in here." I didn't know what else to say to this handsome stranger.

"I wouldn't go that far, but I'm okay. I work out every day. It's a long haul."

We mostly talked about Randy, but when a guard strolled past our table, Arturo asked about his mother. I made up some small stuff to keep talking.

We kept it going for about fifteen minutes until time to go.

"Are you ready?" he asked.

I held my breath, "I guess so." My eye twitched rapidly.

"Hold me close, kiss me long, and pass it."

"Hold on." I centered myself, trying to calm my cramping stomach. I scooted to the edge of my chair, my hands hidden under the table, and leaned into Arturo.

He whispered in my ear, "Okay, kiss me, and hand me the balloon. They'll be watching, so keep them focused on the kiss."

I refused to look at the guards, afraid they'd see my guilt. My hands rested in my lap, trembling. I slid my hand under my dress.

A guard walked nearby. I jerked my hand out, sat up straight, and pretended to smooth my dress. The guard ignored Arturo and me, winking at Mary Lou. She gave him a tiny nervous smile, and he moved on.

The guard appeared more interested in my sister than what I did under the table. At twenty, Mary Lou looked like a woman-child sitting on the other side of the table. She leaned back in her chair, one leg crossed over the other, making her slim frame appear even longer. She used her fingers to comb through her wavy hair falling all the way to the wide leather belt she wore with her hip-hugger jeans.

"We're running out of time. Let's do this," Arturo said.

I breathed in big, moving against him and closing the gap between us again. This time, he put his arm around me and pulled me closer. His other hand rested on my knee. I grabbed the back of his neck to steady myself. With my other hand, in one smooth motion, I retrieved the balloon from inside my panties and pressed it into Arturo's hand. At the same time, I kissed him so hard, he nearly choked.

Arturo secured the balloon somewhere because it disappeared. Whatever. I didn't care what happened to it anymore. I wanted out of there. Knowing the guards watched us now, I hopped up and gave him a quick hug goodbye. I restrained myself from banging open the door and running down the freeway waving my arms all the way home.

We signed out, not saying a word. The guard squinted at my illegible handwriting. We headed to the door, ready to escape.

"Miss," the guard bellowed behind us.

"Shit," Mary Lou said under her breath.

An icy rush passed through me, like cold water down the back of my neck. I turned in slow motion, my heart thrashing furiously against my ribcage.

"You forgot something." He held up our purses.

I couldn't move. Mary Lou hustled around me, retrieved our purses, and thanked the guard.

I commanded myself to walk, not run, but Mary Lou rushed past me again and pushed open the exit door. Outside, I inhaled a giant breath of free air, like the first breath you take after diving underwater.

"Don't start running, Mary Lou. They could be watching."

"Forget it! I'm outta here." She tore across the parking lot, clomping in her platform shoes, hair flying behind her like a flag, and me on her tail.

Randy merged the car into freeway traffic in somber silence.

I turned around in my seat and faced Mary Lou. "We did it! God, I'm shaking so hard."

"Don't ever ask me to do anything crazy like that again, Charlotte. I almost peed my pants. We could've got in a lot of trouble."

"Everything went exactly as I described, right?" Randy's hands trembled on the steering wheel.

"Are you okay?" I asked Randy.

"Yeah. I got a reaction from getting so close to that place. It brings up a lot of bad memories. It's a nightmare in there." He blew out a long stream of air. "I ain't never going back."

The day after the San Quentin drug smuggle, I hurried back to the safety of Mike, appreciating him as never before. Mike, so discreet with his business, he'd never take a risk like that. He still lived in the hill house and had plenty of room, so Mary Lou and I spent the next several days with him de-stressing. Randy objected, but discussion of Mike was off-limits.

For my Halloween birthday, Mike and I threw a costume party and invited eight or ten of our friends. At the party, I introduced Mary Lou to Mike's friend, Roger, who was recently divorced. Roger and Mary Lou spent the evening flirting and dancing in our living room. Mike had introduced me to Roger and his wife several years earlier, and I'd always thought highly of them both.

I spotted Mary Lou and Roger sitting close to one another on the deck, their backs to me, gazing out at the moonlight reflecting a heavenly runway on the Pacific.

I opened the sliding door and poked my head out. "Don't get up, guys. I'm going to bed."

"Are you okay? It's only one thirty," Mary Lou said.

"Yeah. Everyone else is still here. See you tomorrow." To Mike, I whispered, "Good night."

About five o'clock in the morning, Mike stormed into the bedroom, ripping the covers off of me.

"Get up," he hollered.

"What the hell?" I wiped foggy sleep away.

"What's this shit about you smuggling drugs into San Quentin for that little punk you're fucking?" Mike yelled. "And you involved your sister in your crazy scheme!"

"I—"

He stood over the bed glaring at me. I pulled the sheets under my chin. His face flushed crimson. His mouth appeared to foam.

"Randy needed a favor—"

Mike clenched his fist. "Shut the fuck up!"

I kicked the sheets off and rolled away.

He swung at me but missed.

I lay on my back and bicycle-kicked at him. I'd fought Mom like this so many times, I defended myself from Mike with no problem.

His two fists swung back and forth through the air, missing my legs every time.

I pedaled the air hard, almost kicking him.

His blows never connected with my fast-moving legs. He got tired and quit swinging, arms dropping to his side. He stomped to the bathroom.

"I got away with it. I knew I could," I called out.

He leaned out through the bathroom door, his toothbrush in hand. "You're so stupid. Sneaking drugs inside a state prison is just plain stupid. What pisses me off most is you would have called me to get you out of trouble, and we'd both be involved in your shit."

The first light of dawn filtered through the vertical blinds.

He stared at me, shook his head, straightened the messy covers, and slid into bed. I moved close to him. "I'm sorry. You're right, but I—"

He scooted away, making waves move across the king-sized waterbed.

The next day, Mary Lou and I laid our towels on the warm sand and rubbed baby oil over each other's back and shoulders. Exhausted from last night's party and my fight with Mike, I lay back in the sun and closed my eyes.

"I don't get it. Why did you tell Roger about San Quentin? I've never seen Mike so pissed."

"Yeah, you said he almost hit you. He'd never hurt you. You know that. I'm sorry. I bragged about getting away with it, and Roger promised not to tell anyone."

For spring break, Randy and I drove my VW bug south to Big Sur. Foam stuck out of the cracks in my car seats and faded red paint rusted off the exterior, but the car chugged along on Highway 1 without stalling.

We camped inside Pfeiffer State Park and hiked all day through magnificent redwoods, across clear running streams, and past waterfalls. Here and there along the trail, people sunbathed on huge, warm river rocks. Randy and I found a flat one and stretched out on it. The sun toasted my skin as I listened to the water trickle and splash. I absorbed the natural beauty and gave thanks.

My faith had evolved from my Catholic school days. Like Mike, I believed the energy of God existed in everything from the smallest molecule on earth to the empty space in the universe, all part of one energy.

Randy brought me out of my prayer of appreciation. "Tell me about the hot baths. You said it's a yogi retreat?"

"Esalen's a place that offers courses for advancement of spiritual and personal growth. Hot baths built on the side of the mountain collect the sulfur water, which naturally flows down to the ocean. Since we're not attending a course, the baths are only open to us, the public, from 1:00 a.m. to 6:00 a.m. Oh, and we'll take the acid at midnight so we'll come onto it about the time we get there, okay?"

"Have you dropped acid before?"

"Yeah, you?"

"Yeah, but I can count the number of times on one hand," he said.

Later that night, snuggled beside the campfire in our sleeping bags, we startled awake to the clanking sound of our cheap wind-up alarm clock around 12:30 a.m.

"Oh man. This better be worth it," Randy said, his hair sticking straight up.

I splashed water on my face, and then we shuffled to the car. After dropping a hit of LSD, we concentrated on the road, knowing we wouldn't feel the effects of the acid for about a half-hour. The VW headlights were barely strong enough to pierce the dense fog as we puttered around the tight curves of Highway 1. One side of the two-lane road hugged the mountain while the other fell straight down to the rocky shore below. I glanced at Randy, who focused on the hairpin turns.

"I hope we don't come onto the acid too soon. I can barely see as it is," he said.

The discreet, softly illuminated Esalen sign came into view through the fog.

Towels in hand, we descended the dimly lit path down the side of the cliff, listening to the waves crash on the rocks below. The veil of fog lifted to reveal a dark sky full of stars. The beauty rendered me speechless as the effect of the acid took hold. We had a wonderful night ahead.

We got closer to the baths, and a deep harmonious chant grew louder. I inhaled the aroma of frankincense as we entered the changing area.

The co-ed baths, built of weather-worn redwood from floor to rooftop, teetered on the mountain ledge above the ocean.

A single candle lit our way into the baths. I tripped on the acid fully now. My attention rested on the candle's flame, and when I looked away, it caused everything to glow in yellow hues, like an aura. The men's chanting softened to silence.

Esalen visitors bathed nude, but the pitch darkness provided privacy. People were in deep meditation and prayer.

I saw nothing other than a curtain of yellow paisley patterns over a black background. Although obscured by my hallucinations, I sensed the hot tubs nearby. Smears of light blue watercolor joined the yellow hues, forming a braided spiral moving upward with the baths' steam before fading into the dark ceiling. The colorful spiral hallucinations emerged from the tubs and fell into sync with the rhythm of the surf hitting the rocks below.

Randy guided my hand to touch the side of the tub. "Give me your towel."

I heard but couldn't see him through the colorful paisley curtain moving in waves.

Sliding into the hot bath, I reached for his hand under the dark water. I closed my eyes, rested my head back, and sank lower into the steaming bath, marveling at this incredible magic carpet ride.

Soft chanting, faint at first, grew richer, deeper, and in perfect harmony. The men's voices rose and fell like the waves, faded, and stopped. So perfect.

Hours later, I whispered, "I'm ready to get out. Will you get my towel?"

I wrapped the soft towel close and found my way to a massage table at the open edge above the rocky cliff. I saw a little better in the dark and now experienced the most intense hours of the LSD trip—"peaking" is what we called it. Everything still moved in fluid motion like undersea kelp, and the Pacific breathed in and out, filling me with rhythmic waves.

Sitting in a lotus position on the end of the massage table with my towel around me, I faced the ocean, the starry night, and closed my eyes. In tune with nature, I entered a deep, meditative state of gratitude and remained there, taking long slow breaths.

Then something happened.

An all-encompassing spiritual wind, an almighty breath from far away, rose like a universal tidal wave. A long, silent roar blew through me—an enormous swoosh through my entire life and my very soul. A great and awesome love permeated every thought, every breath I took. I heard—no, I felt—a sound. An "Aum," a holy rhythm, the heartbeat of eternity. The deepest boom accompanied the cosmic breath. The most beautiful deep, rich sound and the feeling of infinite love reverberated through and overwhelmed me. I experienced the touch of God.

The long wave passed, followed by a quiet benevolence which beamed down on me, carrying the message, "Everything is okay."

Joyful tears streamed down my face. I rested in the tranquility of bliss. If I could have moved from my stunned silence, I would have fallen to my knees and bowed in humble adoration.

My life's journey—the problems, the mistakes—were all embraced by this enormous love. A love so great it made me cry with gratitude.

Indescribable with language, I couldn't articulate the experience properly. Words only hinted at it.

Randy moved next to me. "The sun will be up soon."

Let me stay forever. Speechless, I followed Randy to the changing room, then up the path.

A gasp escaped my throat.

Randy looked around. "What's wrong?"

Brought out of my perfect solitude, not wanting to utter another word for fear of losing this indescribable euphoria, I reluctantly answered, "Nothing's wrong. It's perfect. Something—I can't explain—something happened."

"What?" he asked.

"A spiritual experience, Randy. I'm overjoyed."

Several hours had elapsed at the baths, and the effects of the acid lessened.

Randy drove us back to our campsite. The fog returned with the dawn, but we saw better with daybreak.

We crawled into the tent instead of sleeping outside. The forest awakened, and nearby campers stirred. Now I understood why monks and yogis spent their lives in caves meditating to reach nirvana.

Randy reached for me. I declined. I tried to hold on to my amazing gift. I didn't want any distraction for fear of losing this feeling. I wanted to keep saying thank you to God for the rest of my life. I limited my words for the next few days, trying to preserve my diminishing state of bliss.

The experience has remained with me, and I yearn for it again, but without the LSD.

Over the next few weeks, I shared my joy, telling people what happened. Everyone quietly and politely rejected my declarations. No one understood. Someone said I needed a long rest, and another friend said the LSD had given me the illusion of something happening.

"It wasn't the acid, Mike. I received a blessing, a kiss from God or something. It's way beyond words. It sounds crazy, but it was the most incredible—"

"Back up. You said you went to Big Sur with who?"

"Why are you stuck on that? I'm trying to tell you—"

"I'm busy. I don't want to hear about you and your punk boy going to Big Sur."

The memory of the event consumed me, and I frequently cried with joy remembering the overwhelming love. After several weeks, the blissful feeling faded, and I gave up telling people about it. But I will never forget it.

DESPERATELY SEEKING

O n the last day of the semester, my art history instructor clicked off the overhead projector and looked up from the center of the stadium-style seating.

"My parting advice to each of you in this auditorium today is scrape together what money you can and spend the summer exploring museums and cathedrals in Europe. That's where you'll get your real art education. Have a fun summer and be safe."

His words touched me. I imagined a trip through Europe to see the art, meet new people, and get a fresh, drug-free look at my life. That was the way to free myself from my addictions—by traveling far away from the things that had seduced me.

The following weekend at Mike's house, after we partied together late into the night, I told him my intention to go to Europe. A few days later, we were running the dogs on the beach, and he asked if I still thought about it.

"Yeah, I called my grandparents yesterday. I'm going to see them first and fly to London from there. I plan to make my way down the continent to the Greek Islands by train and ferry."

"What's in the Greek Islands?"

The frothy end of a wave rolled over our bare feet. The dogs leaped through the retreating surf for their stick.

"Just a destination. Mary Lou has a friend who worked in a coastal tourist town in Crete last summer. She said I might find work there."

"How long you going for?" he asked. "It'll be good to spend more time apart. I want to wrestle my demons under control too. Maybe we could meet in Europe at the end of your trip."

Would it be counterproductive to meet Mike when I planned, at least in part, to get free from the life I shared with him?

We planned to make contact via the main post office in Athens in six months, on January 1.

Randy drove me to the San Francisco Airport for my flight since Mike had gone back east on business.

At the boarding gate, I watched Randy through the plexiglass partition. We waved goodbye, and a pang of regret passed through me. We'd shared a lot of fun, and I knew I might never see him again.

I'd miss him, but I'd miss Mike and our life together far more. Mike represented the security of a big ocean liner, and I was setting out alone on a rubber raft. Our routine together had changed since I'd moved out, but my bond with him ran deep, and no one could touch the special place in me where he resided. We'd lived and cared for each other for six years. Although he saw other women now, his love still ruled my heart.

Yet my desire to find my own way—to discover new things—outweighed my concern about being out of touch with Mike. The same tunnel vision I'd had when I'd run away from home as a kid dominated my thoughts, and I saw nothing but possibility ahead.

"Why do you have to go so far away by yourself?" Mommy Burr asked.

"Lots of kids my age travel alone to explore the world. There's no need to worry."

At the boarding gate, Mommy Burr wrapped her long, thin arms around me, like covering me in a blanket of love. Daddy Burr's smile widened, carving creases into his tanned, leathery face. His gentle hug always lit something inside me, and the weight of the world lifted away under his kind, supportive gaze. I craved his approval over anyone else's in the world.

I boarded the plane in San Antonio and was off to travel alone through countries I knew nothing about. My legs vibrated as if stepping too close to the edge of a high cliff. The plane engines roared, and my excitement built as we lifted off.

Arriving in London, I asked people on the street for directions and found a youth hostel, which turned out to be more like a small dormitory. Already feeling worldly, I proudly showed my passport at check-in. Three sets of bunk beds furnished my room and slept five other female travelers from around the world—all close to my age, twenty-four, except one woman in her late thirties. I took a top bunk and noticed the freckled woman across from me reading a book.

The money I'd budgeted to spend each day, even with a bit extra for padding, didn't go far in England. The hostel alone ate up a third of it, so to stay there was a luxury I couldn't afford. Every dime needed to be spent carefully until I made it to the Greek Islands to find work. At least my student Eurail Pass permitted me to sleep on the train if necessary. I put aside concerns about money. Things always managed to work out.

From London, I rode a train to Dover, caught the ferry across the English Channel to France, and traveled on to Paris, loving every minute of my journey.

After a few days in Paris exploring the Louvre, I boarded the train to the Netherlands. In Amsterdam, I met a Dutch girl my age, who invited me to stay on her houseboat for two weeks. Susie's independent nature impressed me. She spoke several languages and worked at one of the embassies. I watched her remodel her houseboat, swinging a hammer as well as any man. She even sang the lead in a rock and roll band, which impressed me the most. We hitchhiked to the northern Netherlands and spent a few days at the home of her friend who was away on business.

After Amsterdam, I traveled south through Germany, Switzerland, and Italy, taking pictures everywhere and meeting lots of people. I stayed for days, sometimes weeks, in each country.

My problems in California slipped further behind me. I wrote to my grandparents, and I guessed they'd told my mother about my travels through foreign countries by myself, inviting her to worry with them. At my age, Mom would have done it too if given half a chance. No one and nothing held me down now.

Even memories of my sons grew distant. I never told Mike about them because I didn't want to change his opinion of me. My mother convinced me to keep my life a family secret, starting with my stepfather not being my real father. Like the guardian of a dangerous vault, I kept my secrets buried deep and pretended they'd never happened.

I learned the ropes of traveling and discovered many cool places to stay. I figured things out on my own, such as getting by eating yogurt, granola, and anything else I could get cheaply. When Europeans learned I traveled solo, they often bought me wine, cheeses, bread, and moussaka, thinking I must be hungry. I didn't spend much money, but I ate very well. Soon, I barely squeezed into my jeans.

After befriending a young German woman on the ferry from Athens to the island of Crete, we spent a month hitchhiking around the island. We backpacked into the Samaria Gorge on Crete, where we discovered an ancient, crumbling village. We threw our sleeping bags into one of the stone huts and spent an unforgettable night. We also spent a few nights in the Matala caves. The caves, carved out by ancient people, towered over the ocean. In earlier times, the caves housed lepers.

When my friend returned to Germany, I searched for work.

The sun warmed my back as I strolled beside the tourists along the slightly elevated walkway built next to Chania's curved port. The water reflected sheets of sunshine, and the breeze carried a salty fragrance. Small leather shops and patio restaurants lined the curved walkway on one side, and small fishing boats and rowboats bobbed and knocked against the docks on the other. Above the boats, seagulls cawed, searching for discarded bait.

The bars, cafes, and shops stirred to life after lunchtime siesta. A thirty-something Greek guy stopped ahead of me, then unlocked a massive set of glass French doors. He folded them back to face the harbor. He caught me watching him.

"Hello. I'm from America. I'm looking for work," I said brightly.

His expression remained blank. Clearly, he didn't understand me. After a moment, he gestured me inside, saying, "Come."

He stood behind the polished bar, pointing where to drop my backpack. He retrieved a ledger and popped open the cash register. Confused about what to do, I sat on a barstool and looked around until an older man walked in with the calm authority of a prince. When he saw me, he moved his Ray-Ban sunglasses to the top of his head and took in my appearance and backpack. He spoke in Greek to the younger man who'd let me in.

The older man wore a halo of gray curls and a healthy tan, pressed slacks, and a long-sleeved white linen shirt rolled above his wrists. He topped off his style with a gold and silver watch.

Too bad he's so old, probably in his forties.

"I'm Thomas. I own this place," he said in perfect English. "This is Stephanos, my son-in-law. What is your business here?"

"I'm looking for work. Someone told me Chania bars hire foreigners."

"Ah yes, true. Have you tended bar?"

"I worked in an oyster bar in the States—in America."

"Oyster bar? They have bars for oysters in America?" Thomas's soft expression crinkled into a smile. "Your timing is good. One of my girls went home yesterday, and I must replace her. Scorpios is a busy bar. Can you work fast?"

"Yes, sure."

"Okay. I'll give you a try."

"Really? You'll give me a job?" I slid off the barstool.

"Yes. The pay is low, but the tips are good. The job is pouring drinks, no oysters." He grinned, showing shimmering white teeth not common in Europe.

"Great! Thank you." I reached out to shake his hand.

He looked at my outstretched hand and took it. He told me about a place to stay and gave me instructions on how to find it. Following the curved port back along the water's edge, I inhaled the smell of seafood cooking on an open grill and took in the colorful village.

Good fortune shone on me today.

The two-story whitewashed apartment building Thomas described was framed by bright fuchsia bougainvillea. A stone archway invited tourists to peek into the courtyard full of red and white potted flowers crowding around a center fountain.

I located the landlady. "My name's Charlotte. Thomas from Scorpios sent me." I offered my hand to the short, stout lady who wore an apron and a long, gray, one-sided braid.

She quickly checked me up and down and took my outstretched hand. "Ah, Thomas, yes. You want room? How long you stay?"

She led me up a walkway of stone steps to the second floor, unlocked a door, and waved me in.

The towering ceilings, painted light blue with faded white clouds, seemed to include the Mediterranean sky. Old French window-doors invited me out on the balcony where I watched life move about on the port below. Dance music floated up, signaling the early evening festivities were underway. I spotted Scorpios on the other side of the harbor.

The landlady showed me the bathroom directly across the hall from my room.

"Is there a laundry for my clothes?" I made a scrubbing motion on top of my jeans. *Please let there be a washing machine.*

"Ah, *ne*. Here wash clothes." She pointed to the bathtub. "Dry." She pointed to the balcony. Hand-washing heavy, waterlogged jeans in the tub didn't dampen my enthusiasm, but where were the washing machines in Europe?

I rented a bicycle for six weeks, barely able to stop myself from whistling while I rode back to my apartment. I had a new job and a new place to live. I savored the taste of strength and my new independence.

The next evening, I pedaled along the port to Scorpios, anticipation driving my legs to go faster. Tourists strolled hand in hand or chatted with shop owners. Everyone looked happy—my kind of town.

"Hotel California" by the Eagles poured out from Scorpios's open French doors. I locked my bike around the corner in an alley and paused before stepping inside. The entire length of the bar and the tables were already crowded with cheerful patrons hollering in various languages above the music.

Twenty feet of open doors created the ambiance of sitting outside on a large, covered patio. Strings of small red, white, and green lights draped along the exteriors of the portside businesses. Their colors reflected off the water and created a party atmosphere.

Standing outside the bar, a warm breeze blew from behind, as if the island's angels urged me forward. They didn't need to push hard. I wanted to work there.

Three female bartenders worked quickly, pouring mugs and pitchers of frosty beer from the tap. If dressed alike, two of the three—identical twins—were impossible to tell apart. They even styled their shoulder-length red hair the same way.

The third bartender looked about eighteen. She'd tied her wavy brown hair back with a red ribbon, and a sprinkle of freckles crossed her nose. Setting a mug of frothy beer in front of a gentleman customer, she said something that made him throw his head back and belly-laugh.

The patrons at the tables stepped up to the bar to order their drinks, so the three bartenders never left their stations.

Stephanos, Thomas's son-in-law, was bent over a sink washing glasses. He spotted me, dried his hands on a small towel, slung it over his shoulder, and summoned me.

One of the twins shouted above the music, "I'm Coreen. She's my sister Rylee, and that's Raquel. Thomas told us he hired you today. Come around. I'll show you what we do."

Around 1:00 a.m., the music softened, the night wound down, and people left. I wiped the bar while Stephanos lifted the chairs to the tabletops.

"Now we can talk," Coreen said. She cleared and cleaned the tables ahead of Stephanos. "Rylee and I are from Ireland—"

Raquel giggled as she untied the red ribbon holding her hair back. "Like she couldn't tell by your accent."

"What accent? You're the one with the accent, Señorita." Coreen grinned. "Raquel's from Spain."

All three young women spent the summer working at Scorpios during the high season, and they would return home for college at summer's end.

"Why does Thomas hire foreigners instead of locals?"

"Greek girls who work in bars are prostitutes. The tourist clubs in Chania don't want them giving the port a bad name," Rylee said. "And no one but Greek citizens can work in Greece legally, so technically, we're breaking the law."

"The police don't enforce it though." Coreen twisted her hair in a loose top bun she secured with a pencil.

I hadn't seen an American in months, so I found it fun to talk to the GIs and tourists who partied at Scorpios. Customers didn't notice or care whether I drank with them, and I seldom thought about cocaine anymore. No one ever mentioned drugs in Greece.

On many nights after we closed, the club owners invited us—as well as other bartenders—to join them at all-night clubs. Thomas never came along. Instead, he went home to his family. These out-of-the-way clubs were patronized by Greek locals and their guests but never tourists. Bazooka players and Greek singers entertained us in the dark, smoky clubs. Everyone drank ouzo straight from tiny glasses—no ice, no soda.

"Tradition says if you enjoy the entertainer, you throw a plate and let it crash at the performer's feet," Coreen said.

The server placed more stacks of white plates and bottles of ouzo on our table. Our hosts, the club owners, paid for everything.

I spun a plate like a frisbee and watched it smash to bits at the foot of the singer. Soon, broken dishes littered the stage. At break time, the help used a wide patio broom to sweep the broken pieces into a pile behind the entertainer.

I pedaled to work every night and made enough money to live on. I even saved a bit, but I still needed more to buy a ticket home.

Interesting people from around the world patronized Scorpios; however, a Greek man named Spiros unnerved me. Tall and wiry, Spiros wore the same dirty army jacket every night. He often got drunk, stared intensely, and used obscene words in broken English—just loud enough for me to hear. His obsessive interest in me grew night after night.

"American girls no come," he said.

Oh my God, did he really say that? My face and neck burned hot. *Did anyone else hear him above the music?* I held steady while pulling beer from the fountain, pretending not to hear him.

I finished my shift and scooted a stool to the customer side of the bar to chat with my favorite regulars. After the GI sitting next to me left, Spiros grabbed his seat.

I sprang up. "Get lost, Spiros," I said over my shoulder, grabbing my daypack and rushing outside to the dark alley around the corner of the building. I knelt to unlock my bike.

A shadow swished behind me. I turned and peered through the dark but saw no one. I fumbled with the lock and heard another sound. I jumped up and swung around. Spiros's black eyes glittered in his pale face, barely visible in the dark.

Keep cool. Don't panic. "Leave me alone or I'll scream."

I hoped someone would exit the bar and walk by the alley, but there wasn't a soul around. I turned back to the bike, but my hands vibrated so hard, the lock kept moving away from the key.

Everything went black until white bubbles circled and popped in my head. I regained consciousness.

Why am I sprawled in the dirt on my back?

I lifted my head, saw my disheveled blouse and jeans come into focus, and remembered Spiros. His silhouette, fists clenched, wavered above me like a mirage. He mumbled something in Greek, then slipped into the shadows. Did he hit me? Oh my God, he tried to kill me.

I managed to sit upright. Dirt granules scratched across my face when I wiped my tears.

I grabbed my keys and crawled to my bike on all fours, then vomited in the dirt. A whiff of sour beer assaulted my nostrils. I swayed against my bike for a moment before regaining my balance and pedaling back to my flat, tears streaming down my face.

Worried Spiros might follow me, I kept looking back through the dark. I ran up the stairs, then slammed, locked, and wedged a chair against the door. From my balcony, I searched the vacant port for any movement, then latched the window-door and dove into bed. I squirmed under the covers and screamed into my pillow.

Lying in bed the next morning, I gingerly touched my temples and found lumps on each side of my head. Had he used rocks to hit me?

For the first time since coming to Europe over five months ago, homesickness rolled through me. I wanted to go back to California. I missed the safety of Mike's arms and our dogs chasing sticks in the surf. The world was not always a welcoming place for an independent woman trying to spread her wings.

After a hot bubble bath made of laundry detergent, I stepped onto my balcony to feel the sunshine radiating on the peaceful little fishing port. I listened to the seagulls call each other and watched them glide over the harbor, but the happy birds magnified my nightmare.

I scrutinized every breezeway and doorway below me on the port, terrified Spiros might be hiding there, ready to spring out. I needed help. I grabbed my bike key and daypack and raced downstairs.

Outside my apartment building, a barefoot boy, eight or nine, stood by a crumbling stone wall as if waiting for someone. He meandered toward me, dragging a thin stick across the cobblestones behind him.

"You live." He covered his eye with the back of his dirty hand.

I unlocked my bike, ready to ride. "What do you want? I'm in a hurry."

"Spiros."

"Did you say *Spiros?*" I caught his eye.

"Last night," the boy said.

I squatted in front of him, my face level with his, and touched his little hand. "Where? Near me?"

The boy stared at his bare feet but said nothing.

"Please talk to me. Did you see what happened?"

Still looking down, he nodded and put his dirty finger in his mouth.

"He hit me, didn't he?"

"*Ne.*" He nodded. "Two times."

Oh my God. My rage swelled.

"He came back of you. Hit you both sides." The boy made a fist with each hand and swung them wide in front of him, one then the other.

"He hit me in the head from behind using both his fists?"

"*Ne*, two times. Spiros run. You dead."

I guessed the kid waited outside my flat to see if I'd survived. I thanked him, pressed a coin in his palm, and pedaled to Scorpios to find Thomas. Thomas was well-liked and respected by everyone on the harbor. I trusted him. He reminded me of a younger version of my grandfather.

Inside Scorpios, the cleaners mopped the floors with the French doors wide open. Greek music poured from the powerful sound system. The place smelled of Clorox.

"I've got to see Thomas, please." The cleaning man stared at my twitching face.

Without responding, he laid his huge mop aside and walked to the back.

I rubbed my open palms on my jeans, fidgeting and waiting.

Thomas emerged right away, removed his reading glasses, and maneuvered between the tables toward me. "What's wrong? What happened?"

I told Thomas everything I knew about the night before and about the boy.

"Are you okay? Do you need a doctor?" he asked.

"No doctor. I'm okay except for a couple of big lumps on my head and bruises from falling, I guess. I'm so scared, Thomas. I'm afraid he'll come for me again, maybe follow me home."

"I know who you're talking about. Spiros creates many problems for us in Chania. Everyone thinks he's crazy."

"Maybe I should leave Crete." I hadn't earned enough money to pay my way home yet, but I felt desperate.

Thomas sighed, wiping his reading glasses with his handkerchief, his eyebrows knitted together. "I understand your fear, but don't let Spiros chase you away from Chania. He's the one to leave. I'll look into it and talk to the police. But remember, if they question you about Spiros, do not mention your job. They know you work here, but don't bring it up."

"Thank you, Thomas." I sniffled. "Even riding over here today, I kept thinking he might be hiding, waiting for me."

"If you need the night off—"

"I don't want to be alone. I want to be here."

"I'll make a call to the authorities and provide someone to walk you to and from work. Spiros will not be permitted in Scorpios again. He'll hear about the police involvement, so I don't think he'll come around anyway."

"Thank you."

"I'm sorry this happened to you, Charlotte, and to think it happened at Scorpios. It's troubling."

15

BIG TROUBLE IN LITTLE CHANIA

When I arrived for work later, the women bartenders had already heard what happened with Spiros. The police never questioned me about the incident, but Thomas assured me Spiros would be picked up if he came back to Chania.

Problems in or around the harbor seldom occurred, so several days later when a commotion erupted at the entrance of Scorpios, my nightmare came true.

Thomas stretched out his arms to stop Spiros from entering the bar.

Spiros easily pushed little Thomas aside, causing Brody, an American GI and bodybuilder, to get involved. He jumped in front of Spiros and placed his open palm flat on Spiros's forehead before shoving him backward, hard.

Spiros staggered off balance. Anger flashed in his beady snake eyes. He waved his arms, bellowed something in Greek, then lunged at Brody. Another man, a German tourist, sprang from his seat and body-blocked Spiros. All three men scuffled to push Spiros back outside.

I ducked behind the bar, terrified he'd fight past them, find me, and beat me to death.

Rylee laid her hand on my head. "Stay down. Thomas will take care of it."

Frustration built inside me. I fantasized about leaping over the bar and attacking Spiros with a bat. Instead, I hid my face in a dish towel.

Rylee brushed the top of my head. "Okay. They're outside now."

I pushed back my hair and peeked over the bar.

My customer looked around and asked, "What's going on?"

"Thomas doesn't want that guy in here," Rylee said over her shoulder as she pulled the tap handle.

I went to work but watched the door. An hour later, Thomas came back inside. I dried my hands and rounded the bar to speak with him. He gestured me back to work. Perspiration glistened on his forehead, and he pressed his lips into a tight line across his face. He weaved his way through the tables of customers to his office. Most of the patrons remained oblivious to what happened.

After closing time, Thomas and I sat together while the others cleaned up.

"We kept Spiros pinned until the police arrived. I gave them the details and reminded them about your trouble last week. I don't want this new incident to make a problem for any of us."

"Yeah, I hope this doesn't cause a bigger problem, Thomas. I'll do whatever you suggest—give a statement, file a complaint, whatever. Will they keep him in jail?"

"Yes, yes. Other complaints have surfaced against Spiros. Local police are not tolerant of violence—especially against tourists. Laws are different here than in America. He will be punished."

Weeks later, Thomas approached the bar and bowed his head to speak privately. "An officer with the Chania police is here. Will you talk with him?"

"About Spiros?"

"I think so, but I'm not sure. He's not my friend, and he likes to throw his weight around. See what he wants."

I scanned the crowded club and spotted a man in his forties sitting alone. He was dressed in business attire and watching me. A smug look of entitlement appeared on his face when I walked through the tables to join him.

He remained seated but reached across and pulled out my chair.

"Hello, Charlotte," he said in a friendly tone, but his eyes darted from side to side, never looking directly at me. He hid something.

"Hi." I reached out to formally shake.

He took my hand and covered it with his other. Goosebumps traveled up my forearm. I suppressed a shudder, kept cool, slid my hand out from between his, and sat down. I leaned back, sitting straight but creating distance.

Something isn't right.

"My name is Ari Papanikolou, official for Chania police. You heard of me?"

"No. What do you want?" My stomach quivered.

"I want to know you."

With those five words, I realized he was a pompous old man who used his authority to bring me to his table under the guise of official business.

I stood. He reached for me, but I jerked back. "I'm going back to work."

"Come now. We're both adults. I can make things difficult for you."

I stared into his rheumy eyes. This guy was another Spiros trying to bully and control me. Instead of an army jacket, he wore a fancy suit and shiny shoes. I felt like knocking his teeth loose. Instead, I turned and walked to the bar.

"Who is he? What does he want?" Rylee asked while operating the cash register.

"He's a slimy reptile who crawls out at night to party on the waterfront," I said. "Some kind of official cop. He actually hit on me. I think he wants to make trouble for Thomas more than me. He knows about Spiros."

"He probably thinks you and Thomas have something going."

We went back to pouring drinks. Later, she said, "Yeah, I got hit on too—not by him. A different cop. Chauvinist pigs."

Accustomed to men attempting to control me through their authority or violence, I learned, as every woman does, that sometimes I could sidestep my way out of it. Other times, I wasn't so lucky.

My youthful energy and blind faith in life continually trumped my fear and propelled me forward, sometimes right into danger.

I inherited that daring gene from Mom and considered it a gift. My mother was strong, lived by her own rules, and influenced me with her independent attitude. Unfortunately, she didn't teach me the importance of achieving a skill to support my independence.

The turmoil arose when my carefree attitude butted against a world where women were expected to behave a certain way. If I followed my heart and violated societal expectations, I shouldn't be surprised if a man puts me back in my subordinate place. Common thinking is that women invite trouble if they exercise too much freedom.

The same can be seen in the courtroom when a female rape

victim must explain, in public, her behavior prior to the rape. While sitting on the witness stand, she is expected to defend herself for drinking too much, dressing a certain way, or being married to the wrong man. It's no wonder why the majority of rapes are never reported.

I'm lucky I didn't get killed by some guy who took it as his personal challenge to control my independent attitude—though I came close more than once.

After closing time, Ari Papanikolou entered the bar trailed by a uniformed officer. The two men stomped toward Thomas's office. A few minutes later, they emerged and left.

Thomas came out and turned down the music. "I need your passports, everyone."

"What? Why?" Raquel asked from the other end of the bar.

"It's a formality, but I must deliver all four passports to the police station tonight. You cannot work tomorrow night without them. We'll all go to the station in the morning and get them back."

"But—"

"Please, it's been a long few days. I need your passports now."

The next morning, we met Thomas in front of Scorpios. The other bartenders and I then strolled through the village with Thomas. Children played soccer in the street, dogs sniffed around trash cans, and shop owners swept their storefronts. As our small group walked by the shops, many paused, leaned on their brooms, and greeted Thomas as an old friend.

I fell in step beside him. "Is this happening because I refused to go out with that Ari guy?"

"Yes, but there are other things too." His mouth made a grim line.

"Let's report him. Tell his boss what's going on."

He kept his stride and looked at me from the corner of his eye. "He *is* the boss."

"Crap. Any chance he'll arrest us?"

"No, but I must warn all of you"—he stopped and looked at the other women—"if you argue with Ari at the station, he will deport you. He will say you're working illegally in Greece and are no longer welcome. Say nothing and let me talk. I think he wants to make a little problem for me, not so much you."

We entered through a screen door. A floor fan worked furiously to fight the rising morning heat in the dirty waiting room. Scuff marks and dried liquid spotted the gray linoleum floor. Six metal chairs sat side by side against the dull white wall. The room smelled like sweat and ancient cigarette smoke. I heard Ari in the next room talking loudly to someone, probably on the phone. We waited almost an hour in the suffocating heat.

Ari poked his head out and summoned Thomas. We squirmed in our seats as we listened to Ari and Thomas yell at each other in Greek behind the closed office door. When Thomas finally came out, he exhaled audibly and wiped a bead of sweat running down the side of his face. He waved us to follow, our passports in his hand.

No one spoke as the group trudged back through the village.

I arrived early before work that night and found Thomas in his office doing paperwork. I tapped on the open office door. He raised his eyebrows in question and waved me in.

"I'm leaving Greece," I blurted out.

He closed the ledger and peered up at me. "Are you leaving because of Spiros?"

"Partly, yes. I'm a target for him, and now this Ari cop, for them to work out their hatred of Americans. I mean, they didn't bother Raquel or the twins but singled me out."

"I think you're mistaken, but I understand your concern."

"Besides, my boyfriend is meeting me in Athens soon."

It was time to sell out and go home to the safety of Mike. Who was I kidding about finding freedom and independence? The world showed me my naïveté.

Drug-free for nearly six months, I hoped Mike had wrestled his problems under control too. Maybe we could start over. At least that much made sense.

Thomas woke me from my thoughts. "Come back to Scorpios to see us."

"Thanks for your kindness, Thomas."

I circled around his battered desk to hug him goodbye. I hoped his children realized how fortunate they were to have a father like him.

The next morning, I looked around my room and up at the sky-high ceilings. The flowers I'd bought three days ago sagged, and the wicker basket for collecting fruit from the farmer's market was empty.

I passed through the tall, glass window-door on the balcony one last time and took in the sight of the seagulls sailing over the fishing boats. Couples and families walked hand in hand along the water's edge, enjoying the fresh energy of a new day in Chania. So many times, I'd relaxed on this balcony in the morning sunshine, drinking Nescafé and watching the villagers bring their wares outside for the day ahead.

Mike would love this little Greek village.

At that moment, I realized I still loved him.

I had so much to tell him about my travels and new friends. I no longer had a biting urge to run away and search the world for elusive answers to unknown questions. I'd learned the answers I sought weren't out in the world.

I jumped off the ferry and hauled my backpack into downtown Athens. The scene hit me like a tsunami. Gone was the cool, coastal vibe of Chania, with colorful flags sailing valiantly along the water's edge of the little tourist port. In its place, cars honked, people hustled, and garbage piles crowded the curbs.

At the main post office, two letters from my grandparents asked me to write. Nothing from Mike. Only four days before our rendezvous.

Why haven't I received word saying where to meet him?

I found a youth hostel, checked in, and leaped into my bunk.

I wanted to show Mike my new self, free of drugs and a bit more independent. Not that he cared about the independent part, but I wanted to impress him the way he impressed me. After all, I'd learned to travel alone on almost no money. He probably expected to pay my way home, but I intended to buy my own plane ticket. First, I needed to find a way to earn enough money to do that fast.

The young people in neighboring Yugoslavia wanted blue jeans, but restrictions by their government left their desire unfulfilled. I formed a plan to meet their need and simultaneously earn money. I'd sell the jeans to students in Belgrade, triple my investment the way I'd seen Mike do, then return to Athens in time to meet him.

I used a portion of my tip savings to negotiate the price for two identical brown suitcases, thirty pairs of jeans, and a round-trip train ticket from Athens to Belgrade. I managed to get a rock-bottom price for the jeans from an Athenian shop merchant, careful not to tell him why I bought so many pairs. He might attempt to dissuade me if he discovered my plan to enter Yugoslavia.

The pants fit perfectly folded into the two suitcases, and

I protected my 35mm camera and precious photo canisters by wedging them between the jeans.

A communist country, Yugoslavia had a frosty relationship with the United States. Although not exactly behind the Iron Curtain, they weren't friendly to America either, rather sort of indifferent. This knowledge didn't deter me. What could they do to me? No one searched women's suitcases anyway.

Something jarred me awake at the railroad border crossing into Yugoslavia. The other passengers were alert, sitting upright and looking out the windows.

Two uniformed soldiers carrying machine guns stormed onto our rail car and questioned passengers in the first row. I figured they were searching for someone in particular, maybe a criminal. But when they moved down the aisle, their tone sounded harsh toward every passenger. They got closer to my row, demanding passports and papers from everyone—and searching suitcases! I felt a surge of adrenaline.

They're looking for smugglers like me!

My panic rose almost out of control. I whipped my head around, desperate for someplace to run.

If I charge through the exit and leap off the train, the guards might shoot me in the back.

Communist laws are made to control people, not protect them.

Grabbing the armrests, I pushed myself against the seat to still my vibrating body. The soldiers moved closer. They asked questions, and if they didn't like the response, they opened the person's suitcase.

A young guy seated across and facing me, riding backward, wore a tan-colored fringed leather jacket. Fringe Guy kept twisting in his seat to watch the guards work their way closer. He squirmed, head jerking one way then the other, spastic-like.

The other passengers wore blank expressions, but they all fidgeted. A little girl cried. I almost cried, too.

I'm an American smuggling thirty pairs of jeans into a communist country. What the hell am I doing?

My turn came to show my passport. The guard glared from beneath the shiny brim of his hat and leaned toward me, causing my legs to vibrate even more and make me look guilty. My limbs refused to obey my mental command to stop shaking.

"Passport," he said in clipped English.

His scrutiny traveled down my braids to my bell-bottoms, which I'd embroidered with butterflies. I was a quivering flower child ready to be stomped on by dictator boots.

Fear of him searching my suitcases and finding piles and piles of jeans made me sick. No one wears thirty pairs of jeans on one trip! I imagined my arrest and torture as an American capitalist pig—maybe they'd drag me to a dark dungeon and stretch me.

He motioned again. I shook my head, indicating I didn't understand. He snapped his fingers twice in front of my face, and his nostrils flared. "Passport!"

"Yes, yes," I squeaked. Handing it to him, my hand made the passport tremble.

He looked at it closely, held it next to my face, and carefully compared the picture. I attempted to match the happy travel photo, but my eye kept twitching and my mouth wouldn't smile.

He snapped my passport closed, handed it back to me, then waved to my suitcases in the overhead bin.

"What? Yes, mine." *This can't really be happening.*

He moved his machine gun around to his back, pulled one

of my bags down, and laid it on the floor, blocking the aisle. Kneeling on one knee while fumbling with my suitcase buckle, he grunted, pointing at the lock. He waited, eyes piercing into mine like he knew I was stalling, guilty. I shook my head, pretending not to understand.

In a flash, his lips pulled back in a feral snarl showing teeth too big for his mouth. I caught my breath and imagined saliva dripping from the corners of his mouth. I reacted fast, trying to force my shaking hand inside the tiny outer pocket of my backpack where the key was hidden, but my hand wouldn't hold still.

Meanwhile, the other guard joined us and said something to Fringe Guy sitting across from me. Fringe Guy sat frozen and unresponsive. In one big yank, the guard jerked him out of his seat. Fringe Guy wrestled him. Big mistake. My guard stood up to help. He grabbed the guy on the other side and gave him a shake. The three scuffled, and Fringe Guy tripped over my bag, almost falling back, but the two guards held and lifted him. His feet trailed the floor as they dangled him like a rag doll down the narrow aisle. They disappeared off the train.

I breathed out as shock hit me. Every instinct said to run, but where?

Like other passengers, I pressed my face against the window and watched. The flat landscape with gray skies, bare trees, and puddles of rainwater completed the bleak atmosphere. The guards pushed Fringe Guy back and forth between them, their voices inaudible. Then the ruckus moved out of our line of sight.

I grabbed my suitcase off the floor and slid it back into the overhead compartment. In a flash, I stripped off my jean jacket and stuffed it in front of the suitcases, hiding them.

I sat down, wishing for the train to take off and leave the

guards behind. A short time later, two new guards marched down the aisle toward me.

Oh shit. I sank low, head down, and pretended to be asleep.

Holding my breath, I heard them shuffle past and start with the row behind me. They worked their way to the end of the car and disappeared off the train. Fringe Guy never returned to his seat. When the train moved a little, I popped up from my pretend sleep and asked the older lady sitting next to me if she spoke English. She stared ahead and didn't respond.

Her male companion looked across her. "I speak English," he said.

"What happened to that guy?" I asked.

"He from Yugoslavia. Buy jacket in Greece. Pay no import fee. Guards destroy jacket."

"What happened to the guy?" I repeated, afraid of the answer.

He shrugged and looked out the window. The lady next to me remained silent. No one spoke again.

I didn't pay any import fee for my jeans!

A cold rush passed through me. I leaned back and prayed I wouldn't get arrested. This was crazier than my San Quentin smuggle.

At the busy Belgrade station, people rushed everywhere. Loaded down with a suitcase in each hand and a backpack on my back, I wobbled through the crowd, stopping frequently to set the bags down and catch my breath.

A young guy, his coat collar upturned, showed bushy brows and sprigs of short, frizzy hair sticking out from under a beanie cap. He looked up from his conversation with an elderly couple, excused himself, and walked toward me.

"Do you need help?" he asked in good English.

"Wow, English. Yes, I need directions. I want to find the Belgrade university dorms. I brought clothing the students will want to buy," I said, faking confidence.

He searched my face, the corners of his mouth curled up a little like I must be kidding. "American here to sell something. Yes, yes, of course. What kind of clothing?"

"Jeans."

"Jeans. My name Viktor. Come, I help you."

Viktor hailed a cab just as it began to sprinkle again. So grateful for his help, I didn't question his motive. We rode through the city toward the university dorms.

The cold, musty-smelling cab matched the look of Belgrade, gray and forbidding like it was hiding something terrible.

Real winters fell on this country that were unlike sunny California winters.

Let me unload these jeans and return to Athens to meet Mike as soon as possible.

Viktor, curious about me as an American girl traveling alone, asked several questions. I answered him but wondered silently why he wanted to help me.

"You have man jeans—my size?"

"No, women's," I answered.

We stopped in front of a long, narrow, two-story brick dormitory. I exited the cab and stepped right into an icy mud puddle. The cold water seeped through my canvas Keds. At least it'd stopped raining. I shivered off the frigid air penetrating my bones, pulled my jean jacket closer, and reminded myself this was an adventure that would end soon.

Viktor moved ahead to enter the dim, sage-green hallway. A gust of air blasted in before he muscled the door closed.

He knocked on the first dormitory door.

A young woman with dark hair pinned up in a bun slid the chain lock aside and opened the door halfway. As Viktor spoke to the woman, he pointed to my suitcases. She scanned me up and down, and her brown eyes widened and rested on my baggage when he said the word "American." By the time he finished talking, her guarded expression softened, and she opened the door all the way to reveal another female student standing behind her, listening to our conversation. They invited us in.

A bit warmer, the tiny dorm room offered a welcome relief from the frigid hallway.

I knelt on the floor, clicked open one of the suitcases, and proudly handed each girl a pair of jeans. Viktor stood back.

The first girl examined her pair, said a few words to her friend, and handed the jeans back to me. She spoke to Viktor.

"What did she say?"

"She say these not American jeans. These Greek jeans," he said.

"Well, yes, but—" I hated hearing the tremor in my voice.

"They want American jeans," Viktor said.

The floor rolled like a wave under me. I'd made a colossal mistake, but I held my composure. "Let's ask some other students. Maybe—"

Viktor spoke at length to the girls before we left. He was helping me as an excuse to meet all these college girls, but I didn't care. I owed him.

We knocked on the next door and the next one, but all the students said the same thing. My plan had fallen flat.

DEAD ON ARRIVAL

16

O utside the building, dark clouds obscured the setting sun.

"I must go home now," Viktor said. "Where do you go? A hotel?"

"No. I planned to sell the jeans and take an all-night train back to Athens."

"You go to train station now? I show you bus stop and speak to driver for you."

"Yes, yes." I couldn't wait to leave this country.

After thanking Viktor and bidding him goodbye, I boarded the crowded bus and dropped into an open seat next to a young couple. They turned out to be sister and brother. Both spoke good English.

"My name Vesna. This my brother, Bojan."

Weary from the day's events, I pushed down my despair and answered their questions politely. The deep cough I'd developed during the last few hours kept interrupting our conversation.

Bojan, an animated talker, held a fixed grin on his face. His mouth appeared packed full of crooked, yellow teeth, and his reddish hair stuck up and out like he'd just woken from a fitful nap.

I asked him about the train to Athens.

"No more trains tonight," Bojan said.

"Oh no. Are you sure?"

Neither of them understood my question.

Unbelievable. Mike will think I've lost my mind when I tell him about this trip. "Sounds about right for my luck today."

"My luck?" Vesna asked.

"I'm very tired. Will I be permitted to sleep at the train station tonight? On a chair?"

They waited while I got control of my hacking cough.

"No. But you can put your bed in my shop," Bojan said. "My shop not far. If you like, we go."

"Yes. Very nice. Thank you." My chest clenched tight, making it hard to breathe without coughing over and over. I struggled to lift my bags.

The siblings each picked up one of my suitcases, and Bojan helped me off the bus with my backpack. I stumbled, weaker by the minute.

To my surprise, Vesna reboarded the bus and waved goodbye.

"Come this way," Bojan said.

We walked the road in the dark for about twenty minutes, then cut across a field. He carried my suitcases, but I could barely stand under the weight of my backpack. I swooned, dizzy. Water sloshed from my shoes with every step.

Bojan unlocked his shop just as it started to rain again. The bare concrete floors kept the temperature low, but at least it was warmer than outside. He flipped on a single light. Bicycles hung from the ceiling, and French racing posters covered the walls. Bike parts, arranged in neat rows, hung on hooks above the workbench.

Bojan pointed to a folded blanket. I rolled my sleeping bag over the blanket, pulled off my wet shoes, dried my feet on a shop rag, then crawled into my bag, coughing and delirious with exhaustion.

Bojan perched on a stool at the bench, clicked on a small overhead lamp, picked up some screws, and worked. I forced myself to stay awake as long as possible, waiting for him to leave, but I drifted off fantasizing about a seafood dinner with Mike in Athens. When had I last eaten?

Something jerked me out of a deep slumber. Bojan's face was two inches from mine, his body stretched out parallel next to me on the floor.

Keep calm. "I fell asleep." I eased back from him.

"I stay for you," Bojan said in a throaty tone.

Don't panic. "What time is it?" I asked, controlling my rising fear.

"Morning. Four o'clock, five o'clock. Come, move closer."

My sleeping bag and clothes were flimsy barriers between us. He was so close, I smelled his sour breath.

He reached around, pulled my head to him, and puckered his lips to kiss me.

I pushed him back hard. "No, please. I'm sick and need sleep."

He mumbled something I didn't understand and jumped up. In the dim light, he snarled. "Get up. Get out."

"What? I don't know where I am. Let me stay until sunrise."

"I say go—now."

I gathered my stuff. He opened the door to snowflakes floating down like feathers.

At least it's snow instead of rain.

"Go."

I had the choice to sleep with this asshole or get lost in the frigid night—possibly die in the snow. I'd rather die in the snow.

"Will you point me toward the bus stop? Please."

He indicated a direction before shutting the door.

Snowflakes scattered in swirls of wind as I trudged along, squishing water from my wet Keds. I heaved my belongings along a few steps at a time before my hacking cough forced me to stop.

In a daze but not crying, my resolve deepened. I knew my survival depended on my will to go on. I had to find the damn bus stop.

I waddled beneath the weight of my bags, dragging myself through the frigid dark until, finally, the dirt changed to hard pavement under the shallow snow. The road!

About twenty minutes later, in the dawning light, I spotted a group of about six people huddled together, all dressed in boots, heavy coats, and round hats. One of them noticed me, and they all turned. The bus stop! Thank you, Universe!

"To Belgrade?" I pointed to the old bus lumbering toward us on the slushy road.

An older, heavyset lady, dark-tanned with deep lines webbing out from her eyes, nodded once. "Belgrade," she said through her face scarf.

In truth, I didn't care where the bus went. I got on to survive. Thank goodness the driver accepted Greek Drachmas for payment.

The bus driver waited while I heaved my clumsy luggage aboard one piece at a time and found a seat. It had stopped snowing, and morning light tried to pierce the thick, gray sky. The buildings, landscape, and even the people appeared gray. Steamy clouds blew from my mouth. By the looks on the passengers' solemn faces, I imagined they worked backbreaking factory jobs.

At the terminal, I learned the train to Athens was ready to depart. I huffed along the platform, lugging my backpack and suitcases toward my train. Unable to lug everything a step further, I dropped one suitcase and ran to board with my other two bags. I dumped everything on the first empty seat, jumped off the train, and ran for the bag I'd left behind.

Halfway there, the whistle blew, and the train rolled a bit. I slid to a halt. My suitcase sat in plain sight where I'd left it on the platform.

Clutching a handrail for support, a uniformed man leaned out from the train, watching me.

"No! Wait! My bag!" I yelled. He followed my pointing arm to my bag sitting about thirty yards away.

"Passport?" he yelled.

I pointed to the train.

He waved his hand in a rolling motion to run to him. I charged after the train, grabbed his free hand, and he pulled me aboard as the train picked up speed.

People crisscrossing the platform in front of my bag obscured my line of sight as we chugged away. The bag held worthless jeans, anyway, so what the hell? But when I checked my other suitcase, I discovered the bag I'd left behind contained my camera and my European photos from the past six months. I plopped heavily into my seat. Every inch of my body ached, and my head and chest felt ready to explode from the pressure. I didn't care about the expensive camera, but I had to go back for my irreplaceable pictures.

The same uniformed man who'd helped me board now weaved side to side from the rocking movement of the train as he punched tickets. I handed him my return ticket to Athens.

"Sir, I must go back to Belgrade for my bag."

"Very difficult," he said.

I dismissed his remark. "I'm getting off the train at the first stop and taking another train back."

He stared at me. "First stop, mail stop. No tourist stop."

An hour later, we arrived at a tiny mail depot located in the countryside of Yugoslavia. I got off the train alone and stood under an overhang. No signs of life could be seen through the veil of rain except for a lone mailman on the deserted platform who exchanged a large, canvas duffle bag with the train conductor. They both looked my way.

The weather-worn, pitted-wood station looked like the Hollywood backdrop for an old Western movie. I expected to see horses with thick winter coats tethered to a hitching post and standing strong against the winter.

The mailman opened the creaky door and motioned me inside. Four tiny round tables, each with two chairs, furnished the small cafe. I dropped my bags on the hardwood floor and positioned my chair near the crackling fire in the potbellied stove.

The mailman strode behind the three-foot length of counter and poured coffee into two tiny ceramic cups from a long-handled copper pot. When the grainy black liquid hit my flaming throat, I thought it the most delicious brew that had ever touched my lips.

"Coffee good," I said.

My cough wheezed up from my chest again. Heavy with exhaustion, I willed myself not to lay my head on the table. I didn't want to appear rude.

I asked the man what time the next train came through going back to Belgrade, but he shook his head, unable to understand my question.

His gray overalls and bushy gray hair matched the sky outside, but his fatherly face looked gentle like my grandfather's, steady and calm.

The same door swung open, and a new man slipped inside.

Flakes of snow gusted in behind the large man. He pushed the door closed and greeted the gray-haired mailman without taking his eyes off me. His slouched shoulders made him look tired, like he'd recently plowed the fields. He stomped off his weather-beaten boots and removed his snow-dusted coat.

His gaze followed my braids, my thin jean jacket, and moved down to my wet Keds. I imagined a farmwife cooking over a big iron pot and a bunch of kids waiting for him at home.

The fire snapped and popped. The man sat, pulled out tobacco, rolled a cigarette, and offered it to me.

I declined with a shake of my head. This man had far fewer luxuries in his life than I had, yet he'd offered to share his. The gesture touched me.

I rested my head on my hands. The two men murmured in hushed tones like they didn't want to disturb me.

I jolted upright when the depot door banged open, and the mailman poked his head inside and waved me to come. The other man was gone. *How long had I slept?*

I stood outside on the platform and listened to the train whistle its approach before the exhaust caught up and flooded the platform making me choke out a cough.

A uniformed ticket-man leaned out from the train and greeted my mailman host but stopped when he saw me. I thanked the mailman in Greek for his hospitality. He touched his fingers to his forehead and nodded a small salute goodbye.

On the train, I peered out the window thinking about my pictures. My fierce determination to retrieve them kept me going. I considered them the most valuable and irreplaceable possession from my trip, documentation of my six-month journey through Europe, learning and searching.

At the Belgrade station, my turn came to speak with the ticket seller perched behind a scratched, yellow, plexiglass window. Her hair color matched her dark-rimmed cat-eyed glasses, and her deep red lipstick had bled into her lip lines.

"Ma'am, do you understand English?"

"Little," she said without looking up from a document.

"I left my bag here this morning, early. It's brown, about this big."

"No bags here," she said.

"Please, is there a lost and found?"

Uninterested, she pursed her lips and peered over my shoulder to the person behind me. My time was up. The ache in my bones doubled the weight of this loss.

I never saw my bag again, but I still lugged around the rest of those damn jeans.

I boarded the train and fell quickly to sleep. Several hours later, I woke when the train crossed the border to Greece with minimal commotion. Greek guards came on board, but none carried machine guns or hateful dispositions. They checked our tickets and passports in a calm, routine manner and sent us on.

A glint of daybreak shone as we reached the outskirts of Athens. I thought of nothing except finding dry socks and a warm bed.

A day after leaving Belgrade, with burning behind my eyes and a painful, mean cough, I stepped off the train at the Athens terminal. Stumbling a few steps, I drop-sat on my suitcase and covered my hot face with my hands.

Dear God, help me. I'm scared and I'm sick. Give me strength.

I centered myself and remembered my spiritual experience in Big Sur. *Whatever happens now, even if I die, I'll go out with the faith that love embraced me, and we are all destined to be okay.*

Knowing this comforted me, but feverish teardrops rolled from between my pressed lashes.

Nearby, someone cleared his throat. A slim man with dark, thinning hair stood a few feet away. "Can I help you?"

He introduced himself as Hypatos and showed a wide gap between his front teeth when he spoke. He wore a wrinkled white dress shirt and business slacks. Underarm sweat rings dampened his shirt.

I wiped my face on my jacket sleeve. "I need to find a warm place to sleep. Cheap."

"Come, I show you." He lifted my backpack and my one suitcase. I forced myself to shuffle after him.

"My place not far. Can you make it? You go to hospital?"

"No, I'll be okay. Where's the post office?"

"Post office? Post office closed now. Open tomorrow. Come."

We walked past a junkyard of rusty buses and burned-out industrial buildings with broken windows. I coughed so hard, I stopped to dry-heave.

Hypatos scurried back to help me. "You need hospital."

"No hospital. Just need rest."

We entered a quiet residential area of two- and three-story buildings made of white stucco, common in Greece. He ascended the stone steps. It took all my will to follow, hunched and slow like a dying old woman.

His tiny apartment lit up when he pulled back the living room drapes, and the morning sun poured in. He offered me a chair at the yellow, Formica kitchen table, heated a can of chicken noodle soup, and set out bread. He left me while he ran water in the bathtub. The hot soup slid warm down my throat, but the smell made me queasy even though I was famished. I grabbed my napkin to spit out pieces of chicken and poured the remaining soup down the sink drain. A violent cough left me barely able to breathe.

Hypatos rushed in. "Go now, take hot bath. You stay here. I make bed for you."

Throbbing pain ripped through my chest. I nearly accepted his offer. *Is this another weird situation about to happen? I haven't the strength to fight this time.*

"I can't stay. I'm sorry."

I braced for his angry reaction, but he only nodded.

"You no understand me. Go now, take bath."

I locked the bathroom door and eased into the sudsy water, so grateful for the warmth. I mustered the energy to wash my hair with bar soap and use the rattling hair dryer for as long as I could manage. I pulled on an almost-clean T-shirt and a pair of the worthless new Greek jeans, but my only shoes still squished out water when I walked. Stronger from the bath, I entered the kitchen.

"I must go now. Thank you for your help, Hypatos."

"Where you go?"

I felt light-headed. Instead of answering, I eased into a kitchen chair and looked away, trying to think past the pain in my chest.

After a few moments, he said, "I show you place. Come."

I dragged myself behind Hypatos across the busy square.

The alley hotel door stood propped open by a dead potted plant. I paused at the entrance to let my vision adjust to the dark lobby lit only by a small lamp on the clerk's desk. Clouds of old and new cigarette smoke slammed me. Torn faded wallpaper decorated the walls, and two stuffed purple chairs furnished the lobby.

A dark-skinned clerk sitting at a low desk noticed us and

turned down the radio playing Turkish belly-dance music. When Hypatos said something in Greek, the man crushed out his cigarette and grunted a response before sliding a skeleton key across the desk. Wheezing for air, I followed Hypatos up the shadowy staircase.

We stood at what looked like the dark mouth of a cave. Hypatos flicked a switch, and the bare lightbulb hanging over the bed flickered on. The swayed bed was dressed in clean white sheets and folded blankets. I dragged myself across the squeaky floor, eased back on the starched pillowcases, and tried not to jolt my painful chest.

Hypatos walked to a grated wall heater and turned the knobs until it gurgled to life. I kicked off my Keds, hearing them thump the floor.

Hours or days later, I woke and squinted through the dark. Lying on top of the bedspread, fully clothed and covered with blankets, I shivered and my memory cleared.

I squinted at the light bulb hanging above me in the dark. I tucked the covers around me, trying to get warm. I thought of Mommy Burr and Daddy Burr, then Mike. Why hadn't I told my grandparents I loved them more often? So wrapped up in my fast life, I'd seldom stopped to appreciate them. Now it was too late. Death summoned me, promising escape from this grungy life.

Mike's face and the sound of his voice drifted through my mind. I pictured him and the dogs, remembering the small, kind things he did for them and me.

"Miss Charlotte, can you hear me?"

The weak bulb provided enough backlight for Hypatos's silhouette to come into view through my fluttering eyelids.

Someone stood beside him. He placed a cool washcloth on my forehead.

"This my good friend, Aigle. She is nurse. We brought more water, soup, and medicine."

Aigle helped me sit up and pushed the sweaty hair off my forehead. Around Hypatos's age, mid-50s, she wore her blonde hair twisted back in a bun. She smelled like fresh air, reminding me of Mommy Burr. Aigle took my temperature and pulse. She spoke Greek in low tones to Hypatos as she unwrapped a stethoscope and listened to my chest and back.

"Miss Charlotte, Aigle thinks you carry pneumonia. This medicine stop infection in your chest, but if you no good tomorrow, we go to hospital."

"How long?" I whispered through my wheezy cough.

"How long you sick? I don't know, but you here three days. Try, drink water."

"Bathroom," I said.

They helped me to the bathroom and left me for privacy. I pulled back the ripped curtains to find it dark outside. The chipped mirror reflected my half-open burning eyelids, cracked lips, and my hair sticking out in knots all over my head, like Phyllis Diller.

Dizziness overcame me, and I sank to the linoleum floor. Aigle entered to find me gripping the side of the sink. She ushered me back to bed and fluffed my pillows.

"You need hospital. You too sick," Hypatos said.

"I need rest." I didn't want to tell him I couldn't afford a hospital. Sleep descended on me and promised comfort. "Hypatos—"

"Yes, Miss Charlotte? I'm here."

"Thank you for helping me." Grateful sniffles escaped, and I reached for his hand, but not finding it, I gave in to deep sleep.

I slept all the way through the rest of the night and the next one. For the first time in days, I was able to sit up by myself. I reached for the water jug and medicine.

The dark room had no windows, making it impossible to tell the time of day. I eased from the bed and tested my strength.

I'm meeting Mike soon. How long did Hypatos say I'd been here?

Finding my hairbrush and toothbrush, I shuffled across the hall. I sensed the worst was behind me.

PART III

HOMECOMING QUEEN

I organized my luggage, ran out of energy, and crawled back to bed.

Sometime later, Hypatos knocked, and I popped upright.

He clapped his hands in front of his face. "The American girl is better? Thank Jesus for answering my prayers."

"Yes, much better. Are these pills antibiotics?"

"Yes, for infection in your chest. Can you eat today? I brought fruit, crackers, yogurt." He held up a banana.

"I think so." Sitting cross-legged, I searched for the right words. "Why did you help me like this, Hypatos? I'm a stranger to you, but you saved me—maybe saved my life."

"You were sick, lost, and needed help." He shrugged.

I pressed my hand over my chest. "Thank you from my heart. How much do I owe you for the room, the food, and the medicine?"

"You owe nothing, Miss Charlotte."

"Oh no—"

"My reward is God answered my prayers." He stood and interlaced his hands like he was praying.

"You're an angel." Emotion swelled in me.

We talked more, and I discovered he was a religious man.

His efforts had shown genuine benevolence. He was a real-life Good Samaritan who lived by his faith.

The next day, I left the suitcase full of worthless jeans in the hotel room, wishing I'd ditched it a long time ago. Hypatos carried my backpack down the stairs. Outside in the crystal-bright sunshine, I took a deep breath, which caused another hacking spell that had me searching for my cough drops.

"I've never witnessed such a good person as you," I said. "I'm blessed to call you a friend."

I hugged his bony frame, and then he helped lift my backpack. He spotted my tear of gratitude and smiled shyly, looking downward as if embarrassed.

Hypatos had held the power to seriously damage or abandon me in my vulnerable condition. Instead, he rescued me. He gave me his time, money, and care, and asked nothing in return—a rare breed of man, indeed. He helped me glimpse the real meaning of love, the kind that's achieved by helping someone with no hidden motive or payback expected, just gracious love. He probably didn't realize the enormous impact his kindness had on me, but I hoped on some level he did.

I carried a skepticism of strange men, as all women do, a wariness borne of so many dangerous encounters. Women are in danger when they're alone in a parking lot at night or when they get cornered by a lecherous co-worker in an empty office. Our freedom is limited by the behavior of men. But there are those special times when I've crossed paths with a man who harbored no intention other than what he presented. Good fortune beamed on me when I met such noble men as Thomas and Hypatos.

"Can you show me where the post office is located on my map?"

"Post office? The big post office is three blocks that way." He pointed. "Not far."

"Goodbye, Hypatos. Thank you again, my dear friend."

Later as I waited in line at the post office, I turned to the lady behind me.

"Excuse me, do you speak English?" I asked.

"Yes, I'm British," said the petite woman in her sixties. Her white shirt collar peaked out the neckline of her navy-blue sweater.

"Do you know today's date?"

She blinked, searching my face as though I might be joking, but then she peered at her watch. "The 7th. January."

My breath caught in my throat. Mike and I had agreed to meet on New Year's Day. I was six days late.

My turn came slowly. My heart beat rapidly as the postal lady emerged from the back, clutching my mail. She stopped to chat with a co-worker, a letter and postcards in her hand.

"Ma'am, please."

She glanced at me, but her face registered annoyance at my interruption. She turned back to her friend. Standing ten feet from me, I pictured myself leaping over the counter and grabbing my mail from her hand. At last, she sauntered over and asked for my passport. I scrambled for it, knowing those cards must be from Mike.

The woman took her time checking my passport against the name on each card and letter before handing me everything.

I moved aside and read two cards from Mike.

Charlotte, I arrived in Athens yesterday, the 28th, my birthday, remember? You can find me at the Athens Empire on Socrates. Ask any local for directions. Hope you're well, Mike.

He sounded so formal.

The next card read, *Charlotte, Today's the 3rd. Been here almost a week and still no sign of you. My flight's tomorrow, but I can change it if you contact me. Mike.*

I pulled off my backpack, leaned against the post office wall, and slid down to a squat. He'd flown out of Athens three days ago.

I ripped open the letter from my grandparents and read through their loving words. It contained a money order for a hundred dollars. They asked me to come home.

I rearranged the weight of my backpack and set out to find a bank to cash the check. I bought a cheese pie from a street vendor, checked into a youth hostel, and went straight to bed, exhausted. A church bell rang at three o'clock in the afternoon.

I reread the letter from Mommy Burr and Daddy Burr, feeling their love reach across the ocean and embrace me. Gnawing homesickness and my lingering cough spurred me to leave the hostel in search of a call center.

The call attendant took my grandparents' phone number, and I waited outside for their call back. Sitting against the building, I let the sunshine heal my body and spirit until I dozed off. Late in the day, I finally got a call back.

"Mommy Burr, can you hear me?"

"Charlotte, my gosh, how are you? When are you coming home?"

"Now, Mommy Burr. I'll fly back as soon as I can get a flight. I received your letter and the money order today. The money really helped. Thank you so much."

I called Mike the next morning and waited several hours until I exhausted my energy and left. I phoned him twice more during the week while waiting for an open flight home to the States, but he didn't call back.

He must be back east on business.

Once freed from lengthy customs in San Antonio, I ran to Mommy Burr and Daddy Burr, who waited with the crowd. I hugged them both, refusing to let go. Mommy Burr's giggles in her soft, throaty tone was music to my ears.

The next day, I called Mike again. "Mike, I'm in Fredericksburg. I got your postcards in Athens. There's so much to tell you. Please call me back. I love you."

He didn't call back.

Mommy Burr brewed teas for my cough, and I took a long nap each day. She fixed wholesome foods from their garden, and my cough eventually disappeared.

My grandparents and I sat outside on lawn chairs at night, stargazing and talking about various topics—my travels, current politics, and alternative sources of energy. They spoke against the Vietnam war and didn't trust Richard Nixon. I loved the way Daddy Burr spoke to me, respectful and patient. I don't know if he realized he was teaching me, but I listened carefully to every word he said.

"When I was growing up, a farmer who lived a few miles from my folks developed a way of harnessing sunlight to run his whole farm. He got local recognition from other farmers, but he disappeared, and nobody heard from him again," Daddy Burr said.

"What do you think happened to him?" I asked.

"People speculated all sorts of things. Some people said big energy companies didn't want knowledge of his discovery to spread, and they 'took care of him.' But I don't know if that's true. The timing of his disappearance strikes me funny. You never know whom to trust."

Back home in Santa Cruz, Mike and our friends often conversed on these topics. The war raged on, and many people suspected we were fighting for oil rights in Vietnam on behalf of energy companies.

The topic of our conversation changed when Mommy Burr asked, "Have you thought more about going back to school?"

"No. I've had enough college."

"You can't do much with two years of school. We want to see you finish and get a good job."

I pictured myself spending a sunny day inside a stuffy building doing tedious tasks for a grouchy boss. Not for me. Mommy Burr and Daddy Burr meant well, but they were out of touch with reality. Eventually, however, time taught me that I was the one out of touch.

After a week, Mike finally called me back.

"I'm so glad to hear from you. I missed you in Athens by a few days. I got sick—"

"When are you coming back?"

"Thursday. I have so much to tell you—"

"Me too. I'll meet your flight. We'll talk then." He sounded distant and stressed.

After six months apart, we just needed a night together to get reacquainted.

I'll make him feel so good, his eyeballs will roll back in his head.

After getting off the plane in California, I raced up the jetway, filed through the double doors, and spotted Mike searching for me. He'd cut his long beard and now wore a goatee. His light brown hair was shorter too. I nearly pounced on him. He saw my emotion and broke eye contact. I read him as angry, and he had every right to be. I hadn't met him in Athens as planned.

We waited at the baggage claim, and I reached for his hand. He looked at me, a question in his expression. He slowly accepted my outstretched hand, not saying a word.

Our dogs jumped and yipped with joy when we arrived at the van. I had missed them so much. On the ride home, I chatted on and on about my recent illness in Athens and touched on the adventures of my trip.

Something isn't right. A dreadful sensation crept through my body.

Mike broke his heavy silence. "We need to talk." He cracked the back windows for the dogs. "I met someone."

His words didn't register at first. When they did, I shuddered. A big ball of grief stuck in my throat and threatened to suffocate me.

I must have heard him wrong. "Wha—When?"

"We met a few months ago after a concert at the Catalyst."

"What about hooking up in Athens?" My throat constricted even tighter.

"Yeah, what about that fiasco? I flew over to meet you, but you never showed."

"Yes, but—"

He held up his hand. "I don't want to hear it. You didn't call or write—not once."

I rushed my words. "I got sick."

He'd stopped listening, and I stopped groveling. He looked different. Where's the guy who loved me so much? Embarrassed and in shock, I floated in a dark stupor for the long ride home.

"Where do you want me to drop you?"

My head spun. "I guess Felton."

While traveling, I'd sublet my mountain cabin to Mary Lou. It was located in Felton, outside Santa Cruz. I had assumed I'd start over with Mike, and Mary Lou would be able to keep my place permanently.

Mary Lou welcomed me home with sisterly hugs and curious questions. Over the next few months, I shared the place with her on money I'd stashed away before leaving for Europe.

At night, I went to clubs and drank myself drunk. Sleeping most of the next day nursing my hangover, I repeated it all over again the next night. I escaped from obsessing over Mike by talking and joking with guys who bought me drinks, but I didn't give anyone my phone number. I had no interest in them beyond those moments in the bar. Thoughts of Mike remained in the front of my mind, and regret haunted me. I foolishly believed our love was so strong—that he loved me so completely—I could disappear in Europe for six months and he'd be home waiting. I imagined turning back time to write him letters every day, but my fantasies vanished, and I returned to the reality of losing him.

Mary Lou attempted to intervene, but no comfort nor care touched my self-loathing. She grew increasingly impatient, telling me to look for a job instead of sleeping all day. Sometimes her words pierced through my foggy mind and made sense. My money steadily decreased. Who wanted to hire a twenty-five-year-old who'd only ever worked part-time at a library, a bar in the Greek Islands, and a short stint in an oyster bar?

After closing time at another dance club one night, I drove home drunk. I wound my way up the mountain road, taking the curves too fast in drenching rain. I hated myself and felt lonely even though I'd danced with a dozen guys that night—every one of them buying me a drink. Through the thousand showers of rain, a blurred, yellow caution sign loomed ahead. It was the last thing I remembered.

A black curtain came down like someone splicing the memory from my brain. I regained consciousness but couldn't recall what had happened. I pushed against the steering wheel crammed into my chest, but it didn't budge. Branches were crushed into the broken windshield. The foot-well beneath the steering column was mashed metal against my knees, wedging me in tightly. I worked open the mangled door enough to squeeze out and drop into the shallow creek on all fours. A waterfall trickled nearby. The smell of clean, wet pine and damp earth helped me gain clarity. I dragged myself out of the two-inch-deep water, knees bleeding, and tried to stand.

Were my ankles sprained or broken? The steep, slippery bank made it impossible to crawl to the road above. My car was a folded accordion against the tree. Evidently, the car had gone airborne off the road at the hairpin turn, hit the redwood tree, then bounced down the embankment into the creek.

Through the woods, a cabin porchlight glowed faintly. I stumbled and crawled toward the light, disgusted with myself, wishing the accident had killed me.

I woke lying on a strange couch in an unfamiliar place. My knees and ankles throbbed. A young man and woman stood nearby in the firelight.

"You're awake." The woman pulled her white bathrobe tighter around her.

"How did I get here?" I touched my head.

"You don't know? We heard sounds, like thumping, and found you lying on the porch. Do you want an ambulance?"

"Um, no. Please don't call an ambulance or the cops. I'll get in trouble for drinking and driving. Give me a minute. I'll call my sister."

The one person I really wanted to call was probably in bed next to his girlfriend. My self-esteem had fallen below nothing.

"I'll call her. What's her number?" The woman held up the black receiver, waiting.

I told her the number.

A while later, a sharp knock startled me awake.

I heard Mary Lou say from the door, "I'm here for my sister. Sorry if I sounded short on the phone, but I've been putting up with this crap for weeks. Her late-night partying, drama, depression. And now this."

Mary Lou stomped on the hardwood floor toward me. Her face softened when she took in my ratty appearance, bloody knees, and swollen ankles.

"We're going to the hospital," she said.

"No. I'll get busted for driving drunk."

"They're not going to call the cops. Let's go."

The three of them helped me into the car. On the way to the hospital, we talked.

"You've got to pull yourself together. Your hard partying isn't helping." Mary Lou steered the car toward the emergency entrance and got a wheelchair.

The last thing I wanted to hear was my sister bitching at me. *What am I supposed to do? Magically get over my empty yearning for Mike and move on? Why did I leave Greece? At least I had a job there and people who liked me.*

A few days later, Mary Lou watched the tow truck haul my Honda from the creek bed on a long, steel cable. She confirmed my fear. I'd totaled it.

Without a car and on crutches, I was confined to the house, where I did a lot of thinking. Weeks passed, and I healed enough to limp around. I took the bus to Santa Cruz and asked the oyster bar owner for my old job back, but he didn't want me. He said I wasn't dependable, that I showed up to work stoned or not at all.

I made my regular weekly phone call to my grandparents and told them some of what happened.

"We'll help you, Charlotte, but we want you to come live here."

"I don't know, Mommy-Burr. I've got to think about it. I need to find a job, and there are no jobs in Fredericksburg. And the closest college is too far to drive each day."

I loved my grandparents, and I struggled with the guilt of knowing I'd always chosen a life of fun and excitement in California over a life of peace and love in the Texas countryside.

Additionally, I didn't want to live off my grandparents. But their advice, after years of suggestions, finally made sense. I had to go back to school, or I'd end up waiting tables at Denny's for the rest of my life.

After my stepdad moved the family to Okinawa, Mary Lou and I occasionally wrote each other letters, but I didn't hear from the others during those years. When they returned from Japan, Dad retired from active military service, and the family moved to Louisiana. Dad landed a job flying helicopters on and off oil platforms in the Gulf. Mom worked as a real estate agent. We talked on occasion, but I shared limited information about my life. Mostly we talked about her art projects and my siblings.

More days passed, and my desperation increased as my money supply dwindled. I faced a hard reality. If I called her, hat in hand, would Mom know what I should do?

It was one of the hardest phone calls I'd ever make. If I opened the door, she'd walk through to help me—if it weren't too inconvenient. Selfish and tyrannical as she was, she wouldn't let me drown if she could easily toss me a lifebuoy.

"Mom, Mike and I are finished. It's over. I want to finish my degree so I can get a decent job."

"Oh, Charlie, I'm sorry," she said. "Come see us. Be with your family. We'll think of something when you get here."

Sleep eluded me that night. Memories of childhood horrors and the possibility of new ones plagued me, but I had few options.

I secretly hoped that going home would heal my relationship with my mother. I fantasized about sitting face-to-face with Mom, holding hands and looking deeply into each other's eyes. We'd see our convoluted, painful history behind us, and Mom would say, "Charlie, I'm so sorry for causing you, the other kids, and my parents so much pain. My inner demons tormented me, but I have no excuse. Please forgive me. I love you."

I would tearfully respond, "Thank you, Mom. Thank you for recognizing me, seeing me as your daughter, as someone you value. Even though I fought you and even hated you at times, deep down, I've always loved you."

This accountability would go a long way toward healing me and our family. It would be the start of a real relationship with my mother, but it never happened.

I didn't consider the possibility of healing anything with Dad since a solid relationship had never existed in the first place.

The night I arrived, Kathy and Suzie, my two youngest sisters, told me all about life in Louisiana. We sat in Kathy's bedroom talking until Mom called me from the kitchen.

"Charlie, come sit. We want to talk to you."

We? I'd hoped to talk to Mom alone about my school plans.

Mom used her natural flair for interior design to make her homes comfortable yet stylish. I walked through the family room furnished with three dark leather couches arranged in a U-shape. A gigantic TV hung over the fireplace framed by a massive bookcase. Cream-colored carpeting offset the dark couches, and multi-colored modern art covered the walls. Mom's furniture and art pieces reflected more money now since five of the eight kids had grown up and moved out. Only the three youngest—Jacquie, Suzie, and Kathy—remained.

I shuffled to the kitchen where Mom and Dad waited for me at the dinette table. I hoped my face didn't reveal my fear. They offered the chair between them, flanking me.

"Do you want coffee?" Mom asked.

"No thanks," I said, rubbing my thighs over my jeans.

Mom got right down to business. "Charlie, what are your plans for the future? We want to help you."

"I've talked to Mommy Burr and Daddy Burr about going back to college."

A shadow passed over Dad's face, and the air grew heavy at the mention of my grandparents. Mom and Dad stared at me. I had made the mistake of mentioning that my grandparents wanted to help me.

Dad reached for the pull cord on the ceiling fan above the table. I flinched at his quick movement. His mouth curled upward at my response. My face flushed. I hated that I feared him so much.

"Did you think he was going to hit you?" Mom asked incredulously.

I didn't respond. *Why did he act that way toward me? Because I was born from another man?*

No matter what I did, Dad had never loved nor respected me. I accepted that. I craved Mom's love and always wanted her to see me as her amazing daughter who lived life to the fullest like she did.

I'm not a helpless kid anymore, and I have nothing to hide. I can leave anytime. But where will I go?

I'd given birth to two children, one in my own bed at home, gotten married, divorced, overcome drug addiction, navigated a six-month solo trip through Europe escaping rape, violence—even death—all by the time I'd turned twenty-six. Yet to them, I remained a disappointment, a dependent little girl, back in their home begging for help.

Mom poured herself a second cup of coffee.

I sat up straighter and held my head up like Daddy Burr always told me to do. Seconds ticked by.

"You have two years of college completed, right?" Dad asked.

"She could live here and finish her bachelor's degree." Mom carried her coffee to the table.

I visualized life with them after living on my own for ten years. My hands squeezed the chair arms.

"She won't need to finish school if she gets a good job." Dad looked at me. "You have no real work experience. What do you want to do for a living? What do you like doing?"

"I love to travel." I guess bartending in Greece and working part-time at the library and oyster bar didn't count as work experience, but I said nothing. I almost spoke up in support of school, but I didn't know the first thing about interviewing or student loans.

"Travel? Then work in the travel industry," Dad said.

Mom looked at Dad, her eyebrows raised as if something had occurred to her. "There's a travel agency next door to the real estate office where I work," Mom said. "I'm on good terms with the owner. Maybe she has an opening."

Having no idea how to stand on my own two feet without Mom's help, I gratefully accepted her olive branch. It was as close to making amends as she got. I was on her radar now, but she had three other kids left at home attending college, plus her own successful real estate business. She needed a quick solution to my problem. Dad also was busy, flying for the helicopter company.

Mom spoke to the agency's owner, and I went to work as

a travel agent. Mom and Dad pointed me in the direction of self-reliance, but other than a one-month travel agent course, school was forgotten.

FATHER KNOWS BEST

During the years since I'd left home, Mom and Dad had learned to parent without physical abuse—or maybe we were too big to beat now—but the emotional torture persisted. Mom seemed happy with her career, fewer children, and more money, or maybe she was happier because Dad stayed around and helped. Memories of my childhood hung just below the surface of my mind, an undercurrent of discomfort.

Another interesting development had occurred since I'd left home. Mom no longer hid her resentment of Dad. She dominated and contradicted him openly, humiliating him in front of us. Previously, Mom and Dad had shown a united front. But now that she no longer needed him, she clearly held the position of control. And she was merciless.

My sisters told me Mom had engaged in an affair with a top general—Dad's boss in Okinawa. Dad had known about the affair since Mom had taken no steps to hide it.

I kept my head down, not daring to lose this last chance to stand on my own. I missed California and living in the Deep South didn't fit me. I met people who hunted animals for fun and threw beer cans out of their pickup trucks. Peaceful moments and water-colored sunsets occurred in the marshes, but mostly it echoed decay to my spirit because I wasn't happy. At least I took advantage of my travel benefits and flew from New Orleans to San Antonio to visit my grandparents often, much to my mother's chagrin.

I worked hard at the travel agency, proving my ability to handle my first full-time job. Day after day, I answered phone calls, booked reservations, and daydreamed about going back to the west coast.

Mom loaned me the down payment for a small house a half hour outside of Lafayette and paid for the installation of central air-conditioning. I was grateful, but it anchored me to an area where I didn't belong. I took in a roommate, but I still couldn't save enough for a fresh start in California.

I sent people to the west coast on vacation and even thought of visiting there myself, but I feared if I went back even to visit, I'd never return. I'd made this commitment to work, and I needed the experience.

After five years as a travel agent in Lafayette, I landed a job as a gate agent for TWA at the New Orleans airport. The airline provided flexible hours and unlimited air travel. I sold my house, barely broke even, moved to New Orleans, and rented a room from a fellow employee who lived near the airport.

My friends from TWA and I frequently partied on Bourbon Street in the French Quarter. One night I met Martin, an engineer for the local utility company, nuclear division.

Martin and I jumped into a whirlwind romance. He lived on one side of an antebellum home divided into two units. We chased each other up and down the apartment's spiral staircase, listened to jazz, and slowly revealed our life stories while lying next to each other, exhausted from making love. As always in my life, I refused to reveal too much. I hid information about my abusive childhood and my two kids. Family secrets remained safe with me.

My indoctrination of shame and secrecy had rooted deep, and my history was complicated. How could I share my jumble of confusion with anyone, even a therapist?

Six months later, while spending an afternoon at Martin's place, the sky broke open in a furious downpour.

"Oh no, Kona's in my backyard," I said. "I have to go. He's probably getting soaked."

"I'll go with you."

The wipers worked frantically to battle the blinding rain flooding the roadway as we drove toward my house a half hour away.

I found my Siberian husky, Kona, in the backyard, shivering under a narrow overhang trying to escape the rain. My wet shirt stuck to my skin and Martin's hair dripped as we towel-dried Kona, put him in the backseat, and headed back to Martin's place.

Stripping off my sopping-wet clothes, I wrapped myself in a thick towel, embraced Kona, and apologized to him over and over for leaving him trapped in the rain. Martin peeled off his sweatshirt and jeans, quick-rubbed himself dry, and bounced into bed naked. I dove in behind him. Kona lay peacefully next to the bed as the rain peppered then pounded the windows so hard, they almost broke. Kona, Martin, and me, my little family, all safe together in one place.

On occasion, Martin shared bits of his childhood. His father, a gruff, controlling man, owned a hardware store where young Martin had worked every day after school.

"As a kid, I worked hard for my dad, but he was moody and unpredictable. Never satisfied," Martin said.

As it turned out, Martin inherited that moodiness, making life with him uneasy at times. But on that day in the rain, he represented the embodiment of a responsible man, a safe harbor for Kona and me. I'd never met anyone who'd contributed the maximum to a 401K starting in his early twenties. Now in his thirties, Martin's investments were growing, and he had the prospect of a great career in the nuclear industry ahead of him. Subconsciously, he fit my idea of the perfect guy, a solid practical counterbalance to my happy-go-lucky nature.

Lying naked beside each other, full skin-to-skin contact, Martin and I got into playful sex. Afterward, sitting up and straddled across him, my hair hanging in damp strings, I pushed his hair back from his forehead and gazed into his face. Overwhelmed with gratitude for his care of me and Kona, I heard the words "I love you" slip out of my mouth.

"I love you too." He cleared his throat. "If I asked you to marry me, would you say yes?"

Taken off-guard, I searched his face for sincerity. Silence grew and crowded the moment. He filled the silence.

"I want a family, Charlotte. I'll buy a house big enough for all of us—with a yard." He motioned toward Kona, who raised his head from the floor. "I know how important he is to you. What are you thinking? You look confused." He brushed my hair back, tucking it behind my ear.

I didn't want the moment to get away, but words escaped me. I needed time to process the notion.

"Are you asking me to marry you?"

"No, I'm asking if you want a gooey slice of pizza." He grinned. "Yeah, I'm asking you straight up, will you marry me?"

"Yes!" I bounced up and down on his belly, hunched forward, and kissed him, happy and terrified at the same moment.

I loved Martin and knew he could provide a stable home. It's what every woman who's in love wants from her man, right? I said "yes" and felt excited about his proposal. So why was a seed of doubt buried under all my excitement?

We flew to Boston and picked out my engagement ring from a jeweler friend of Martin's, a stunning two-carat solitaire. He bought a house in the New Orleans suburbs but refused to let me take part in his decision about which house to buy. Although nothing was said, we agreed he controlled the decision-making because he controlled the money. We moved into the new house together, all within the first year of knowing each other.

We acquired another husky, followed by three rescue kittens, two of which Martin had found abandoned in a field while walking the dogs.

While later waiting for a stoplight, Martin saw someone throw something small and furry from a pickup truck into the intersection. Martin snapped on his emergency blinkers, jumped out, and rescued our third cat, a cowering tabby kitten covered in dried poo. Martin's sensitivity made me love him even more.

I fed our new kitten using a child's doll bottle until she got big enough to eat on her own. Her personality, so vibrant, even while starving and abandoned, earned her the name Sassy.

I didn't make enough money at TWA to contribute much to our household, so Martin paid for everything and seemed comfortable with it. He paid off my Visa card each month and bought me a sports car to drive. After a few years of living together, I cut back to part-time at TWA while retaining my travel benefits.

When my friends from work complained about money worries or their emotionally abusive husbands, I appreciated Martin even more.

Never having solid parental role models, Martin provided the compass I needed to navigate my way to a "normal life" in the suburbs.

I'd left hard drugs behind years earlier but still smoked pot on occasion. Martin forbade me from keeping marijuana around.

One night, he stormed into the house, slamming the door behind him. "What the hell is this shit?" He waved a baggy of marijuana in the air.

"Oh, I'm sorry. I forgot I left—"

"I've driven around for days not knowing I carried this shit under my seat."

"I'm sorry."

"Sorry? I pass through a security checkpoint every morning when driving into the nuclear plant. They randomly search vehicles. If they'd found this, I'd have gotten fired! Goddamnit! I told you. No drugs of any kind around here."

I understood his point but seldom gave thought to the consequences of my actions. Looking back now, I see how irresponsibly I behaved, always falling back into the role of the naughty little girl who depended on Martin to rescue and/or reprimand her.

On another occasion, I drove Martin's beloved Camaro to the local dry cleaner's where I routinely dropped off my airline uniforms. Leaving the engine running and door wide open, I'd hop from the car, toss the uniforms on the counter and rush back out to the waiting Camaro. The last time I did that, a guy loitering nearby saw his golden opportunity. By the time I turned around and exited the open door, he'd already launched himself into Martin's car and sped off with my purse in the backseat. I telephoned the police and Martin at work and waited for the avalanche of trouble to come.

"Goddamnit, Charlotte!" Martin later yelled as he bolted from my car. He kept hollering, and a few onlookers even backed away.

I covered my face and bawled. "I'm so sorry. I didn't—"

Martin went on and on about my careless behavior, arms waving in the air. I didn't argue with his badgering. He kept yelling until one of the cops interrupted.

"Hey, man, you've said enough. Can't you see she's sorry?" the officer asked.

"She's a dingbat!" Martin said, frustrated.

For the next week, night after night, we drove through the poorest neighborhoods in New Orleans, hoping to spot Martin's car. He yelled at me and pounded my steering wheel continuously.

Looking back, Mike and Martin each provided safety nets and a secure setting for me to act out my missed childhood and absent father-daughter relationship. I had no idea what a healthy relationship with a man looked like.

"Didn't you tell me a while back you never wanted to be like your mom?" Martin said. "You're proving to be exactly like her."

I bristled and recalled the three times someone had stolen Mom's car from our driveway. It happened every time she left the keys in the ignition overnight.

A few days later, the cops found Martin's car abandoned but in good shape.

Weeks later, the incident forgotten, I brought dinner to Martin and watched him finish painting the kitchen in one of his several rental houses.

"There's a new musical playing in London, *Phantom of the Opera*. Supposed to be great. Let's fly there for New Year's Eve and go see it," I said.

"You go. I want to work on the houses."

"Come on. We can make it a short trip." I lifted the Tupperware lid to show him the chicken and gravy I'd brought.

"Isn't Richard flying the London route now? Go with him."

"Can't you leave the renovations for a few days?"

"Here, help me finish." He handed me a paintbrush.

Richard, a flight-attendant friend, visited our home several times for dinner or barbecues. Richard was gay, so Martin never got jealous of our friendship. Traveling with Richard was like traveling with a considerate girlfriend. We took care of each other.

Richard and I flew to London in December of 1987 and saw *Phantom of the Opera* in Piccadilly Circus on New Year's Eve. The following night we saw *Les Misérables*.

Flying first class, Richard shook loose a white cloth napkin and lay it across my lap with natural finesse. He served me wine and hors d'oeuvres, treating me like any other first-class passenger. I adored him but missed Martin, wishing he'd come along.

I used my benefits to fly to San Antonio every month to see my grandparents for the weekend. I also flew to Paris to get my hair cut, to Seoul, South Korea to go shopping, and to Germany to buy a Mercedes on the gray market at a time when the U.S. dollar stood strong against the German mark.

The gray market is a method to purchase and bring a foreign car into the U.S. without using a licensed dealer. At that time, American laws permitted military personnel to bring home one vehicle per family when they completed their tour of duty in Europe. Civilians pressed the government to change the law and extend the same benefit to every American family.

Working for TWA allowed me to fly to Germany and test drive the Mercedes, which I ultimately purchased from a German citizen. We created a win-win situation because I bought the car far below U.S. market value, and I paid the German man far more than he'd get by selling it locally.

My siblings lived in different states, so I traveled to various cities around the U.S. whenever one of them gave a party. Most of my sisters flew for a major airline at that time, and my brother piloted for Delta. My flight benefits extended to Martin, but he seldom traveled. His primary interest involved his investment houses.

My parents got to know Martin when we attended Christmas gatherings or other events at their home in Lafayette. One time, Mom whispered that Martin felt like a timebomb ready to go off at any moment. Secretly, I agreed.

The desire to escape Martin's moods and the mundane routine of suburban life caused the shine of security to wear off, bit by bit. Martin and I grew apart while our comfortable daily routine turned into weeks, and months turned into years.

One evening at home after dinner, we relaxed on our cream-colored L-shaped sofa watching the end of the evening news. Martin's arm rested behind me on the back of the couch.

He faced the TV when he said, "I talked to my folks today. I'm getting tired of telling them we still haven't set a wedding date."

I sighed. *Here we go again.* I hated this ongoing talk about marriage. "I don't want to live in Louisiana for the rest of my life, Martin. What happened to the idea of finding a job on the west coast?"

"I checked it out. My income goes a lot further here than on the California coast. I have a future—we have a future here.

We've been living together five years. Let's get married and start a family."

"I don't want kids. I've said it many times."

He pressed on. "I don't get it," he said. "Don't all women want kids?"

"My mother didn't. She had kids to please my Catholic stepfather. I can't do that."

He snorted but fixed his gaze on his running shoes.

I owed him the whole truth. "There's something I've wanted to tell you for a long time."

He stiffened at my serious tone, then looked directly at me. "What?"

Our kitten, Sassy, walked across the back of the couch. I admired her dark stripes and stroked her small body, stalling.

"Out with it. What do you want to say?"

"I gave birth to two kids as a teenager. I don't know where they are and will never know because I signed papers forbidding me to find them. It isn't right to have more kids when I already have two that I didn't take care of."

His mouth dropped open. He stood from the couch and choked out a short cough. "Why didn't you tell me this before?"

"Because I thought you'd think badly of me, and—"

"I don't know what to think." He coughed again and walked out.

An even deeper division separated us now.

Why don't I want kids? What's wrong with me? Do I have a disconnect somewhere inside?

Lying in bed that night, I thought back to my siblings and all the bottles, diapers, and babysitting I did every day. Mom wanted the outward image of the perfect *Brady Bunch* family, but I didn't know what that looked like in real life.

Ours was never the kind of family that celebrated children by proudly hanging Crayola drawings on the refrigerator. Kids meant hard work and were an unwanted nuisance, according to Mom, and she proved it by pulling me close beside her where I worked and witnessed it firsthand. We lived in a constant state of drama and chaos.

Too often, Mom seemed overwhelmed. She forced me to co-mother starting when I was about seven years old. Later, she handed me the role of sole mother while she took off for Vegas. It robbed me of the joy of having my own kids. I'd already raised a family, her family, and the experience taught me that raising kids wasn't fun—at least not for an ill-equipped kid in a dysfunctional family. The cost of having children was simply too high.

Now I faced a hard choice. I could live a comfortable life married to Martin and raise a family in Louisiana or move out and struggle alone without sufficient education or direction.

In addition to my aversion to raising kids, I couldn't picture myself happily married to Martin for the rest of my life. His moodiness disrupted our harmony. It felt like the surface of anger. I didn't fear violence from him, but his unpredictable moods drained our happiness.

I drifted into an uneasy sleep.

Several weeks later, a handwritten letter arrived in the mail. "Diane Rossler" was on the return label. Rossler was the mystery family name on my birth certificate. My heartbeat pattered like a snare drum. I ripped open the envelope, hands quivering.

Dear Charlotte,

You don't know me, but I think after we meet, we'll be friends for the rest of our lives. We're sisters. I recently learned of your existence from our father.

Please call me when you read this. I hope I hear from you soon.

Love, Diane

I sank into the dining room chair, head spinning. My real father. And another sister? My other family had reached out! These were the people I'd wondered about my whole life.

I picked up the letter again, staring at the last name, "Rossler." It held the answer to the question that had forever plagued me: Who was my real father?

Mom said she'd protected me from my biological father's violent temper by making him promise not to contact us after they divorced. Never permitted to ask about him, I buried this secret with all the others and hid my shame for having a different father from my siblings. I was close to my sisters and brother and didn't want separation from them in any way.

Cut off from my sons and biological father, my chance had finally arrived to meet the father I'd wondered about and the family I'd never known.

My hand vibrated as I dialed.

"Hello?" a female voice answered.

"Hello? This is Charlotte, your…your sister. I received your letter."

"Oh my God, Charlotte."

Moments passed as the silence thickened. I didn't know what to say.

"I found out about you last week when Dad told me I had another sister. This is so strange."

I regained my voice. "The return address says you live in Austin, Texas. I'm in New Orleans and work for TWA. I can catch a flight; come see you."

"Yes! When's the soonest you can come?"

"Tomorrow?"

"Perfect. I'll meet you at the airport."

The next day, I walked off the Jetway and scanned the waiting greeters. We spotted each other at the same time. Around us, the crowd of people faded from my vision. Only she and I remained.

I embraced her then pulled back to look at her closer. "This is amazing."

"Yeah, I can't believe it."

Her golden-brown hair fell loose down her back and curled at the ends. Three years younger than me, she was thirty-three, the same age as Mary Lou. She wore her jeans tight, tucked inside her cowboy boots, and her large, shiny belt buckle flashed when it caught the light.

Dimples appeared on the sides of her grin. Her diamond-blue eyes twinkled mischief. We walked excitedly out of the airport, side by side, stealing glances, our arms brushing against each other.

"Why didn't I get cute dimples like yours?" I exclaimed.

"I don't know. Why didn't I get platinum-blonde hair like yours?" she replied. She studied me while she started her late-model Lincoln. "How about some lunch?"

"Sure. Anything. How did you find out about me?" I asked.

"Dad reminisced about his past while we were on a long flight back from Germany recently. In a melancholy mood, he confessed he'd fathered another daughter before me."

"Oh, wow. How did you get my address?"

"Our Aunt Evelyn—she's Dad's sister—knew your mom in high school. I called her, and she gave me your mom's phone number. I called your mom a few days ago. I guess she didn't tell you."

"No, she didn't, but I can't believe she gave you my address," I said.

"It took some gentle persuading, but yes, she did."

After years of concealing information about my birth father, Mom gave Diane my address knowing she'd probably put me in touch with him. Maybe Mom decided she had nothing to gain by keeping me from my biological father anymore. She'd relinquished control of my life. I guess time softens everything, even anger and revenge.

"When I was little, I asked Mom about my real dad. She said he was mean." Dreading Diane's response, I cracked the window a bit.

The forest rushed by as we sped up to merge into the fast lane.

Diane giggled. "No way. Dad's a good man. He said he made mistakes, but remember, they got married at eighteen." We exited the freeway and turned into a restaurant parking lot. "Dad loves you, Charlotte. You're his first child, and I'm his second. His third wife gave birth to his third daughter, and they adopted a fourth daughter. The fact is your mother wanted no contact with him after they divorced."

Why did Mom keep my birth father a secret from me all these years? Was she afraid he'd take me from her? Or was it because her previous marriage and divorce didn't fit our perfect, big-family image to the outside world?

How would my life be different if I'd known him? I don't want a life without my brother and sisters, but I could have known both families without hurting anyone.

THE PROBLEM

Diane and I met frequently over the next few months. She flew to New Orleans or I flew to Austin. I discovered we shared an adventurous spirit, but she drank hard, partied late, danced Texas two-step on the weekends, and described fierce fights with her boyfriend. Listening to her stories made me realize how much I'd mellowed since my party days in California.

Stirring gumbo on the stove in her apartment, she looked up. "Dad keeps asking about you. Are you ready to meet him?"

"Yes, but I'm nervous."

"No doubt he's nervous too. Do you like flying in small planes?"

"Sure. I've flown in a few," I said.

"Good, because Dad is passionate about flying. He flies by himself a lot. He'd love to take you with him."

"He has a plane?"

"He's got four planes and a private runway on his 2,000-acre hunting ranch—in addition to his home ranch. About fifteen years ago when he was forty, he began an oil-service company. Now, he's got thirty employees and the company is nationwide plus Puerto Rico. He does well."

The next week, my father flew to New Orleans to meet me.

Arriving at his hotel parking lot, I turned off the engine and pulled down the makeup mirror. I checked my face and brushed my hair for the umpteenth time, then got out of the car and smoothed down my cream-colored slacks.

Early like me, I recognized my father sitting on an upholstered lobby chair. He stood slowly as I walked toward him.

I embraced my handsome, six-foot-one father for the first time and cried like a little girl. At thirty-six years old, I grieved for all the years I missed out on having a dad who loved me.

"My dad," I whispered, holding him.

He sniffled a bit.

Mesmerized, I sat and took in my real father. His blondish-gray hair was thin on top. He wore a starched western-style shirt and shiny cowboy boots. He looked like an old-fashioned Texas cowboy.

"In answer to your question about what to call me, you can call me Dad or Walter or whatever works."

"I like Walter," I said.

With a lifetime to catch up on, I wanted to tell him about everything—even my abusive childhood. Although digging around in the past—reporting things he was powerless to remedy—wouldn't change anything. It might satisfy something in me, but it would possibly cause him frustration and pain. I put myself in his shoes. If I discovered my sons were mistreated by their adoptive parents, I would reel from not having protected them. I didn't want to lay that burden on my father.

He brought me out of my thoughts when he said, "My sister, your Aunt Evelyn, introduced me to your mother in high school. They were best friends."

"I remember Mom referring to Evelyn a few times, but she didn't tell me very much."

"She probably mentioned Evelyn around Christmastime because she wrote your mom every year and asked about you, then relayed to me anything she'd learned."

"Wow. Mom said bits and pieces about Evelyn on occasion, but nothing about you, ever. I was about five years old when Mom told me Dad wasn't my real father. She forbade me from telling anyone our dark family secret. I guarded it my whole life. My siblings and I never talked about it, and my stepfather never adopted me."

Walter's face flushed in spots, and his lips tightened.

"My parents said if it were important, I could pay for the adoption with the babysitting money I earned from neighbors. I wanted to fully belong to my family, but I only made twenty-five cents an hour, so I never saved enough."

"Good Lord," Walter said, shifting in his chair. "I asked to see you, but they refused. I thought about pressing it legally but wasn't sure how you felt. You were my first child. And so you know, I would never have consented to your adoption anyway."

A long silence fell between us as I absorbed his words. Once Mom decided something, no one dared to cross her. So many hazy questions in my life sharpened into focus.

Walter watched me, and I hoped he liked what he saw. Did he suspect I was a wild California girl from what my mother told his sister? Probably, but I wanted him to like me anyway.

"Charlotte—" He hesitated. "Evelyn said you had a child."

Oh, God, I didn't want to have this conversation so soon. "Yes." I looked away and dug my fingernails into my palm. "Actually, two." *Let me crawl away and hide.*

"Two? I never heard about the second baby." He swallowed this new information with a sip of his sparkling water. "Do you see them? Your children?"

"No, never met them."

"You've never met them?" He leaned forward. "Do you want to?"

"Yes. But my mother and the adoption agency said I'd be breaking the law if I contacted them. I signed papers releasing my rights."

"Breaking the law? I don't know if that's true anymore."

"I signed up on two different lists which make biological parents available if the kids want to find their parents—" My voice trailed off.

My mother had denied Walter and me relationships with our respective children. Why?

Mom resented her parents for expressing their concern about the way they saw my stepfather treating me. She claimed her parents interfered with our family dynamic, so she kept them away from us for years. She did the same thing with Walter. She used me to hurt him by keeping us apart. She prevented anyone from objecting to the way she raised me by simply eliminating their presence from my life.

"Diane said you're engaged to be married. What does your fiancé think about all this? The kids, I mean?"

"Well, I don't know." *Please don't ask any more questions because my answers don't make sense even to me.*

"Have you told him?"

"Yes, but it's complicated. We've lived together five years, but I don't think we're going to stay together." *Walter loves kids and wouldn't understand if I admitted part of my problem with Martin is I don't want kids.*

"Oh? Sorry to hear that." He squeezed lime into his water. "Has your mother offered to help find your children?"

"She'd be horrified if she knew I even thought about them. We went through a lot back then."

Thankfully, Walter dropped the subject, and we made plans for me to come meet his family in Texas.

Martin listened while I recited the gist of my first meeting with my real dad.

Exhausted, I entered our bedroom and leaned against our four-poster bed. I viewed the backyard through the large window, but my mind stayed fixed on Walter and our conversation about my future plans.

Walter expressed confusion about my indecision and emerging desire to leave the relationship. The general expectation that women will jump at the chance to marry made me wonder, again, why I didn't share that value. I desperately wanted to fit in somewhere, and marriage to Martin provided me the inclusion I desired.

Martin offered me status in the community, respect as his partner, material comfort, and the opportunity to be part of a family, our family. I loved him for his intelligence and easy laugh. So why was I unfulfilled?

Years earlier, I'd moved out of Mike's house to search for something more. Every time I thought I'd found what I searched for, it turned out not to be enough. In my early years, I searched for a father figure to rescue and validate me. The men I loved had, indeed, taken care of me, offering a predictable, safe harbor. But along with safety came confinement of my spirit and growth. I wanted to make my own decisions and not exchange the possibility for a safe life.

I inherited itchy feet from my mom. Her gutsy, outgoing personality, creativity, and determination to feel free were passed down to me, but I took it a step further. Her possibilities were derailed by the choices she made to fit her gender role and meet the expectations of others.

I, too, felt the enormous pull of society's mores. Mom helped me escape a destiny of raising kids too young by searching for an abortion doctor and then locating the adoption agencies.

Had I created another layer of distance from raising a baby by marrying a man who wasn't the biological father and who wouldn't pressure me to keep the child? I even created a back-door out of the marriage. The night I asked Jerry to marry me, while we sat on the porch swings, I said, "I'll put the baby up for adoption and annul the marriage. I won't hold you to it." I framed the statement to make the marriage commitment easier on him. I also gave myself a way out, never fully committing to him.

In Mom's day, society insisted women fall in line and play their role as mother, or take acceptable jobs such as secretary or waitress, always under the control of and subordinate to men.

As I came of age, the women's movement trudged further along, and women spoke out against the layers of sexism in the United States. The women's movement, as well as ideas emerging from the counterculture of the 1970s, had influenced me deeply. Traditional family units, religious beliefs, politics, drugs, sexism, racism, and war were all questioned by my generation through demonstrations that cried out for change. The Vietnam war, the epitome of violence, served as a wake-up call to young people. The slogan, "Make love not war," showed the mindset of the anti-war movement and the insistence for change from old ways of thinking about violence and sex.

Women had not yet broken boundaries by attending law school, becoming doctors, or holding positions of power other than in minimal, practically token numbers.

Women doctors are no longer uncommon—nor are female members of Congress—and now we've elected a Black woman as vice president.

As society claims to accept a woman's choice to achieve more than motherhood, we still see many obstacles that disprove the claim. Even with these changes, sexism is so blatantly woven throughout our lives, and women are discouraged and controlled at every turn starting with the opponents of *Roe v. Wade*.

I increased the number of visits to Texas to care for my aging grandparents, and at the end of each visit, Walter flew one of his planes from Corpus Christi and picked me up at Fredericksburg's tiny private airport.

Leaving my elderly grandparents standing on the Fredericksburg airport tarmac and flying away, even to Walter's home, tore at me. I watched my grandparents wave goodbye as we ascended into the clouds and saw Daddy Burr hand Mommy Burr his handkerchief to wipe her nose. My heart broke. I never wanted to make them sad.

After a short visit with Walter, I'd catch a commercial flight home to Louisiana.

Months later, I punched the button on my blinking answering machine.

"This is Daddy Burr," Daddy Burr's message clicked off.

Something must be wrong.

I dialed him. "Daddy Burr, what is it?"

"Mommy Burr fell in the kitchen, and she's in the hospital." His voice caught.

I flew to San Antonio the next day and sped the seventy miles over the rolling hill country to Fredericksburg.

At my grandparents' home, I helped Daddy Burr into my rental car.

"How does she look?" I asked on the way to the hospital.

"Tired."

"You look tired too."

He appeared on the verge of tears. "I can't sleep. I'm worried about her," he said.

What would happen to my grandfather if we lost Mommy Burr? How will he survive without her?

A vacant atmosphere echoed in the hospital, and an astringent smell hung in the air, like sickness covered up. I supported my grandfather's arm while he held his cane in the other hand to *tap, tap, tap* along the hospital corridor. Daddy Burr slowed his pace when we got closer to Mommy Burr's room, as though he feared what he might find.

I let go of his arm, sprang ahead, but halted at the door.

I didn't recognize the frail, pale-skinned person who slept on her side in an iron bed surrounded by instruments and tubes. Her tiny white head and one hand partially showed from under the covers. Her frame, withered so small, barely lifted the blanket. Breathing deep for control, I moved next to her, stroked her head, and smoothed her sparse hair.

The late afternoon light streamed in through the sheer curtains to warm and illuminate her, making her glow. It seemed angels waited patiently nearby.

"Mommy Burr, can you hear me?" I whispered.

"She can hear you, Charlotte. I told her you were coming. She's been waiting," Daddy-Burr said, a tremor in his voice.

I held her hand and thought about all the work she'd done in her lifetime to care for my grandfather, my mother, and for my siblings and me. She'd given us so much time, energy, and love. A giant ball of grief stuck in my chest.

I watched my grandmother breathe, listened to the monitor beep steadily, and more memories surfaced. I'd spent hours beside her cooking, sewing, and canning garden vegetables. Mommy Burr was a true gentlewoman who'd often told me how much she loved me and how she wished things had turned out differently with my mother.

My grandmother loved my mother deeply. For reasons I'd never understood, my mother resented her. Mommy Burr often expressed her sadness about Mom and hoped she'd come around to a different way of thinking one day. She showered her love on me as a substitute for Mom, but I could never replace the hole Mom left in Mommy Burr's heart. I tried to ease my grandparents' pain, but nobody could replace my larger-than-life mother.

My grandmother and I clung to the comfort of loving each other, but we always felt Mom's absence, the missing link between our generations. She loved Mom the way I wanted Mom to love me.

In earlier years, I forced myself to imagine my grandparents eventually dying. Maybe facing their deaths in my heart would lessen the impact when it actually happened. Now, as I watched Mommy Burr lying there, practicing for this inevitable event didn't make it any easier.

Daddy Burr stood beside the bed on his old, bowed legs. He lay his cracked, weathered hand on Mommy Burr's head and spoke softly to her.

"Charlotte's here, Mommy Burr," he said.

Heavy with grief from seeing the two people I loved most in the world in this condition, I prayed for their peace and for mine.

In deep meditation, a stillness descended on me. I recognized a glimmer of the joy I'd experienced at Esalen Institute in Big Sur so many years before. When it happened, the experience comforted me, and now as I stood by my grandmother's bed, it blanketed me with calming compassion. I wept, fearing the loss of Mommy Burr's presence in my life, my motherly anchor of love. I owed her my sanity.

The ride home from the hospital seemed so long. "Did you call Mom?"

"Yes. She said she'd come," he said.

We wound our way along the driveway as the sun set. The trees cast long, winter shadows, and squirrels sprung from tree to tree. Life went on all around us, oblivious to our grief. The black wall phone rang in the kitchen. My hand hovered above it, afraid of what I might hear if I answered.

"This is Nurse Catherine." She paused. "Mrs. Beerman passed away a few minutes after you left."

I thanked her and hung up. In a daze, I turned to my grandfather, who leaned on his cane. His eyes met mine expectantly, unrealistic hope etching his sorrow-creased face. He waited for me to say she'd woken up and called for us. Instead, I told my old grandfather his lifelong partner had just died.

I braced myself against the same counter where my grandmother had often stood and cooked for hours.

Daddy Burr plopped onto a kitchen chair next to the picture window. "She held on until you got here, Charlotte."

I covered my face with my hands and wept like a child who'd lost her mother. I came around the table and held Daddy Burr. His scarce gray hair looked disheveled the way my grandmother's hair had looked on her deathbed. His bony shoulders shook as he grieved in my arms.

He'll be lonelier than ever now. He lived in the country seven miles from town and had no close neighbors. *How will he cook and clean and do all the things my grandmother did?* "I'll come stay with you for a week out of every month," I said with conviction, but I knew it wouldn't be enough.

I hadn't thought of my grandmother as old at eighty-three. My mother, stepfather, a few siblings, and several of my grandparents' friends showed up to say their goodbyes at the funeral my grandfather and I arranged. My mother greeted everyone, but I didn't see her shed a single tear.

For the eulogy, Mom made it a point to sit beside Daddy Burr, to hold his hand, and show her support. Glad that Daddy Burr had his daughter next to him during this time, I sat a few rows back to give them space. I wanted to be alone while thinking about Mommy Burr in the quiet, respectful manner she deserved.

Once the funeral ended, everyone left, including Mom. I stayed another week to attempt the impossible task of getting Daddy Burr comfortable without my grandmother.

My problems with Martin shrank in comparison to my grandfather's broken heart.

TWA permitted employees to trade or give away our scheduled work hours. I flew to San Antonio each month using my flight benefits and spent a week with Daddy-Burr as promised.

I also hired a local lady, Marie, to come to my grandfather's home three times a week to cook, clean, and take him for rides in the country.

Several months after my grandmother passed, Daddy Burr and I enjoyed our regular sunset ride through the Texas hill country. Trees canopied the road, and herds of grazing deer scattered for cover in the tree-spotted hills when they heard us coming.

My mind drifted to Martin, and Daddy Burr guessed my thoughts.

"How are things between you and Martin?" he asked.

"I wanted to talk to you about that." I steered the car to the side of the winding lane and parked under a shade tree.

"Since I stopped wearing my engagement ring a year ago, our relationship has deteriorated even more. His moodiness changes to anger because I keep dodging our wedding plans."

"He's angry because after living together five years, you told him you aren't going to marry him, but you're still living there." Daddy Burr opened his palms as if not understanding.

"It's a hard situation."

"Tell me again why you want to leave him. Is he violent?" He retrieved his white hanky from his pocket and wiped his face.

"Oh no. Never."

"What about your job?"

"If I transfer to LA with TWA, I won't make enough money working part-time to support myself."

"I've always said you should finish school for this very reason. You've got to stand on your own and not depend on anyone."

"I finally get it. I kept trying to find a shortcut or another way to achieve independence. I can't see myself tied down and raising kids. It never made Mom happy. Earning my own way is the key."

"Maybe your upbringing has spoiled your ability to be content raising a family." He gazed out the window toward the hills.

He was right. I wouldn't be content raising a family in Louisiana or anywhere. Taking on the responsibility of small children sounded unpleasant at best.

"I want to leave Martin and go back to the west coast and attend school, court-reporting school."

"You'll be a lot further away from me in California."

"It's a further plane ride, nothing more. I'll still come every month and spend a week, but I hope you'll consider letting me move you to California."

"No, this is where I belong. Mommy Burr's buried here. We built our home and our lives here," he said, conviction clear in his voice.

I touched his hand. I loved my grandfather so much my heart ached. He was my surrogate father, but we'd lived so much of our lives apart. My stepfather represented a powerful male figure in my life, but he was never loving and never fully identified as my father.

The more time I spent with my biological dad, Walter, the more I discovered what I'd missed. I tagged on a few days to spend with him in Corpus at the end of each visit to see my grandfather. Walter expressed genuine interest in me. We'd stroll around his company grounds or go flying. Semiretired, he didn't do much work, but he liked to walk the company property to show me this part of his life.

I soon discovered the many differences between me, my Texas siblings, and the other people I met in Texas. As proud deer hunters, many people carried high-powered rifles in their pickup trucks. The sight of dead deer hanging upside down in the trees—sweet brown eyes staring, bellies cut open and bleeding out—saddened me. I didn't see the fun in killing those beautiful animals.

I was the unadopted half-sister in my first family, and to this family, a strange Californian half-sister who brought her own Kashi to eat for breakfast. Walter made light of our obvious differences, but I didn't quite fit in.

"Have you figured out what you're going to do?" Walter asked.

"About Martin? I'm moving out and enrolling in court-reporting school."

"Good to hear. About school, I mean. But why court-re-porting? Why not law school—be my family lawyer?"

"I'm not finished with my bachelor's degree."

"Not a good enough reason. Think about moving here and going to law school. I'll help you."

"I don't know, Walter. I'm a California girl. Mommy Burr used to say I could never shake the sand out of my shoes."

Law school seemed a daunting task at which I'd probably fail. I wasn't even sure I could handle court-reporting school but figured it must be easier than law school. Wrong again.

"Where do you want to live in California?"

"Southern part. Ventura." *Living in Santa Cruz without a job might tempt me back into old party habits.* "There's a woman in Ventura I used to work with at the travel agency in Lafayette. She offered to rent me a room in her house."

I returned home, closed my bank account, and made arrangements to send boxes of my belongings to California. I dreaded the face-to-face with Martin.

"I put in my two-week notice at TWA. I'm moving out and going back to the west coast."

Martin's face darkened. He stomped out and banged the front door closed behind him. Over the past months, I'd told him several times about my plans to leave, but it didn't help alleviate his anger and confusion.

Am I doing the right thing?

Martin proved generous even at the end when he could have hurt me out of revenge. I left with the car he bought me, his gasoline credit card, which I'd used during all the years we'd lived together, and cash to start over. He also let me keep my costly engagement ring to sell.

During the long hours on the road, I thought about why I didn't want to marry and have kids like people expected. Martin offered a safety net, a quiet harbor, but marrying him meant my happiness would forever be conditional on his happiness. I would be trading my joy for stability if I allowed him that much influence over my life.

Martin was a great dad in the making, but his dreams differed from mine. Our life choices stood at opposite ends of the spectrum, but neither was wrong. My decision took five years to make, but I'd finally made it.

I swore on my grandmother's grave that I'd never let myself get in this position again. The decision to go back to school must develop into a good job, or I'd live my life searching for another safety net, dependent on the generosity of men, or become a coke-snorting bag lady. The road ahead allowed no room for failure.

DEARLY DEPARTED

By the time I arrived in Ventura, the fear in my gut had turned to determination so deep my teeth ground together. Like a racehorse at the starting gate itching to break out and run, I planned to charge through school.

I qualified for school loans and landed a part-time job at a beach espresso shop called Latte on the Pier. Working interfered with my vigorous steno-practice schedule and my monthly visits to Daddy Burr, so my job lasted less than a year. I survived on student loans, and Walter sent me a little money each month to pick up the slack. Daddy Burr covered the cost of my monthly flight to Texas.

During my first year of school, trouble found me. I got plenty of sleep each night, but no matter how much coffee I drank, I nodded off in a drowsy stupor in my afternoon classes. I could barely focus on the dictation or my English and law classes. I fought a throbbing headache and foggy mind from the time I woke until I fell into bed each night.

I hired a hypnotist to teach me to hypnotize myself. I practiced daily, hypnotizing my crushing headaches away, but the headaches refused to stop. I wanted to tell Daddy Burr, but he'd worry. I called Martin, and he offered to fly to California, but I declined. I needed him to listen and care but leave me to heal on my own.

I lost a lot of weight over several weeks. Weakness finally prevented me from getting out of bed for school. I telephoned my landlady, and she drove me to the doctor. With her support, I walked from the car to the doctor's office door. My blood pumped fire.

The doctor examined me, drew blood, and read the results. "You must be admitted to the hospital and put on antibiotics immediately. Your tests indicate your body is fighting a severe infection. We already called and got you a bed."

"No! I can't miss school." My words echoed in my brain, and I reeled thinking of the consequences of my absence.

The doctor ignored my objection and spoke to my landlady. "Use our wheelchair. My receptionist will help you push her across the street to Memorial. Go now. They're expecting you."

My delirium increased every day. Even after five days of intravenous antibiotics, my condition was still deteriorating. My doctor called in a specialist.

The new physician stood next to my bed. "I've reviewed your records and tests. I should have been notified on your admission." He squinted at my original doctor, who looked away. "We need to perform exploratory surgery now, immediately, to find out what's going on."

Someone put a clipboard in front of me and lifted my hand to help me sign. The room buzzed like people running late for something. I wanted to call my grandfather and tell him not to worry, but he didn't even know I was in the hospital.

Someone jabbed a syringe in my drip bag. "Good night, Charlotte."

My vision returned, leaving me blinking against the brightness.

Dr. Myers, writing on a clipboard, appeared at the foot of my bed.

He looked up when I shifted. "How are you feeling?"

"Okay."

He removed his glasses. "We had to perform a total hysterectomy."

"No, what?"

"Your organs were black and covered with lesions caused by the IUD. I've practiced medicine a long time, and I've never seen worse. Your kidneys were dangerously weak. We thought they'd shut down any moment during surgery."

His words garbled from there. My mind kept going back to the hysterectomy. I lived my life not wanting the burden of children, but now, at thirty-seven, disappointment braided through my relief.

The doctor touched my arm.

I turned my head to face the wall, tangled in tubes and my thoughts. *Please leave.*

The doctor said something about checking on me later.

I'd never have a family now, but what did it matter? Daddy Burr and school are what matters.

I drifted off to sleep thinking of Martin. My hysterectomy would have destroyed his dreams of becoming a father if I'd married him. In a way, it helped alleviate my guilt for leaving. Now he was free to find someone who could give him children.

I woke and called Daddy Burr to tell him what happened and report my stable health. Next, I called my school director.

"Ms. Borrelli, this is Charlotte Gulling."

"Yes." She sounded annoyed.

I blurted out, "I'm in the hospital. I've been here a week, and they aren't going to discharge me for several more days. They gave me an emergency hysterectomy. Please don't drop me."

Silence crowded the moment.

"Hmm. Sorry to hear that, Charlotte." Her voice was a bit softer. "Student loans for living expenses have guidelines for attendance."

"Yes, but—"

"Come see me when you get back."

During the second year of school, my grandfather showed signs it was time to move him from the home he and Mommy Burr had built.

Marie called weekly to update me on his condition. "We'd go for more rides in the country if I didn't spend so much time cleaning the house," she said. "It's too big for him now."

She expressed my very thoughts.

On my next visit, while driving Daddy Burr through the hill country for our evening outing, I broached the subject.

"The house has become too big for you by yourself, and I can't be here more than a week each month. Also, it's too much for Marie. We've got to move you to a smaller place closer to town."

"I'm not leaving my home. I've told you that before." He almost stomped his foot on the floorboard.

"Please, let's look at some apartments. We don't need to make a decision yet."

I needed to navigate these waters carefully so not to pressure Daddy Burr. I loved him too much to overrule his will. We needed a mutual agreement.

I swung open the hall closet in the third place we'd seen that day. "This apartment is adorable. What do you think, Daddy Burr?"

He looked around the bright yellow kitchen, the new carpet, and the clean, shiny bathroom. He liked the place but covered up his approval.

"This can be my bedroom when I come to see you." The breeze moved the starched white curtains in the light blue bedroom. "Think of the new friends you'll make living here."

The realtor came by to see us the next night and estimated how much she thought we'd get for the house.

When Daddy-Burr heard the number, his face lit up. "Oh?" he asked in surprise, revealing his approval.

That sealed the deal. He agreed to sell it and move to the bright little apartment in town. I planned to make his big move seem fun.

He signed the real estate contract, and we made plans. Marie and I hired a few locals to move his furniture and hosted a garage sale for the remaining stuff that wouldn't fit in his new place. Plans and dates were set in motion.

Exhausted but relieved, I flew home to California. I entered my apartment and saw my answering machine blinking. Marie had left three messages. Panic washed over me.

Daddy-Burr must be in trouble.

"Charlotte, your mother's here. She showed up today after you left for the airport. She's upset because we're selling the place, and she's got your grandfather all worked up."

I called Daddy Burr, but Mom picked up the phone. It'd been months, maybe a year, since she'd come to see Daddy Burr.

What timing. I got right to the point. "Mom, what's going on there?"

"What is this about you selling Dad's home without my knowledge? And who is that Marie woman?" she asked.

My temperature rose, but I told myself to step carefully around this rattlesnake. "If you'd come see him more often, you'd know who Marie is. You'd also know Daddy Burr can't live so far from town anymore."

She felt my soft accusation and shouted, "My father is upset because he doesn't want to leave his home!"

"He'd accepted the idea and was even excited about it when I left this morning," I said, my voice fast and shaky. "We've already rented him an apartment for when the house closes escrow."

"I'll be damned if I let you do this to Dad!" her voice dripped with contempt.

The irony of her words hit me like a tsunami, and I hated that I still feared her so much. "He's lonely out there by himself, and it's dangerous, Mom."

"You'll run him out of his home over my dead body!"

Protecting my grandfather's well-being from anyone causing him problems—even his own daughter—summoned a murderous fury in me.

"I can't let you interfere, Mom." I spit out the words in a low tone, using all my control not to scream.

She smashed the phone into its cradle.

I lay in bed that night thinking about Mom. Sassy purred next to me as I stared at my apartment ceiling in the dark. I worried about my grandfather in her hands. She'd leave him out in the country by himself and forget about him in a week. Legally, I could trump her because I held power-of-attorney, but I dreaded the battle. A formidable opponent, I pictured Mom spinning a tale to support any crazy claim she'd come up with.

I fluffed my pillow again and turned over, agitated. Sassy

jumped off the bed. I searched deep for courage and finally found it. Afraid or not, on behalf of my grandfather, I'd fight my mother in court, if necessary. Though battling her would take time and money, and I worried about missing more school.

The next day, I walked into the director's office and found her sitting at her desk buried in papers. The dark paneling and stacks of banker boxes made the generous office appear cramped.

I explained the situation about my grandfather and that I needed to go back to Texas.

She listened and said, "Your grandfather needs you."

"Thanks for understanding, Ms. Borrelli." I turned to leave.

"Hold on." She set her pen down, rubbed her temples in circles, and looked at me. "I've made special allowances for you to miss a week of school each month, and now you're missing more." She came around the desk, leaned back, and crossed her arms. "Maybe this isn't the right time for school."

I sucked air and held my breath. "I can't quit."

"Of course, but maybe—"

"The truth is I have nothing else." The tension in my shoulders hardened like solid rock, and my eye twitched spastically. "My grandfather's getting old, and he needs me; otherwise, school is my priority. I've got to make it through this course and get a job, Ms. Borrelli. My grandfather's one wish is to see me stand on my own feet before he passes. I have to finish school for both of us. My life depends on it."

Ms. Borrelli lowered her crossed arms. "You're in a tough position, but I am too. This can't go on."

I called Marie to say I'd fly back the next day to help her deal with my mother.

"It's not necessary. Whatever you said to her on the phone

last night satisfied her, and she left this morning. She's really something. What did you say?"

"I don't know why she changed her mind but thank God she did." Tension melted from my neck and shoulders. "How is he doing today, Marie? Will you put him on the phone, please?"

I practiced my steno speed vigorously—even during visits to see Daddy Burr—and made progress. Court reporting requires complete honesty and impartiality. Court reporters are called "Guardians of the Record" because they create word-for-word transcripts. I learned to process events without the lens of my upbringing or society, to strip away my own biases and focus on the facts.

In a way, this helped me redirect ingrained patterns of thinking and build the self-esteem that had been beaten out of me in childhood. That lack of self-esteem had resulted in a natural readiness to escape, to run from life and responsibility. My sense of self-worth and independence developed with my progress in school and the love I shared with my grandfather. My tolerance for violence changed, too. I no longer accepted it as a way of life.

I came to understand that freedom was choosing to make my own way and believing I was capable of it. My attraction to risky thrills and pushing boundaries through drug use and smuggling faded into history.

Between my fear of failure and my deep determination to succeed in school and care for my grandfather, I learned what commitment meant. This knowledge was the very thing I needed to process the ongoing challenges which lay ahead.

Several months later, I received another emergency call. Walter's voice sounded clipped and strained.

"Charlotte, Diane's dead."

"Oh my God, no. What?"

"Murdered. Happened yesterday." He paused and blew his nose. "The funeral's Friday. Can you come? I'll send a ticket."

Enormous, puffy clouds floated beneath the plane on the flight to Texas. I thought about Diane, my half-sister, dead. Murdered. How was that possible? I'd recently seen her in Corpus. In her mid-thirties now and beautiful, she enjoyed a vibrant life riding her horse, line dancing, and working out at the gym to keep her amazing figure.

Walter waited for me curbside in his pickup truck at the Corpus Christi airport. On the drive home, lights from oncoming traffic briefly lit his face. He looked defeated. A vein throbbed in his neck, and he kept blowing his nose. He turned and looked out the driver's side window to shield his vulnerability.

"Are you okay to talk about it? How did she die?" I asked.

He blew his nose again, shoving the white hanky back in his jeans. "Drunk and arguing, her stepfather's girlfriend shot her point-blank using a sawed-off shotgun. They airlifted her to the hospital but too late."

My spirit deflated. "I can't believe this."

At the funeral, lying in her casket, Diane looked peaceful at last. Her clothes concealed her fatal wound. I loved her for trying to piece together our fragmented family by finding me and bringing me to Walter. But her life had been in dire need of repair. Her inner demons had caused her lots of drama and ultimately killed her.

After the funeral, I flew home for school. Several weeks later, I returned to Texas and attended the week-long criminal trial for the woman who killed her. Evidence was presented of Diane and her sister bullying their father's girlfriend, a blackjack dealer he'd met in Las Vegas. Everyone drank excessively and anger ran high. Diane and her sister held the defendant down in the bathtub and splashed water in her face making her choke. After they let her out of the bathroom, they followed the defendant into a back bedroom. The defendant reached under the bed and retrieved a loaded shotgun, cocked it, and pointed it at them. Diane made a move toward the defendant, and the defendant shot her.

When the clerk read the verdict of involuntary manslaughter, I sat in stunned silence with the rest of the Rossler family. The defendant served only four months of her six-month sentence. Diane's gone forever, but the woman who killed her was freed by Christmas. She deserved a conviction of second-degree murder. The verdict was bullshit.

Returning to school, I struggled to concentrate in class when the dictation flew past my best speed. Ms. Borrelli expected to see me that day.

"Charlotte, as you know from previous discussions, our program dictates attendance requirements," Ms. Borrelli said.

"Yes, but I can explain—"

"Let me finish. Frankly, you've missed a lot of school, and history shows that court-reporting school requires—"

Oh, God, she's going to expel me! "My sister was murdered!"

Her lips parted in wordless surprise. "What happened?"

I steadied myself and told her about Diane's murder and the subsequent trial.

"If you take school from me, I'll have nothing. Please. I can't give up. I know you're required to drop students with loans if they don't comply with the attendance requirement. But the rule is for people who aren't fully committed. I am fully committed. I'll prove to you I can make it through."

The stress from my grandmother dying, my emergency hysterectomy, moving my grandfather, keeping up in school, and now Diane's death rushed at me. I crumpled in a chair, covered my face, and bawled like a kid until I got hiccups. The office door clicked closed behind me. Ms. Borrelli lay her hand on my back.

"Frankly, I'm at a loss. You work hard work when you're here, but—"

"I work hard when I'm not here too. I practice daily when I'm with my grandfather." I wiped my nose and looked up.

She appeared to wrestle with her thoughts. "Okay. I'll cut you another break. Finish the program and make your grandfather and me proud."

I worked day and night to catch up fast, but there is no catching up "fast" in court-reporting school. Progress is a slow process of building speed and practicing trance-like concentration. People around me dropped out every month due to the rigorous work the program necessitated. I held on and forged slowly ahead.

"Charlotte?" Marie sounded loud and clear on the phone.

"What's going on?" I stiffened and waited. It wasn't time for her weekly phone call.

"Your grandfather started a fire in the kitchen yesterday."

"Oh my God, is he okay?"

"Yes, yes. He's fine, but the landlord is beside himself. You better come quick."

I left a message for Ms. Borrelli and flew back to Texas the next day, steno machine in tow.

I sprinted into my grandfather's apartment and helped him

struggle up from his easy chair. I wrapped my arms around his old body and hugged him. Thinner than ever, he'd break in two if I held him too tight.

"I'm so glad you're okay," I whispered.

Dark soot covered the ceiling and walls of his once bright-yellow kitchen.

"What happened?" I asked.

"Boiling water. It happened so fast," Daddy Burr said.

The memory of my family's Christmas Eve fire came to mind. That fire had killed my dog, Smokey, my brother's bird, and nearly killed my two youngest sisters. Daddy Burr needed protection from himself. Time for another change.

"Daddy Burr, you've lived here almost two years. I think you'd be safer if we moved you to a retirement center."

"Oh no, not this again," he said.

"You're alone too much and it's not safe."

"I don't want to move to an old folks' home."

"We'll find a place where they'll cook for you every day, take you for rides in the country more often than Marie and I can, and you'll make new friends."

A loud pounding on the door made us jump. I peeked out the window and saw

Mr. Hanson, the landlord, scowling. I swung open the door, said a pleasant word, but did not invite him in. Twice, I'd caught him peeking through the apartment window at my grandfather and me. He gave me the creeps.

"Miss Gulling, it's time for your grandfather to move," Mr. Hanson said.

"Got it. Thanks for stopping by." I gently but firmly closed the door, leaving him standing there.

"Ms. Borrelli, I hope you got my message."

"I did, yes."

"My grandfather—well, a fire started in his apartment, and he's getting evicted. I'm in Texas arranging to move him."

"Look, you've attended school for almost two years, and you're barely halfway where you're supposed to be—"

"If I fly home tomorrow for two days of school, I have to turn around and fly back to Texas immediately. If you let me stay these few days, I'll be back in school on Monday."

"Isn't there anyone else in your family who can move him?"

"No, there's not. My siblings and parents live in different states, and they're tied up with careers and families of their own."

"Hmm, okay. See you Monday." She hung up without a goodbye.

She'd let me off easy this time, but I didn't take it for granted.

Daddy Burr and I climbed into the car for our early evening ride in the hill country, but before leaving town, I turned into the familiar parking lot of Sunshine Terrace.

"I'm not going in there," he said.

"Please, Daddy Burr, let's see what they're doing." I opened his passenger door. "Come on. It'll only take a few minutes."

Stubborn, he continued sitting. Reluctantly, he reached for his cane.

I nodded to a young receptionist with dark, teased-up hair. "We just want to look around," I said.

Elderly people playing bingo occupied about half the tables in the dining room.

The same receptionist offered to show us the private rooms. Daddy Burr's cane tapped the linoleum floor as we strolled along the hallway. We peeked into the rooms with open doors.

"Each guest has their own furniture, TV, and phone. We can

provide those things at an additional monthly fee, but most folks like having their own things."

The backdoor opened to a grassy area where elderly folks sat on benches in the sunshine. Our escort talked directly to my grandfather and told him about the daily activities and the shuttle for church service on Sundays. She made a genuine effort to welcome Daddy Burr as if she understood and cared about our concerns.

On our way back to his apartment, I asked, "What do you think?"

"I don't like it. A bunch of old people waiting to die."

"They played games, ate, and traveled to town on the shuttle. Nobody sat around waiting to die," I said. But in a sad way, he was right.

We arrived back at Daddy Burr's apartment to find Mr. Hanson standing in the driveway.

Before we got out of the car, he said through my open window, "Have you made any effort to find another place for your grandfather?"

My voice sparked and rose louder than I intended. "We're doing what we can. Move back and give us room to get out of the car."

He tsked and grumbled, but he moved. Wrapping my arm around my grandfather's, I guided him into his apartment and closed the door.

"Daddy Burr, I have to go home, and I can't leave you like this. Hanson is evicting you. How about this idea? You come live with me."

"No—"

"Just for a few months in my apartment in California until we figure this out."

"I'll push up daisies from my grave before I move to California," he said.

I chuckled and patted his arm. "Okay, what if you move to the retirement center for three months, and if you don't like it after that, we'll figure out something else?"

He lay his head back on his easy chair and closed his eyes, resigned. "Okay, Charlotte, you win. I'll give it three months."

"I'm not trying to win anything. I want to take care of you."

I hired a repair person to repair and paint the apartment. Marie and I worked hard to leave the place sparkling clean, but Mr. Hanson refused to refund Daddy Burr's cleaning deposit. I sued Hanson in small claims, won the judgment, and handed my grandfather his $500 security deposit while sitting in the courtroom.

He looked at the check and said, "Oh boy, let's go get an ice cream cone!"

MURDER EN MASSE

Moving Daddy Burr went smoother this time because he owned so little.

I crawled into one of the two double beds in my grandfather's new room. Although an acrid smell and strange night noises filled the retirement center, I lay at peace in the bed next to Daddy Burr's, listening to his soft snore.

My mind drifted to my length of time in school. Four years. Ridiculous. *I've got to get back, finish, and find a job.*

Another year passed. It became difficult for my grandfather to move around and bathe himself. He needed more help and didn't object to moving this time. The assisted care facility, located next door to the retirement center, graciously welcomed him.

On our evening ride, we parked the car on a hill above a small lake in a local park. We'd finished eating ice cream cones when I turned up Bob Dylan's song, "Knockin' on Heaven's Door," on the car radio.

Daddy-Burr and I sang the chorus together while knocking on the imaginary door in front of us. The simple joy of being with him overwhelmed me. He saw me giggle through my silly tears and took my hand. I had finally found it. This was the true meaning of love. It sat right beside me.

Three weeks later at home in my own bed, the phone blasted in my ear during the night. A call this late meant trouble.

"Ms. Gulling?"

"Yes?" Forcing myself not to slam down the phone, I braced for the next words.

"This is Jorge from the Fredericksburg Convalescent Home. Your grandfather isn't doing well."

Wide-awake, I bolted upright. "What do you mean 'he isn't doing well?'"

"I don't think he'll make it to morning."

"Oh my God. Why didn't you call me sooner? Put him on the phone!"

"He's not responding, and his breathing is shallow. You should know," he said.

"Of course, I should know. Hold the phone to his ear, please." I slapped back my covers, and Sassy jumped off.

Struggling to control my rising panic, I said, "Daddy Burr, can you hear me? I love you. I'm coming. Hang on. I love you, Daddy Burr."

I hung up and burst into a tearful rage. Why take such a beautiful being from this awful world, God? Where is the love in taking one of the few good ones?

I caught the next flight to Texas, but he was already gone. I'd missed his last hours. The attendant repeated my grandfather's final utterance, "Where's my family?" I was his family, and I wasn't there.

Overwhelmed with guilt, I questioned whether I should have quit school and moved to Texas during his final years.

I hired a local woman to sing the Bette Midler song, "Wind Beneath my Wings," at his outdoor funeral in Fredericksburg. Kathy, my youngest sister, said a few words to the small group honoring our grandfather.

A composed, dignified man throughout his life, Daddy-Burr had carried a gentleman's pride. He left me great wealth when he died—his love. I wished for alone time at his funeral to say prayers of thanks for having him in my life, but people had come to honor him, and he would have been delighted to see everyone there. My mother and stepfather, some of my siblings, and a few of his elderly local friends showed up. I thought about how meager his funeral was for such a gracious and deeply important life as his.

Birds flew overhead across the brilliant blue sky, and others darted in and out of the trees. I remembered the message I'd received in Big Sur. Everything would ultimately be okay. I held that memory close for strength. My grandparents were okay wherever they were, and I would be okay in this world without them. We were eternally connected.

After settling Daddy Burr's affairs, I flew home to California and called Walter.

"I plan to continue coming to see you, but I won't come as often since Daddy Burr is gone." I coughed through the tightness in my throat. "I've got to finish school."

"I understand, Charlotte. I'll send you a ticket whenever you can come. There's something else I've wanted to talk to you about. I'm having lunch with my attorney in a few months, and I'm asking him to include you in my will. Right now, you're not in it. We hadn't met when I made it eight years ago."

"Oh, Walter, what can I say? Thank you for thinking of me with your family."

"There's something else. Are you still thinking of finding your sons?"

"Yes. I consulted a family therapist. She suggested I read

some books on triage and get on a list of biological mothers in search of missing children. I did that years ago."

"What do you think about me asking my attorney to help find them?"

"Yes, yes."

"Don't get your hopes up yet. Without their names or the agency name or anything—well, I don't know," he said.

"Thank you, Walter. Your effort means so much."

Monday morning, I walked the hall to Ms. Borrelli's office.

She looked up when I entered and slapped her pen on the desk. She pointed at the chair across from her. "Whatever you say, it's too late. I'm dropping you from the roster—"

"My grandfather passed. I stayed to arrange the funeral and take care of his belongings and final bills. I won't miss any more school." Resigned and exhausted, I almost didn't care what she decided. Daddy Burr wouldn't get to see me finish school now anyway.

"I'm sorry. I know how close you were to him." She waited politely before saying, "Can I expect you'll be present in class from now on?"

"Yes."

Weeks after Daddy Burr's passing, I pushed the door open to my vintage apartment, dumped my books on the sofa, and carefully set my stenograph machine on its tripod in preparation to practice after dinner. Tired from speed-testing all day, I stroked Sassy, who was curled on my pillow. The answering machine blinked fast, indicating multiple messages.

"This is Marie. I heard an announcement broadcast a moment ago about a shooting involving your father's company in Corpus. You better call them. Let me know if I can help."

The next message came from my brother-in-law calling from Corpus Christi.

"Charlotte, there's been a tragedy." He kept clearing his throat. "Your sisters are sedated and can't talk." He hung up.

I steeled myself and called him back. He told me of the mass shooting which had taken place earlier in the day when a disgruntled employee stormed through my father's offices carrying two handguns. He shot and killed Walter, his wife Joanne, and four other employees of Walter Rossler Company, including himself.

From the airport, I called and left a message on Ms. Borrelli's office phone to let her know there'd been another family emergency. Convincing her again to let me remain in school would pose a challenge, but there was no room in my psyche to think about it now.

On the flight to Corpus, my father's memory enveloped me, but I was numb to the news of his death and unable to process it.

Like a robot on automatic, I rented a car and headed to my half-sister's home where the family gathered. We talked until late about the shooting and the circumstances that led up to it.

Walter had never even met the shooter. Hired and fired by one of Walter's three supervisors, the killer held a grudge against the company. He chose the one-year anniversary of his firing to enter my father's offices and shoot everyone within range before killing himself. He shot Walter's wife, Joanne, in the back of the head when she tried to run down the hallway after seeing Walter go down in front of her.

Violence in my life had started at home and continued through my adulthood, including men trying to control, rape, or kill me, followed by three family members killed by gun violence. My spiritual readings helped me understand that the root of violence is fear. Fear of losing control or not achieving control. Feelings of hopelessness and helplessness are rooted in fear.

My experiences didn't prove that fear drives violence, but I suspect it does. My experience taught me that to exercise my right to freedom meant living with the caution of a mature woman who must resist anyone attempting to take her power.

My mother, an only child doted on by her parents, worked to maintain her self-image as a beautiful, carefree, and happy woman. As long as her children lived up to her idea of a big, fun family, she liked us. Too often, she refused to bend and forgive life or her kids for not being perfect. Life overwhelmed her, and she battled her lost freedom caused by having so many children.

My stepfather must have experienced horrific events during his tours as a helicopter pilot in Vietnam. We, as a country, are still learning about the ongoing problems that PTSD creates. I may have been a source of resentment for Dad, a reflection of my mother, his wife who could never be controlled—not her spending, her affairs, or her disrespect. A difficult circumstance for a high-ranking Marine, no doubt.

A few days later, I attended the funeral for Walter and his wife, Joanne. I stopped in my tracks when I spotted Mom emerging from a group of people gathered at the graveside. She greeted and pulled me close. I inhaled her Chanel No. 5 and clung to the small comfort she offered.

"How did you find out about this, Mom? And the location?"

"It's getting a lot of press. I called you, but evidently, you'd already left California."

"Thank you for coming." Unable to identify my emotions standing there facing my mother, I said nothing more; I felt bled dry.

Expressions passed across her face as if she wanted to say something. She cocked her head to the side like a curious bird and said, "I'm here if you need me."

Her presence didn't surprise me—or maybe nothing surprised me anymore. My heart lifted knowing she had cared enough to fly to Corpus and find me.

"I'm staying at the Holiday Inn. Let me know what you need," she said.

A breeze blew an errant strand of her blonde hair, which she'd twisted into a chic updo. All the anger and all our struggles melted away that moment, and I embraced her again. My mother had behaved like an enemy throughout my life, but other times, she stood by me as my closest ally.

We continued talking. The Rossler family called me to the two black limos reserved for us. They didn't invite Mom to the gathering at Walter and Joanne's home following the funeral, and it wasn't my place to ask her.

Walter and I were in the process of building a father-daughter relationship. So many years ahead to know him, now lost. I grew up with many questions about my identity, not knowing whether the Rossler family even cared about me. Diane connected the missing link by finding Mom and convincing her to allow my contact with the Rosslers.

After Diane's death, and with my grandparents gone, and now Walter, nothing bonded me to Texas. My time in Corpus Christi was comprised of hanging out with my father. I knew his other daughters from my visits, but I always hoped time would bring us closer.

On one of our outings, Walter had suggested I take back his last name. At the time, I'd brushed aside the idea, believing it would create a division between my Gulling siblings and me.

After Walter's death, I reclaimed my birth-certificate name, Rossler, to honor his wish.

My brother and sisters never commented on my using the Rossler name, and I felt it had little bearing on my relationship with them. My sisters were all married and using different last names anyway.

The meeting with his attorney had yet to occur when Walter died. His daughters, my Rossler half-sisters, knew nothing about our conversations regarding his will or finding my sons. The will stood as written before we met. I was verbally mentioned but left out of any benefit.

Hope of finding my sons died with my father too.

In the mid-'90s, after six years of school and three tries, I passed the California State Court Reporter's Exam. That particular year, the pass rate for the California Bar exam was 40 percent, and for the Court Reporters exam, it was 14 percent. Walter was right. I'd chosen the wrong profession.

I celebrated with a mixture of excitement for passing and frustration for not passing before my grandfather died. I shuffled through my anticlimactic graduation ceremony feeling my grandfather's absence.

I called Ms. Borrelli the day I received my passing notice.

"I heard you'd passed. I'm happy for you, Charlotte. I admire your determination. You faced a lot of obstacles."

"Yeah, it was a long haul. I wish my grandfather had lived long enough to know I'd be okay—because of him."

"He knows. Somehow, he knows, and he's happy."

I never got to tell Daddy Burr that Ventura Courthouse hired me with a full benefit package. I'd never be financially dependent on anyone again. A sense of accomplishment for finishing school against all odds helped the healing process of my poor self-image. I even made a down payment on a house and paid off my school loans using the small life insurance policy Walter had left me.

A few years later, I got word my sister Jacquie had lung cancer. Theresa and I flew to St. Louis to support her during her final battle. Jacquie's four small children ran around and played, not yet fully understanding what life would be without their mother.

I was struck by Jacquie's peaceful acceptance of her fate, but her lack of anger at her circumstances didn't surprise me. Instead, it reminded me of her gentle nature. I thought back to the plays we staged for each other as kids and how Jacquie had fit the role of serene princess every time.

Alone in Jacquie's bedroom, we sat cross-legged on the carpeted floor facing each other, talking. Her energy was very low, but the sound of her kids in the background, romping around the living room playing games, brought a gentle smile to her face. In a soft voice, she said she loved me. I refused to take in the finality of her words and automatically told her I loved her too. I smiled like it was any other day, refusing to accept she was so close to the end.

Theresa and I flew home. Jacquie died a few days later with her second husband present and our sister, Suzie, by her side.

I missed her even more over the coming years. She left a big hole in our family.

A few years after Jacquie's death, my parents moved from Louisiana to Florida, where my stepfather died from melanoma. I felt nothing. I felt no sorrow for his death, no satisfaction. Nothing.

I didn't attend Dad's funeral. None of my siblings said

anything about my absence. They knew so little about my relationship with their dad—or maybe they knew more than I realized. Growing up, I didn't know what they saw or believed, and I never spoke a word against their father.

My mother remarried at seventy-two and remained in Florida with her third husband, Pete. At eighty-three, she suffered a double stroke, which rendered her unable to walk or talk.

My brother, Dave, flew to Florida to help Pete, who stayed by our mother's side every day.

"How's she doing?" I asked Dave over the phone.

"Not good. She probably won't make it." Stress strained his voice. "I arrived here a week ago and need to go back to work. Are you coming?"

"Yeah, I want to help. I'll be there soon as I can." I found it impossible to imagine my fiercely independent mother unable to walk or talk.

"I'll be back in a few weeks to take over again," Dave said. "Theresa's flying in too."

I arrived at the assisted living center in the middle of Mom's speech therapy session. With Mom's back to me and her wheelchair facing the therapist, I listened to her recite simple phrases.

"Row, row, row your boat." The therapist coached Mom to repeat it.

Hearing my mother's new whispery voice, I stared at the back of her head, struggling to take in the scene. The therapist waved me in.

I moved to view Mom face-to-face. Kneeling next to her wheelchair, I took her hand in mine. Our eyes locked, and her face crumpled into tears of recognition.

Seeing her like this, it struck me that any possibility to heal our relationship was gone now. I teared up, regretting I'd never connected with her on the level I'd so desperately yearned for. I was never able to share a meaningful conversation with her when she was healthy. Now, in this condition, any hope for that was lost. So many secrets were buried long ago, never brought to the light and set free.

I'd grown a lot since my days living at home. Mom remained the same—or maybe she'd changed—but I saw her the same way. I stayed in touch and visited her every year, but our conversations never dipped below the surface of our respective art projects or the latest news about my siblings. She'd never been capable of a deep conversation—especially one that asked for accountability.

My mother lived in her own world and believed her own stories even when proved erroneous. At times throughout the years, I hoped to bring up the past and fix our broken connection, but I feared attempting it might ruin the fragile relationship we'd managed to salvage. My mother was who she was, and in her own way, she loved all her children, even me.

Kneeling next to her wheelchair, holding her hand, Mom searched my face, but I'm not sure what for.

Then I knew.

To my horror, she'd seen a fleeting twinge of satisfaction pass through me at seeing her helplessness. Our roles had reversed, and she'd caught the moment in my eyes. I wish she hadn't. I loved my mother deeply, good or bad.

Mom's pale skin, thin as parchment, blended with her bleached hair. Her fingernails, manicured short and painted a burgundy red, matched the color of her pantsuit. She opened her mouth to speak, but words didn't form. Mom's only response to any question was, "Oh yes" or "no." Other than those few words and mimicking rhymes sung by the speech therapist, she couldn't talk.

"Mom, can you understand me?"

"Oh yes," she whispered.

"The doctors will get you better." I feigned confidence.

I stayed by her all day, every day, for two weeks, spending the night at the home she shared with Pete.

Their home reflected Mom's artistic gifts as an interior decorator. I took photos of her house, moving room to room using my iPad. I brought my iPad to the center for my daily visit, and I found Mom lying in her single bed in the private room Pete insisted she have.

Pete had gone to the cafeteria, leaving Mom and me alone.

"Mom, can I get in bed beside you? I want to show you something."

"Oh yes," she said, her expression questioning.

I crawled onto the narrow bed, making full contact next to my mother's warm body. Beautiful, even on her deathbed, I rolled toward her to view her appearance that was etched in my mind from years of observing her. We shared identical crooked baby fingers on our right hand, as well as same height and weight.

Lying next to her, I picked up my iPad and scrolled through the brilliant, clear photos I'd taken of her home that morning.

"Mom, this is your kitchen. Do you recognize it?"

"Oh yes."

"I love the green granite you chose. Here's your living room. Look at your artwork. It's all waiting for you. You need to eat and get well so you can go home."

She examined the photos carefully, pointing to certain things in each picture and opening her mouth to speak, unsuccessfully.

I put the iPad down. "There's something I want to tell you."
She met my eyes, our faces inches apart.

Is that wariness in her eyes? "I'm going to hire someone to help me find my boys, my sons."

She blinked in the information and looked downward. A pensive look rested on her face, deep in thought, maybe remembering.

"I wanted you to know."

I don't know what Mom's reaction to this news would have been if she'd been healthy, but at this point in my life, it didn't matter anymore. I carried no more guilt around the pregnancies, or about having a different dad, or for loving her parents—my grandparents—so much. I'd freed myself from the wrath of her shame, which had become my shame and cost me a relationship with my father, her, my sons, and so much more.

Mom died a few weeks after my visit. She gave up and went to sleep for the last time. Dave and Theresa, as well as Pete, stood by her side.

Mom, dressed in a blue designer suit and her hair styled in an upsweep, looked elegant in her casket. She would have approved of her classy appearance.

Of eight siblings, five of us attended her funeral.

Suzie, sitting at the back of the chapel, moved toward the front before Dave gave the eulogy. As Suzie passed me to peer into the casket, she whispered, "I'm here to make sure she's really dead."

During our years growing up, Mom's toxicity leaked into all her children. As a result, we all have our inner demons to battle. None of us escaped our family without scars—some hidden, some not—but we each broke the dysfunctional cycle in our own way. The four youngest sisters chose to have children, and the remaining four siblings decided not to. Those who became mothers created happy, healthy families.

I grew up desperately trying to prove my value by taking dangerous risks. Only after making it through school while caring for my grandfather did I develop self-respect and recognize the true meaning of love—the joy of giving oneself unselfishly.

A NEW DAY 22

With so little information to go on, the task of finding my boys seemed futile. I didn't know their names, the name of the hospital, nor the name of the Catholic adoption agency. I did remember the county and the years I gave birth.

I spent hours every day on the internet searching but got nowhere, so I hired a private investigator.

After hanging up with the private investigator, new hope surged through me. I did the math to figure out their ages: forty-six and forty-seven—if they still lived. Determination tugged at my gut. I needed to find out what had happened to them.

Not even forty-eight hours after hiring the investigator, I received a call.

"Good news!" she said. "I've located your youngest. He's called Andrew, and he's been searching for you for years."

After a moment of stunned silence, I choked out, "Give me his number. Does he—does he sound okay? I mean, is he healthy?"

"Yeah, he sounds fine on the phone. Go ahead, call him."

Shaking, I called, and a man picked up on the first ring.

"Hello," he said.

"Hello, is this Andrew?"

"Yeah, it's me."

I listened intently to him pronounce those few words in his husky voice. Everything became surreal, and a thick silence settled on us.

When he sniffled, I jumped in. "Oh my God, Andrew. It's you. I've wondered about you for years."

"Yeah, me too. I searched for you on the internet a long time."

"Oh, wow. Where do you live? Are you healthy?"

"I live in Oregon, and yeah, I'm healthy, I think. This is so weird talking to you. What should I call you?"

Funny, that's exactly what I asked my real father when I met him.

"Call me Charlotte. What kind of work do you do, Andrew?"

"I was a mortgage broker in Phoenix, but I recently moved here to live near my kids."

"Kids? I'm a grandmother?"

"Yeah, my daughters have kids, and my son will be a father soon, so you're a great-grandmother."

"A great-grandmother? Me? Wow." I let this information sink in. "How can we get together? Do you want to fly down here, stay a few days?" I asked, pacing the floor.

"Actually, I'm flying to San Diego in a week or so to visit some friends. From there, I'll catch a train up to Ventura, if that works for you. I'll email you the details."

After days of anticipation and lying awake in the dark for hours, a hint of dawn finally broke. I leaped out of bed.

What to wear for such an important occasion? I carefully selected a pink cotton blouse, gray slacks, and flats, then glanced at the time again. His train was chugging toward me this very moment.

I poured a cup of coffee, noticed the tremor in my hand, and smiled to myself. *Okay, I admit it. I'm nervous.*

Would he like my cozy home near the ocean? What would he think of me and my dog, Taffy?

I picked up my index cards with their neatly printed notes, reminding me of things to say and things to ask. No card told me how to act. Should I act like a friend? I hadn't even known whether he was dead or alive until a week ago.

I stepped on the accelerator on my way to the train station, and my heart beat faster with the speed of my car. Arriving too early, I shut off the engine and visualized the meeting about to take place. *What if I don't recognize him?* A few benches and a metal awning marked the spot where he'd step off the train any minute. I squinted at my watch for the hundredth time.

A lifetime of twists and turns had brought me here today. Wild travels, all those drugs, the men I'd loved, the children I'd lost, had made me who I am. The meeting about to take place was almost fifty years in the making.

The train whistle pierced the air, and the click-clack grew loud like a drum roll. The sun broke through the coastal fog, spotlighting the tracks.

Oh my God, he's here. I walked toward the train.

I recognized Andrew right away because he looked like his father. He stood around five feet eleven, fair-haired like Tim and me, and had a wrestler's build. He wore a jean jacket and a small duffle bag slung over his shoulder the way Tim would have carried it.

What a tough little boy he was at birth. He'd refused to wait another minute to be born and had fought his way into the world weighing a bit over four pounds after only six months in my womb. Guts, determination, and an adventurous spirit flowed through his blood because those qualities characterized both his parents.

After all these years, I embraced my son, now a man.

During Andrew's visit, we searched the internet for his father. We discovered that Tim had died in 2000, and we never learned the cause of his death. I carried great memories of our high school days together riding his motorcycle through the oil fields and laughing so hard my sides cramped.

Over the next few days, Andrew and I hiked, visited the local islands off Southern California, and slowly got acquainted. We connected in a special way based on an unmistakable bond.

On his scheduled day to leave, I don't know why tears stung my eyes when he picked up his duffle bag. We spoke about remaining in contact and my coming to Oregon to meet his family. I blinked several times, saving my tears for the isolation of the night.

The day after I'd spoken to Andrew on the phone, the PI called again. "Charlotte, I found your firstborn, Mark," she said. "He's not so eager to meet or even talk to you. He asked why you're contacting him after all this time. Don't fret. This is often the first response from sons. I've found many boys are reluctant to jump at the chance to meet their biological mother, but they usually come around."

Although unnerved by the PI's report, I felt emotionally prepared for this exact reaction. "It's okay. I understand why he's hesitant. Ask if I can write him a letter."

She called me back a half hour later.

"He said you can write a letter but send it to my business address, and I'll forward it to him. He's not ready to give you his address."

I immediately sat down and wrote Mark a letter, then drove to the post office to mail it.

> *Dear Mark,*
>
> *It feels like a dream writing to you. I'm so happy to find you at last. My main question is, 'Did you have a good childhood?'*
>
> *I've thought about you over the years and hoped you were out in the world, happy and healthy. I'd regret it if I let my life go by and never learn what happened to you.*
>
> *I was a sophomore in high school when I gave birth to you. A kid having a kid. Your father was my sweetheart. I came from a large dysfunctional military family. My mother had me at eighteen and divorced my father when I was two. After she married my stepfather, they had seven more children. I was mistreated growing up and never adopted by my stepfather.*
>
> *When I got pregnant with you at fifteen, my mother sent me away, shunned and shamed from my family. If I'd been older, things might have been quite different. I put you up for adoption and hoped you'd be raised by a loving family.*
>
> *I will answer any questions you have of me.*
>
> *I hope we can email, text, talk on the phone—anything you're comfortable with, Mark. Please, let's be in contact.*
>
> *Charlotte*

Although Mark had no time to receive the letter, let alone respond, I checked my mailbox the next day, obsessed about getting his response.

When he received my letter, he called the PI and gave me permission to call him after he got home from work.

Waiting all day intensified my anxiety. My leg jiggled out of control when I sat to eat lunch. I refused to pick up the phone when it rang, not wanting to think about or talk to anyone except him. I held Taffy and rocked her back and forth. The hours crept by until five thirty finally arrived. I dialed the number with my jittery hand.

"Hello?"

"Is this Mark?"

"Yes." His voice sounded deep and mature.

"This is Charlotte." Emotion swirled through me. "Thank you for letting me call you. I wanted to talk to you to ease my worries about your well-being. I hope you're happy and your life is good."

I spoke too fast, too stiff.

He responded in a calm but hesitant way. "I guess I'm happy, yes. I've been married for seventeen years. My wife is my rock."

I let out a long, silent sigh. "I want to hear everything, but I need to tell you something first. You have a brother. You're the first of two sons I had as a teenager."

"A brother? Wow. This is all so weird. Why are you contacting me now after all this time?"

I listened for sarcasm in his tone but detected none.

"I've thought about it for years. I feared if I located you, you'd tell me it was too late and your life was none of my business. I searched anyway, hoping to at least hear you were okay."

Again, I talked too fast. I stopped and listened to the empty silence expand between us.

"Okay. There's something else," he said slowly.

"Ask me anything. I have no more secrets."

"Well, um, you got pregnant with me, right? Then you got pregnant a second time. I don't get it. It seems you should've learned the first time."

I clasped my palm over my mouth. Heat burned my face. There it stood before me bare naked, the disgrace I'd run from all my life. To hear my son say those words crushed me.

I inhaled, centered myself, and looked inward for balance.

"Yes, I can see why you'd ask that question." Breathing shallowly again, my voice sounded high-pitched and forced. I stopped talking and fought for clarity. "I don't understand a lot of things about myself. As a kid in search of belonging somewhere, sex made me feel wanted, valued. My relationships with your dad and Andrew's dad were full of joy, and I needed more of that. Sex with each of them became my way of breaking free from the life I lived at home and finding a bit of closeness. I never thought I'd get pregnant a first or a second time."

We talked for another hour and the next night too. He and his wife, Vickie, drove from northern California to see his adoptive mother in a retirement center located south of Ventura. They stopped by to meet me.

I watched Mark and his wife get out of their car in front of my house. A strong, healthy man emerged. He had a straight posture and a look of confidence. Transfixed by his every move, I watched him open the car door for his wife.

Mark, like his brother Andrew, looked identical to his biological father. Mark grew up not knowing he was half-Hispanic. With fair skin like mine and dark hair like his dad's, his good looks were the only characteristic he shared with his father. His real dad, Danny, rebelled and fought against life, whereas Mark worked hard and earned the love of his adoring wife.

Mark, Vickie, and I spent the day the same way I had with Andrew, cruising to the islands off the Ventura coast. On the ferry ride to the islands, leaning over the railing watching the water rush by, I told Mark his resemblance to Danny was uncanny and that his father was a dark-haired James Dean. Hearing this information made him grin, but he didn't ask any questions about Danny. Instead, he turned his face into the wind and looked toward the islands.

The holidays approached. I asked each son to share the season together as so many families do every year.

I drove north to Tracy, California, the day before Thanksgiving and checked into a small hotel Mark had recommended.

The next morning, sitting next to Mark at his kitchen table before the guests arrived, he showed me photo albums containing pictures of him growing up.

I stared at the toddler wearing a diaper and a cheek-to-cheek baby grin. He sat on the kitchen floor next to his adoptive mother. I imagined picking him up and holding him. What did he smell like? Would he feel soft and appear angelic like my little sisters had felt nuzzled in my arms so many years ago? I bit my bottom lip, holding down rising emotion.

The album pages showed the years passing, measured by his growth. The healthy boy matured from baby fat to freckles, then to a handsome young man.

I tore my attention away from the album to look at Mark and cleared my throat. "I need to say something." I waited until my composure steadied. "I'm so sorry I gave you up for adoption. I was sixteen and in high school when you were born. I had no job, no car, no husband, and no family support. I'm not looking for forgiveness, just trying to help you understand the circumstances. If I'd kept you, we would've ended up on the streets, alone and hungry. At least that's what my mother told me. My best option was to let you go to a loving family.

"People said eager families wait in line for years to adopt a baby, and they subject themselves to a rigorous background check to qualify. I don't know if that's true, but it's what the Catholic adoption agency and my mother said to reassure me. I guess I wanted to believe it."

"I don't harbor any resentment toward you for adopting me out," he said.

I choked on his generous words. His acceptance rolled through me like a wave, but I'd missed a lifetime with him. "Excuse me," I said.

An unbearable sadness swept over me. I escaped to the bathroom, shut the door, and tried to clear my mind.

I buried my face in a towel, slid down the bathroom wall, and let my emotions go. I'd never trusted myself to give my sons a loving family. Their chance to find love was better without me. At least that's what I told myself. But the bottom line is I chose to give them away. I chose to delay having more children until it was too late. Already sitting on the floor, I lowered my face to the cool tile and lay there until someone tapped on the bathroom door.

"Charlotte, are you okay?"

"Yes, I'll be a moment longer."

Mark and Vickie's friends arrived for Thanksgiving dinner, and I didn't want my disheveled appearance to embarrass them. I commanded myself to pull it together. The mirror reflected my bloodshot eyes. I called on my deep reserve of inner strength and splashed water on my face.

The living room was filled with Mark and Vickie's friends. I told people an allergy attack caused my puffy appearance.

Their beautiful home took on a festive spirit. An orange and yellow bouquet of flowers surrounded by small pumpkins and pinecones decorated the two tables. Six formal place settings on each table completed the holiday picture of perfection. Coming from the stereo, a jazz guitarist picked a holiday piece on his guitar, setting the mood.

Women worked around each other in the open kitchen. Someone lifted the aluminum foil to check the marshmallow yams while another stirred butter into the mashed potatoes. Vickie, Mark's wife, tossed an enormous bowl of salad while chatting with her friends. They each greeted me, saying, "Hello."

Mark looked for my reaction when he caught me glancing around. Someone handed him a glass of red wine, which he offered me. He looked relaxed and happy.

We sat for dinner. Mark stood at the head of the table. He toasted thanks for his good fortune in life, glanced down at his wife seated next to him, and then his eyes found mine.

Later, after the last guest departed, I hugged Vickie goodbye. When I embraced Mark, he noticed me swallow several times. My heart broke again for the boy I never knew.

"Don't worry, Mom. You did what you had to do. I'm fine."

I pulled away, grabbed my jacket, and bolted through the open front door.

I rushed down the entrance steps, lost my footing, and fell to my knees. Feeling embarrassed and out of control, I pushed myself up, torn pants and all. Mark sprinted down the steps to help me, but I recovered quickly.

"I'm fine, really. I just need rest."

He walked me to the car. I drove away and parked around the first corner out of sight. I let go, crying and pounding the steering wheel, wanting to turn back time, relive my life, and remedy my mistakes. Exhausted, I drove to the hotel. The night drizzled chilly rain, matching my emotions.

I flopped on the bed, fully clothed. I'd lost my sons, my grandparents, my real dad, my mom, my sister Jacquie, and my sister Diane. Stripped down to bare emptiness with nothing left to give, a merciful deep sleep descended upon me.

The next day, I drove home after eating breakfast with Mark and Vickie. When I walked into the house, my little dog, Taffy, yelped, bounced, and darted around, so excited to see me. I took her to bed, held her close, and told her everything that happened. She listened patiently, kissing the salty moisture off my face.

A few weeks later, Andrew called.

"Charlotte, I can't wait for you to meet my family. What time is your flight arriving?"

"I have to cancel our Christmas plans, Andrew. I'm not in a good place right now."

"Oh no! You can't cancel. We haven't talked about anything except you coming for Christmas. Please come."

"I have to think about it."

He kept calling until I agreed.

Driving to LAX to catch my flight, I almost turned around to go home. Emotionally drained, I didn't want to lay my grief on Andrew and his family. No more inner demons tormenting me again like during Thanksgiving. I had nothing left to give them.

I flew to Oregon, bringing Taffy with me. Andrew picked us up. Taffy sat in my lap as I gazed out the car window noticing the patches of Christmas snow on the distant hills. Andrew asked about my Thanksgiving visit to see his brother, Mark. I told him about the lovely dinner but didn't mention my bathroom breakdown or falling on Mark's front steps.

We entered the apartment Andrew shared with his son Patrick and Patrick's girlfriend. Andrew's Chihuahua, Milo, met Taffy and me at the door and welcomed us in. Milo's tiny body wiggled with his wagging tail. Taffy looked huge beside Milo. At ten pounds, she was not accustomed to outsizing other dogs.

Andrew pointed to a stairway next to the entrance and said it went to the bedrooms on the second level. Milo and Taffy led the way into the living room. A Christmas tree stood in the corner with a large flat-screen TV, volume turned down, next to it. A husky young man stood up from the small dining table.

"Hi, I'm Patrick. Wow, you're my grandmother."

We shook hands, awkwardly but friendly.

"Yeah, I guess I am. Call me Charlotte."

Patrick took me by surprise because he looked identical to my deceased sister Jacquie's son. They would be second cousins but looked like twins.

A slim, brunette woman with a wide smile peeked out from the kitchen while wiping her hands on a dish towel.

"This is my girlfriend, Kim," Patrick said. "And this is our new baby girl, your great-granddaughter, Talia."

He gestured toward a car carrier, which held a sleeping newborn swaddled in a pink blanket. Mesmerized by the infant's puffy pink cheeks and tiny fingernails, I watched her for several minutes.

Arranged with dark leather furniture, the living room had a solid, masculine feel to it.

Milo barked once until he recognized the two girls coming through the front door without knocking, each accompanied by a child.

"Charlotte, these are your two granddaughters and your two great-grandsons," said Andrew.

Andrew's daughters each reached around my outstretched hand and embraced me.

A two-year-old boy peered at me shyly from around his mother's leg, chewing his fingers. I felt so vulnerable.

The other boy, around four, stood next to his mother and asked, "Why is she sad?"

I glanced away, determined not to fall apart in this home too.

Andrew mussed the boy's hair and answered before anyone else. "She's not sad. She's happy to meet you kids."

Christmastime allowed me to see Andrew interact with his three grown children and three grandchildren. Watching him tickle his four-year-old grandchild—causing the little boy to shriek with laughter—made me think of the kind of childhood Andrew must have lived. He was a natural father. Soon he involved me in the romping games around the living room. Taffy also got involved in the chasing, but tiny Milo stayed out of the way. Andrew caught the boy and suspended him upside down, making the kid giggle hysterically.

Overcome with joy, I easily participated with Andrew and his family. Many times, I stopped and thought, *This could have been my world.* Then a great-grandchild grabbed my attention and made me laugh again.

(Back row L-R) David, Theresa, Jacquie, Kathy, Mary Lou
(Front row L-R) Charlotte, Shirley, Suzanne, and our niece Caroline

A NOTE TO READERS:

This book was a six-year endeavor to write. Thank you for joining me on my healing ride through emotional hills and valleys.

If you got even a tiny smile or a tear from reading it, please leave a review wherever you purchased the book. Thank you!

And please visit my website:

https://charlotterossler.com